FLAVORS of the
SOUTHERN COAST

FLAVORS of the SOUTHERN COAST

COOKING WITH *Tommy Bahama*

100 recipes

By Rick Rodgers

PHOTOGRAPHS BY PEDEN + MUNK

CHRONICLE BOOKS
SAN FRANCISCO

Published exclusively for Tommy Bahama
by Chronicle Books LLC.

Text copyright © 2016 by Tommy Bahama Group, Inc.

Photographs © 2016 by Peden + Munk.

Tommy Bahama Book Development Team:
Doug Wood, Chief Executive Officer
Rob Goldberg, Executive Vice President, Restaurants
Andy Comer, Vice President, Creative Services
Eric Karp, Senior Director of Brand Marketing
Don Donley, Director of Culinary
Thomas Prowell, Editorial Director
Curtis Smith, Creative Director
Melinda Porter, Director, Creative Projects

Text and recipes by Rick Rodgers
Design by Toni Tajima
Food styling by Alison Attenborough
Prop styling by Amy Wilson and Nicolette Owen
Food assistants: Sandy Ta, Tina Dang,
    and Shelly Petericia Ellis
Prop assistants: Nina Lalli and Nicole Louie
Photo assistants: Rob Petrie and Craig Mulcahy
On-location production assistants: Jessica Fender and
    Curt Leimbach
Camera operator: Thomas Nakasone
Studio assistant: Asmite Gherezgiher,
    with assistance from Marley Wong

All rights reserved. No part of this book may be reproduced in any form without written permission from the publisher.

ISBN: 978-1-4521-5537-1
Manufactured in China.

This book has been set in Seria Sans.

MAKE LIFE ONE LONG WEEKEND is a trademark of the Tommy Bahama Group, Inc.

A.1. Original Steak Sauce is a registered trademark of the Kraft Heinz Co.; Alouette is a registered trademark of Alouette Cheese USA; Angostura is a registered trademark of Angostura Ltd.; Anson Mills is a registered trademark as Anson Mills; Ateco is a registered trademark of the August Thomsen Corp.; Aunt Jemima and Quaker are registered trademarks of Quaker Oats Co.; Brugal is a registered trademark of Brugal & Co.; Bulleit and Captain Morgan are registered trademarks of Diageo North America, Inc.; Certified Angus Beef is a registered trademark of the National Beef Packing Co., LLC.; Clamato is a registered trademark of Mott's LLP.; Cointreau Liqueur is a registered trademark of Rémy Cointreau USA, Inc.; Cruzan is a registered trademark of Cruzan Viril Ltd.; Crystal Hot Sauce is a registered trademark of Baumer Foods, Inc.;

Dröste is a registered trademark of Dröste Nederland B.V.; Frank's RedHot Original Cayenne Pepper Sauce and Frank's RedHot Sauce are registered trademarks of the French's Food Co.; Gebhardt is a registered trademark of Hunt-Wesson Inc.; Goya is a registered trademark of Goya Foods, Inc.; Grana Padano is a registered trademark of Consorzio per la tutela del Formaggio Grana Padano; Grand Marnier is a registered trademark of House of Marnier-Lapostolle; Heinz is a registered trademark of H. J. Heinz Co.; Herbsaint Liqueur and Peychaud's Bitters are registered trademarks of Sazerac Brands, LLC; Hershey's is a registered trademark of The Hershey Co.; Ke Ke Beach Key Lime Cream Liqueur is produced by Ke Ke Beach, Netherlands; LaMonica is a registered trademark of LaMonica Fine Foods; Licor 43 is a registered trademark of Diego Zamora, S.A. Corp.; Luxardo is a registered trademark of Girolamo Luxardo S.P.A. Corp.; Mae Ploy is a registered trademark of Thep Padung Porn Coconut Company Ltd.; Microplane is a registered trademark of Grace Manufacturing Inc.; Midori is a registered trademark of Suntory Liquors Ltd.; Old Bay is a registered trademark of McCormick & Co.; Parmigiano-Reggiano is a registered trademark of Consorzio Del Formaggio Parmigiano-Reggiano Consortium; Pepperidge Farm is a registered trademark of the Campbell Soup Co.; PepperMary Cajun Blend and PepperMary Island Jerk Rub are trademarked products of PepperMary Specialty Products; Pyrat Xo is a registered trademark of Patrón Spirits International AG; Pyrex is a registered trademark of Corning Inc. Corp.; Ritz Crackers is a registered trademark of Intercontinental Great Brands LLC; Ron Zacapa is a registered trademark of Rum Creation & Products Inc.; Sauza is a registered trademark of Tequila Sauza, S.A.; SKYY is a registered trademark of Campari America; Spike is a registered trademark of Modern Products, Inc.; Tabasco is a registered trademark of McIlhenny Co.; Tanteo is a registered trademark of Tanteo Spirits; Van Gogh is a registered trademark of Luctor International LLC; Zatarain's is a registered trademark of Zatarain's Brands, Inc., McCormick & Co.

10 9 8 7 6 5 4 3 2 1

Tommy Bahama
400 Fairview Avenue North, Suite 488
Seattle WA 98109
www.tommybahama.com

Chronicle Books LLC
680 Second Street
San Francisco CA 94107
www.chroniclebooks.com/custom

Tommy Bahama

MAKE LIFE ONE LONG WEEKEND

CONTENTS

Foreword by Rob Goldberg • 9

Introduction: Relax in Style—the Southern Way • 11

CITRUS FRUITS • 17

APPETIZERS 18

- 21 Crab Cakes with Coconut Crust*
- 22 Seafood-Avocado Cocktail*
- 24 Conch Fritters with Red Pepper Jam*
- 25 Super Nachos with Skirt Steak, Black Beans, and Queso Sauce
- 27 Bacon and Bourbon Jam Crostini with Goat Cheese*
- 28 Spiked Guacamole with Fire-Roasted Pepper Salsa*
- 31 Texas Caviar
- 34 Spicy Pickled Okra
- 37 Zesty Pimento Cheese (AKA Zesty Pub Cheese)*
- 39 Savory Tomato and Cheese Pie

LOUIS MICHOT—SEED COLLECTOR • 41

SALADS AND SOUPS 42

- 43 Chopped Chicken Taco Salad with Chipotle Ranch Dressing
- 44 Grilled Chicken and Mango Salad*
- 47 Muffaletta Salad with Olive Vinaigrette
- 48 Horiatiki Greek Salad with Marinated Grilled Shrimp
- 50 Baby Spinach with Lime-Mustard Vinaigrette and Sweet and Spicy Pecans
- 51 Fresh Ambrosia with Sour Cream Dressing
- 52 Coleslaw with Poppy Seed Dressing
- 56 Church Supper Potato Salad
- 57 Shrimp and Sausage Gumbo with Slow Roux
- 58 Tortola Tortilla Soup*
- 61 Crab Bisque*
- 63 Cuban Black Bean Soup with Chorizo Sofrito

LEONARD HORAK—CHICKEN FARMER • 65

CHICKEN 66

- 67 Roast Chicken Asado with Root Vegetables
- 68 Hickory BBQ Chicken with Sweet and Sticky Root Beer Sauce
- 71 Fried Chicken with Iced Tea Brine
- 72 Chicken Breasts with Jerk Marinade*
- 74 Cheese-Stuffed Chicken Breasts with Roasted Red Pepper Cream*
- 78 Tandoori-Style Chicken
- 79 Chicken Fricassee with Spring Vegetables and Chive Dumplings
- 80 Arroz con Pollo y Chorizo
- 83 Grilled Chicken Wings with Mole Rub

FIERY CHILES • 85

RED MEAT 86

- 87 Creole Surf and Turf with Spicy Mustard Sauce
- 88 Smoked and Baked Texas Brisket
- 90 The Ultimate Texas Chili
- 91 Ropa Vieja
- 94 Jamaican Beef Patties
- 96 Picadillo-Stuffed Acorn Squash
- 99 Baby Back Ribs with Blackberry Brandy BBQ Sauce*
- 100 Puerto Rican Pork Roast
- 102 Jerk Pork Tenderloin with Pineapple-Rum Sauce*
- 105 Bourbon-Brined Pork Chops with Peach Glaze and Corn-Bacon Hash
- 107 Jamaican Curry Lamb
- 110 Greek Lamb Souvlaki with Vegetable Kebabs and Tzatziki

GULF SHRIMP • 113

SEAFOOD 114

- 115 Baked Grouper with Dill-Yogurt Sauce
- 117 Caribbean Mahi Mahi with Quinoa Succotash*

119 Crayfish Étouffée
120 Jamaican Fish Rundown
121 Marinated Swordfish with Skordalia and Horta
122 Tuna in Veracruz Sauce
125 Crab Enchiladas in Green Sauce
126 Crab-Stuffed Shrimp with Two Sauces*
129 BBQ Shrimp with Spicy Beer Sauce
132 Shrimp and Andouille with Cheese Grits

JOEY FONSECA—CATFISH FISHERMAN • 135

SANDWICHES AND TACOS 136

137 "Wet" Chicken Burritos with Red Sauce
138 Grilled Chicken Tortas with Chipotle Aïoli
139 Bacon BBQ Burgers*
142 Cuban "Hamburgers" with Chorizo and Shoestring Potatoes
145 Beef Debris Po' Boys with Gravy
146 Pulled Pork Sandwiches with Blackberry Brandy BBQ Sauce*
149 Old-School Cuban Sandwiches with Garlic Mayonnaise
151 Lamb Shanks Adobo Soft Tacos
152 Crispy Fish Fillet Sandwiches with Island Tartar Sauce*
154 Blackened Fish Tacos*
157 Oyster Po' Boys with Mississippi Comeback Sauce
158 Fried Green Tomato and Pimento Cheese BLTs

COLLARD GREENS • 161

SIDE DISHES AND BREADS 162

163 Smothered Green Beans
164 Collard Greens with Bacon and Garlic
167 Southern Vegetable Gratin
168 Baked Grits with Spicy Mushrooms and Cheese
169 Creamy Macaroni and Cheese with Parmesan Crust
170 Quinoa Succotash*
172 Sweet Potato Mofongo*
173 Yellow Rice and Peas
174 Coconut-Almond Rice*
177 Crispy Yuca Oven Fries*
178 Moist Corn Bread with Fresh Corn
182 Jalapeño and Beer Hush Puppies
183 Flaky Buttermilk Biscuits

GEORGEA SNYDER— FARMERS' MARKET ADVOCATE • 185

DESSERTS 186

187 Peanut Butter Cakes with Salted Peanut Frosting
188 Chocolate-Rum Cake
190 Mango Icebox Cheesecake with Gingersnap Crust
192 Tres Leches Strawberry Shortcake
193 Hummingbird Quick Bread
195 Key Lime Pie with White Chocolate Topping*
196 Sweet Potato Pie with Bourbon Whipped Cream
200 Peach-Blackberry Buckle
202 Florida Strawberry Shortcakes with Lime Whipped Cream
203 Pecan-Chocolate Bars
204 Orange-Cinnamon Flan

ANN TUENNERMAN—MRS. COCKTAIL • 207

COCKTAILS

33 Hemingway La Floridita*
33 Key Lime Martini*
55 Hurricane*
55 Margarita*
77 Daiquiri*
77 Leap of Faith*
109 Sazerac*
109 Mojito*
140 Bourbon-Mint Lemonade*
140 Hibiscus-Ginger Punch
199 Keys Breeze Punch*
199 Voodoo Punch*

BASICS 209

209 Crispy Onions*
209 Island Slaw*
209 Basic Rice
210 Shrimp Stock
210 Aïoli*
210 Chipotle Aïoli*
211 All-American BBQ Sauce
211 Jalapeño-Lime Butter*
211 Cilantro Oil*
211 Meyer Lemon Vinaigrette*
213 Roasted Garlic
213 Dry Jerk Seasoning
213 Cajun Seasoning
213 White Chocolate Topping

Acknowledgments • 217

Index • 218

* indicates a Tommy Bahama Restaurants specialty

FOREWORD

In 1996, when we opened the first Tommy Bahama retail store in Naples, Florida, we also debuted our first restaurant. There was no shortage of local inspiration, from the colorful coastline to the incredible seafood to the bright citrus fruit growing all around us; it was clear that if Tommy Bahama could capture the spirit of the Gulf Coast and translate it into a restaurant atmosphere, it would serve as a beacon for living a simple, elegant life.

Since the beginning, gathering with friends and family to enjoy great food, wine, and cocktails has been a cornerstone of the Tommy Bahama experience. Our original restaurant in Naples has been both a touchstone and a benchmark as we've opened other restaurants, from New York City to Tokyo to Maui. While each Tommy Bahama restaurant is unique and has its own sense of place, our early experience on the Gulf Coast will always quietly manifest itself in the offering.

We're thrilled to bring you the second cookbook in a series that celebrates culinary traditions from different parts of the world. *Flavors of the Southern Coast* represents our roots, and you'll find some of our favorite recipes from the Gulf States. We have drawn from the rich heritage of Texas, Louisiana, Mississippi, Alabama, and Florida to tailor a dynamic selection of casual, satisfying dishes rich with the color and flavor of the South. Along the way, we've met some of the region's most innovative farmers, fishermen, mixologists, and culinary stars, whose stories we share in these pages.

We invite you to join us in the kitchen to create satisfying and soulful dishes that will inspire you to Make Life One Long Weekend!

Cheers,
Rob Goldberg
Executive Vice President
Tommy Bahama Restaurants

INTRODUCTION
Relax in Style—the Southern Way

American culture is often referred to as a melting pot. The symbolism is never more apt than in the Gulf Coast states, where a conglomeration of cuisines have simmered into a style of cooking that is as versatile as it is delicious. And it is served up with a big helping of that unique ingredient, Southern hospitality. All of these elements come into play whenever you eat at one of the sixteen Tommy Bahama restaurants around the world—or cook one of the recipes in Flavors of the Southern Coast.

Here you will find the entire panoply of culinary cultures that thrive along the almost seventeen hundred miles of Gulf Coast shoreline. Spiciness runs throughout this unique cuisine as a common thread, illustrated by the aromatic heat of Jamaican jerk seasoning, the bright chile kick of Mexican cooking, and the distinctive herbaceous burn of Cajun dishes. The elegant fare of Southern plantations lives on in the upscale food at seashore resorts and in the stately Creole restaurants of New Orleans. Home-style food is found in such dishes as Puerto Rican pork roast (pernil) and that iconic Southern classic, chicken and dumplings, or the dish that symbolizes Texas in one word: chili.

While these cuisines happily coexist today, they originally developed almost exclusively of each other because travel was so difficult in early days. New Orleans, for example, was the only port in the vast region for many years, and that city developed its personal culinary style from the influences of its various visitors and conquerors: Creoles and Cajuns, Spaniards and Frenchmen, Greeks, Caribbeans, and Mexicans.

Many Southerners believe that what is served in the glass is as important as what is on the plate. With that in mind, we offer some of our favorite cocktails, most of which depend on the spirited Southern, Caribbean, and Mexican trifecta of bourbon, rum, and tequila.

This book also highlights some of the people who make the Gulf Coast region such a special place to eat and drink. These are individuals who grow the vegetables and fruit, provide the meat, catch the seafood, and mix the drinks. Their inspiring work is the foundation of what we do at our restaurants every day.

In Flavors of the Southern Coast, we bring you recipes for classic down-home Southern dishes as well as some more sophisticated fare created by the chefs at Tommy Bahama restaurants, as indicated by our marlin logo . We have carefully tested these dishes for the home cook and have broken them down into components that can be made well ahead and assembled before serving. So, when you have a craving for the Tommy Bahama experience at home, a full range of offerings is now at your fingertips.

It is our wish that the flavors of these mouthwatering dishes will take you on a virtual culinary cruise from the Tex-Mex delights of Texas to the Greek-inspired foods of Tampa and the many tasty ports of call in between.

¡Buen provecho!
Bon appétit!
Kalí órexi!

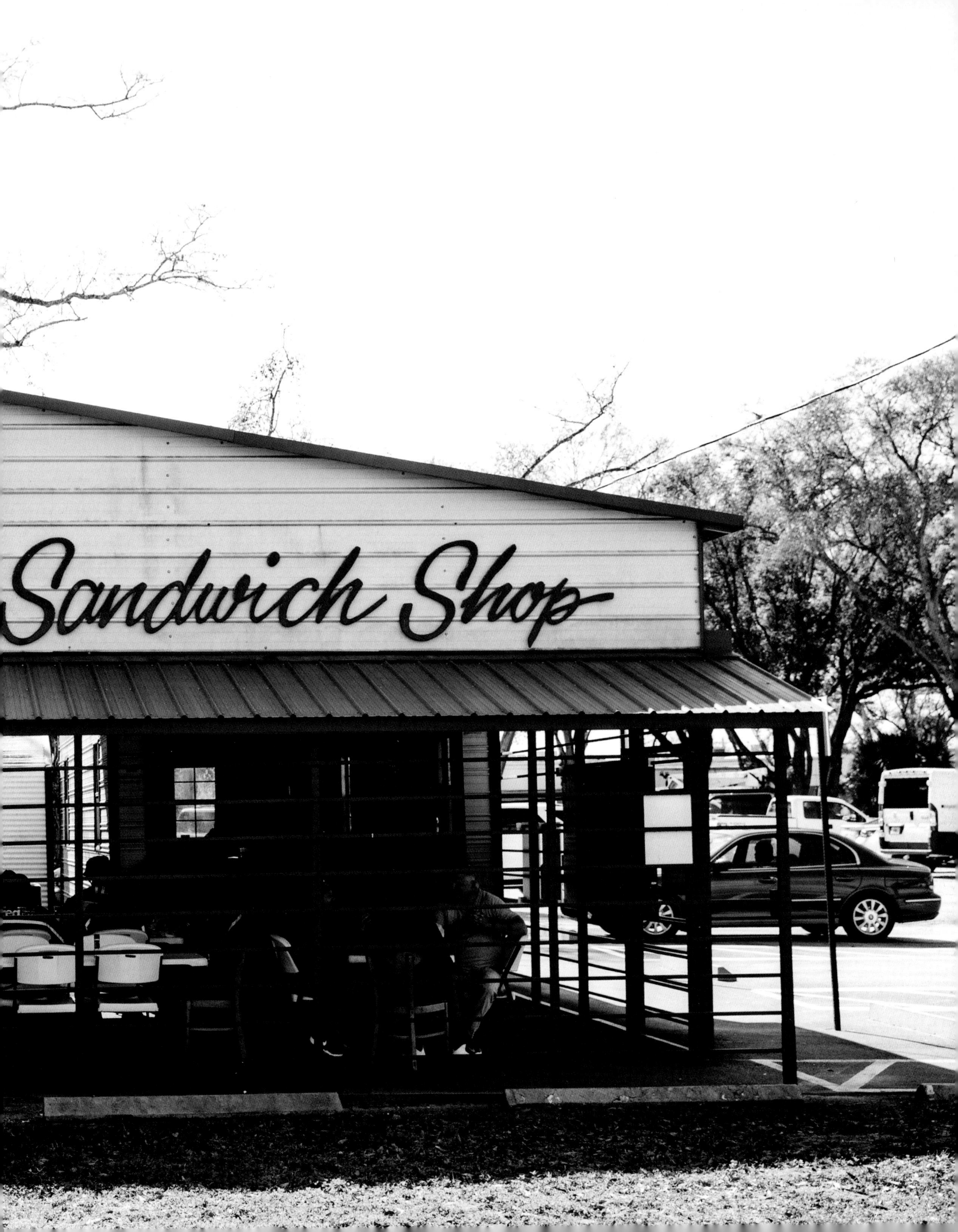
Sandwich Shop

Other states in the Gulf Coast grow oranges, but the fruit is a vital symbol of Florida. You'll find oranges emblazoned on the state license plate and on tourist essentials like T-shirts, postcards, and juice glasses. The citrus industry contributes $9 billon to Florida's annual economy.

    Thanks to its popularity in orange juice production, the Valencia orange is the backbone of Florida's orange economy, representing over 60 percent of the crop. Named for the sweet oranges of Valencia, Spain, it was originally a hybrid from Southern California. Transported to Florida in the 1920s, Valencia oranges greatly benefited from the efforts of Lena B. Smithers Hughes, a botanist who developed virus-free strains that supplied the vast majority of budwood to the state's growers. In 1986, Hughes became the first woman inducted into the Florida Agricultural Hall of Fame.

    Floridians are the primary consumers of the local oranges, and much of the fruit is not exported from the state. Otherwise, the crops go mainly to supply the large markets on the East Coast. Your morning orange juice is likely to come from Florida, as it supplies 90 percent of the fruit for that product.

    Grapefruits, tangerines, and kumquats are other important Florida citrus crops. For most Americans, especially in the winter when these fruits are at their peak, hardly a day goes by without some kind of contact with Florida citrus. But what about lemons and limes, especially the Key limes that give their name to another popular Florida export, Key lime pie? Blight, frosts, and hurricanes have decimated lemon and lime groves in recent decades, and growers simply did not replant. Key limes are now a Florida backyard crop, and most of the Key limes sold in markets from coast to coast are imported from Mexico. In fact, they are sometimes called Mexican limes; larger Persian limes are the common supermarket variety.

CITRUS FRUITS

APPETIZERS

Here is a collection of irresistible snacks in the Southern tradition to enjoy with a beverage of your choice or to kick off your meal. Although these are mostly casual finger foods, you'll also find some sophisticated plated first courses fit for a special dinner party.

21
CRAB CAKES WITH COCONUT CRUST

22
SEAFOOD-AVOCADO COCKTAIL

24
CONCH FRITTERS WITH RED PEPPER JAM

25
SUPER NACHOS WITH SKIRT STEAK, BLACK BEANS, AND QUESO SAUCE

27
BACON AND BOURBON JAM CROSTINI WITH GOAT CHEESE

28
SPIKED GUACAMOLE WITH FIRE-ROASTED PEPPER SALSA

31
TEXAS CAVIAR

34
SPICY PICKLED OKRA

37
ZESTY PIMENTO CHEESE (AKA ZESTY PUB CHEESE)

39
SAVORY TOMATO AND CHEESE PIE

Tips for Grilling

The temperate weather in the Gulf Coast makes this part of the world a prime area for grilling in every season. Barbecue uses low heat to cook and tenderize meats and wood smoke to add distinctive flavor. It originated with the pit-cooking of the Taíno people in what is now called Haiti. The Spanish conquistadores dubbed the technique, *barbacoa*, and took it to Texas and elsewhere. These days, cooks can choose between the traditional charcoal grill or a propane model. In this book, we are not using drum smokers or asking you to dig any pits.

DIRECT AND INDIRECT HEAT

Direct heat means that the food is cooked right over the heat source. This method is mainly used for ingredients that cook quickly, such as steaks, boneless chicken, and seafood. For a charcoal grill, build a charcoal briquette fire (a chimney starter works best) and let it burn until the coals are covered with white ash. Dump the coals into the center of the grill. Do not spread the coals to the very edges of the grill because you want a cooler area to move the food to if it drips and starts to flare up. For a gas grill, simply preheat the grill on high, then adjust the temperature as needed. You can turn off one burner to provide a cooler area.

Indirect heat cooks food by radiant heat, with the food placed away from the source of heat to cook slowly. Barbecue, with its distinctive smoky flavor, is actually an indirect-heat method of cooking. Large cuts of meat, including beef brisket and bone-in poultry parts, are best cooked by indirect heat. For a charcoal grill, dump the ignited, ash-covered coals on one side of the grill and leave the other side empty. Put a disposable aluminum foil pan on the empty side as a drip pan and fill about halfway with water to help keep the heat distribution even. For a gas grill, preheat the grill on high, then turn off one burner. If there is room, put a shallow foil pan or a sheet of heavy-duty foil under the grill grate, but in many models this is not possible, so don't worry about it.

Two-zone cooking is a combination of the direct and indirect methods. We like it for double-thick pork chops, which are first browned over direct heat and finished with lower indirect heat. Set up the fire for indirect cooking (you can skip the foil pan) but scatter about one-quarter of the coals opposite the coal mound. (Or turn half of the burners on high and the others on low.) For skewered food, place the handles over the cooler area.

ADDING SMOKE

Aromatic wood chips or chunks are often added to the grill to smolder and add a smoky flavor to food. Choose your aromatic wood from the many varieties available at hardware and grocery stores. Indigenous woods work best with foods from a particular region. Mesquite has a strong aroma and is an essential flavor in Texas BBQ. Hickory, good with pork and chicken, is a favorite of many cooks in the South. The sweet smoke from fruit or nut woods (such as cherry, apple, peach, and pecan) is very versatile.

Wood chips can be added to either a charcoal or gas grill; wood chunks are used only in smokers and charcoal grills. Soak the chips for at least 30 minutes or up to 2 hours in cold water to cover, and drain the chips well before adding to the coals or to a gas grill smoker box. If you don't have a smoker box, it's easy to rig up an alternative: just wrap a handful of *unsoaked* chips in a sheet of aluminum foil to make a packet and tear open the top to expose the chips. Place the packet, chip side up, directly on the heat source. Once the dry chips ignite and smolder, add a handful of soaked chips.

TEMPERATURE

The key to successful grilling is using the correct temperature. If the heat is too high, the food burns; too low, and it never develops the caramelized surface that adds its special grilled flavor. Some grills come with thermometers built into their lids so you can check the temperature. Otherwise, a grill thermometer is a great investment.

With a charcoal grill, the heat is controlled by vents on the top and bottom of the unit. Fire needs oxygen to stay alive. Open the vents wide, and the oxygen feeds the fire so it burns hot. Close the vents to cut off the oxygen, and the fire burns at a lower temperature. You can also let the coals burn down to reach the proper temperature. Whether your grill is charcoal or gas, always cook with the grill closed as much as possible to keep flare-ups to a minimum and contain the heat.

The heat ranges for grilling temperatures are:

High:	450°F/230°C to 550°F/290°C and above
Medium-high:	400°F/200°C to 450°F/230°C
Medium:	350°F/180°C to 400°F/200°C
Low:	300°F/150°C to 350°F/180°C

These crab cakes have been on our menu in one form or another for many years—they clearly have made a lot of people happy. The recipe has all of the best features of top-notch crab cakes: lots of seafood with a minimum of binder, a light hand with the seasoning to let the seafood shine, and a perfect balance of a crisp crust and tender interior.

CRAB CAKES WITH COCONUT CRUST

SAUCE

½ cup/120 ml Thai sweet chili sauce

1 Tbsp stone-ground mustard

1½ tsp unseasoned rice vinegar

1½ tsp soy sauce

CRAB CAKES

1 lb/455 g lump crabmeat, preferably super lump, picked over for cartilage (see Note)

½ cup/45 g minced yellow onion

3 Tbsp minced red onion

1 Tbsp minced green onion, white and green parts

1 large egg plus 1 large egg yolk, lightly beaten

3 Tbsp plain panko (Japanese bread crumbs)

1½ Tbsp unbleached all-purpose flour

1 tsp Old Bay Seasoning

¾ tsp celery salt

¾ tsp kosher salt

½ tsp freshly ground black pepper

CRUST

½ cup/45 g sweetened coconut flakes

½ cup/45 g panko (Japanese bread crumbs)

½ tsp Old Bay Seasoning

2 Tbsp Clarified Butter (page 154) or vegetable oil

2 cups/400 g Island Slaw (page 209), for serving

1 To make the sauce: Whisk all the ingredients together in a medium bowl.

2 To make the cakes: Put the crabmeat, yellow onion, red onion, and green onion in a large bowl and mix gently. Add the egg and egg yolk, panko, flour, Old Bay, celery salt, kosher salt, and pepper and mix again, taking care not to break up the crabmeat too much—you want to see lumps of crab. Let the crab mixture stand for 5 minutes. Divide into 8 equal portions. Shape and press each portion into a thick cake about 3 in/7.5 cm wide.

3 To make the crust: Combine the coconut, panko, and Old Bay well in a wide, shallow bowl. One at a time, coat the crab cakes with the coconut mixture, patting to help it adhere, and transfer to a baking sheet.

4 Position a rack in the center of the oven and preheat the oven to 200°F/95°C. Line a second baking sheet with paper towels.

5 Heat the clarified butter in a large skillet over medium-high heat. Add half of the crab cakes to the skillet and reduce the heat to medium. Cook, turning once, until golden brown on both sides, adjusting the heat as needed so the crust browns steadily without burning while heating the crab cakes through, about 7 minutes total. Transfer to the paper towels and keep warm in the oven while cooking the remaining crab cakes. Wipe out the skillet between batches with paper towels.

6 Serve hot, with the sauce and slaw.

MAKES 4 SERVINGS

NOTE: Fresh crabmeat should be used when available. Otherwise, canned pasteurized crabmeat is fine; it's sold refrigerated at many supermarkets and wholesale clubs, graded according to the size of the cleaned meat. The most common grades (some brands have slightly different names) are super or jumbo lump (very large pieces in mostly distinct chunks), lump (large chunks with some broken meat), backfin (mostly smaller pieces of broken body meat), special (flakes of body meat), and claw (from the crab pincers). Always pick through the crabmeat to remove any bits of shell or cartilage.

This could very well be the ultimate seafood cocktail, served with a light-bodied sauce instead of the typical red glop. With lots of vegetables to balance the chunks of shrimp and crab, it can be served as a salad as well as a palate- and eye-pleasing appetizer. Toss the ingredients together right before serving, because marinating doesn't really improve this cocktail.

SEAFOOD-AVOCADO COCKTAIL

SHRIMP

1 lb/455 g extra-jumbo (16 to 20 count) shrimp

1 tsp celery salt

SAUCE

½ cup/120 ml Shrimp Stock (page 210)

⅓ cup/75 ml ketchup

¼ cup/60 ml tomato-clam juice, such as Clamato

1 tsp fresh lime juice

1 tsp green jalapeño sauce, such as Tabasco Green Pepper

½ tsp red pepper sauce, such as Tabasco

½ tsp Spike herbal seasoning

¼ tsp granulated onion

¼ tsp granulated garlic

1 bay leaf

¼ tsp freshly ground black pepper

1 English cucumber, cut into ½-in/12-mm dice

½ cup/50 g finely chopped yellow onion

2 Roma (plum) tomatoes, seeded and cut into ½-in/12-mm dice

2 tsp finely chopped fresh cilantro

1 ripe Hass avocado, peeled, pitted, and cut into ½-in/12-mm dice

8 oz/225 g lump crabmeat, picked over for cartilage

6 sprigs fresh cilantro, for serving

6 lime wedges, for serving

Tortilla chips, preferably strip style, for serving

1 To prepare the shrimp: Choose a large saucepan that will hold a collapsible metal steamer basket. Add enough water to barely reach the bottom of the steamer basket and bring to a boil over high heat.

2 Peel and devein the shrimp, leaving the tail segments on 6 shrimp; reserve the shells and remaining tails to make the shrimp stock. Season the shrimp with the celery salt. Spread them on the steamer basket and cover the saucepan tightly. Cook just until the shrimp turn opaque, 2½ to 3 minutes. Do not overcook. Remove the shrimp from the steamer and let cool. Do not rinse the shrimp, or the celery salt seasoning will wash off. Set aside the 6 shrimp with their tails for the garnish. Cut the shrimp into ½-in/12-mm dice. Cover and refrigerate the chopped and whole shrimp until chilled, at least 1 hour or up to 1 day.

3 To make the sauce: Bring all of the ingredients to a simmer in a medium saucepan over low heat. Pour into a medium bowl placed in a larger bowl of ice water and let stand, stirring occasionally, until chilled, about 30 minutes. Discard the bay leaf. (The sauce can be covered and refrigerated for up to 1 day.)

4 Combine the chopped shrimp, cucumber, onion, tomatoes, and cilantro in a large bowl and mix well. Add the sauce. Gently mix in the avocado.

5 Divide the shrimp mixture and its liquid among 6 glass serving dishes. Top each with an equal amount of the crab. Finish each with a whole shrimp with its tail sticking up, a cilantro sprig, and a lime wedge. Serve chilled, with tortilla chips.

MAKES 6 SERVINGS

Conch (pronounced "conk") is an important shellfish crop in Florida. This mollusk, which is known by its Italian name scungilli, has chewy, sea-flavored meat protected by a beautiful shell. The tough meat is usually sold shelled and is often ground before using, as in these crispy fritters. You can substitute 12 oz/340 g crab or chopped clam meat for the conch in this recipe. The sweet-and-sour red pepper dip is delicious. If you wish, serve Island Slaw (page 209) on the side.

CONCH FRITTERS WITH RED PEPPER JAM

JAM

1 tsp olive oil

2 red bell peppers, cored, seeded, and chopped into ½-in/12-mm pieces

⅔ cup/85 g chopped yellow onion

1 cup/240 ml cider vinegar

¾ cup/150 g sugar

½ tsp minced jalapeño chile

¼ cup/60 ml sour cream

FRITTERS

1 lb/455 g conch (scungilli), trimmed of dark parts, coarsely chopped (see Note)

½ cup/120 ml buttermilk

1 large egg, beaten

1 cup/70 g panko (Japanese bread crumbs)

¼ cup/35 g all-purpose flour

3 Tbsp minced yellow onion

3 Tbsp minced green bell pepper

3 Tbsp minced celery

2 garlic cloves, minced

½ tsp minced jalapeño chile

½ tsp cayenne pepper

½ tsp Old Bay Seasoning

1 tsp kosher salt

Vegetable oil, for deep-frying

1 To make the jam: Heat the oil in a skillet over medium heat. Add the bell peppers and onion and cook, stirring occasionally, until the onion is translucent, about 3 minutes. Add the vinegar, sugar, and jalapeño and bring to a simmer, stirring to dissolve the sugar. Reduce the heat to medium-low and cook at brisk simmer until the liquid is reduced by about half, about 30 minutes. Let cool completely. Purée the jam in a food processor or blender. Transfer to a bowl and whisk in the sour cream. (The jam can be covered and refrigerated for up to 4 days.)

2 To make the fritters: Pulse the conch in a food processor until it is very finely chopped but not puréed; do not overprocess. You should have about 1½ cups/340 g. Transfer the conch to a medium bowl, add the buttermilk, and mix well. Cover and refrigerate for 15 to 30 minutes. (This helps tenderize the conch.)

3 Stir the egg into the conch mixture. Add the panko, flour, onion, bell pepper, celery, garlic, jalapeño, cayenne, Old Bay, and salt and mix well. Refrigerate the batter for at least 15 minutes or up to 4 hours.

4 Preheat the oven to 200°F/95°C. Pour 2 in/5 cm oil into a large, heavy saucepan and heat over high heat to 325°F/165°C. Place a wire rack in a rimmed baking sheet. In batches, without crowding, drop 2 Tbsp of the batter (a 1-oz/30-ml spring-loaded portion scoop works best) for each fritter into the oil and deep-fry until crisp and golden brown, about 2½ minutes. Using a wire spider or slotted spoon, transfer the fritters to the wire rack and keep warm in the oven while deep-frying the remaining fritters.

5 Serve the fritters hot, with small bowls of the jam as a dip.

MAKES ABOUT 20 FRITTERS;
4 TO 6 SERVINGS

NOTE: Look for frozen or thawed conch at well-stocked fish markets and Asian grocers. Canned scungilli is a good product, available year-round at Italian delicatessens and specialty foods stores. LaMonica is a reliable brand. Just drain, rinse, and pat the canned scungilli dry before using.

Unlike so many other dishes whose inventors are lost in the mists of time, nachos are acknowledged to have been created by Ignacio (nicknamed Nacho) Anaya. The original dish consisted of fried tortilla wedges topped with melted cheese and jalapeños. Over the years, this simple recipe has been embellished with additional ingredients to create "super nachos" loaded with grilled steak, beans, and the classic Tex-Mex mild cheese sauce.

SUPER NACHOS WITH SKIRT STEAK, BLACK BEANS, AND QUESO SAUCE

STEAK

1 tsp chili powder

1 tsp kosher salt

¼ tsp granulated garlic

¼ tsp granulated onion

¼ tsp freshly ground black pepper

1 lb/455 g skirt steak

Olive oil, for brushing

CHEESE SAUCE

2 Tbsp unsalted butter

2 Tbsp all-purpose flour

1 cup/240 ml whole milk, heated

2 cups/225 g shredded mild Cheddar cheese

BEANS

1 Tbsp olive oil

1 small yellow onion, chopped

1 garlic clove, minced

One 15-oz/430-g can black beans, undrained

One 11-oz/310-g bag tortilla chips

½ cup/65 g pickled jalapeño slices, drained

2 ripe Roma (plum) tomatoes, seeded and cut into ¼-in/8-mm dice

2 green onions, white and green parts, finely chopped

3 Tbsp chopped fresh cilantro, for garnish

½ cup/120 ml sour cream, for serving

1 To prepare the steak: Mix the dry ingredients together in a small bowl. Brush the steak all over with the oil and season with the chili powder mixture. Let stand at room temperature for 15 to 30 minutes.

2 To make the sauce: Melt the butter in a medium saucepan over medium-low heat. Sprinkle in the flour and whisk until smooth. Let the roux bubble without browning for 1 minute. Whisk in the milk and bring to a simmer. Reduce the heat to low and simmer, whisking occasionally, until the sauce thickens and no raw flour taste remains, about 5 minutes. Gradually add the cheese, letting the first batch melt before adding another. Set aside and cover to keep warm. (The sauce can be cooled, covered, and refrigerated for up to 1 day. Reheat in a saucepan over low heat.)

3 To prepare the beans: Heat the oil in a medium saucepan over medium heat. Add the onion and garlic and cook, stirring occasionally, until softened, about 3 minutes. Add the beans with their liquid and bring to a simmer. Reduce the heat to low and simmer until the beans are heated through, about 5 minutes. Drain the beans well. Return to the saucepan; set aside and cover to keep warm.

4 Prepare an outdoor grill for two-zone cooking with high heat (see page 19). (Or position a broiler rack about 6 in/15 cm from the source of heat and preheat on high.)

5 Brush the grill grate clean. Place the steak on the grill over the hot area and cook, with the lid closed as much as possible, turning once, until well browned, 6 to 7 minutes for medium-rare. (Or broil the steak for 6 to 7 minutes.) Transfer to a carving board and let the steak stand for 3 to 5 minutes. (If cooking indoors, preheat the oven to 400°F/200°C. If your broiler is in the oven, open the oven door for 30 seconds or so to reduce the heat.)

6 Heap the tortilla chips in a very large cast-iron skillet or heatproof shallow earthenware casserole. Place the skillet on the grill over the cooler area and cook, with the lid closed, until the chips are heated, about 5 minutes. Remove the skillet from the grill. (Or spread the tortillas in a large rimmed baking sheet and bake until they are heated, about 5 minutes. Transfer the chips to a large serving platter.)

7 Cut the steak across the grain into ½-in/12-mm slices and coarsely chop into small bite-size pieces. Scatter the chopped steak, pickled jalapeño slices, beans, tomatoes, and green onions over the tortillas and mix with your hands to combine the ingredients. Drizzle with about one-third of the sauce. Sprinkle with the cilantro. Serve immediately, with the remaining cheese sauce and the sour cream passed on the side.

MAKES 6 TO 8 SERVINGS

Two iconic Southern ingredients, bacon and bourbon, are happily wed with caramelized onions to make a thick spread that has many uses beyond this appetizer. Because the flavor of bacon is so important here, use the best bacon you can get your hands on, preferably an artisanal product. If you have leftovers, try the jam slathered on your breakfast biscuits or as a sweet and salty condiment for a chicken sandwich.

BACON AND BOURBON JAM CROSTINI WITH GOAT CHEESE

JAM

1 lb/455 g bacon, cut vertically into strips about ¼-in/6-mm wide

⅔ cup/85 g coarsely chopped shallots

⅓ cup /60 g finely chopped yellow onions

½ cup/120 ml bourbon

½ cup/120 ml honey

¼ cup/50 g packed light brown sugar

1 tsp red pepper flakes

16 baguette slices, cut on a diagonal into ¼-in/6-mm slices

½ cup/55 g coarsely crumbled goat cheese

1 To make the jam: Cook the bacon in a large skillet over medium heat just until it begins to render its fat, about 5 minutes. Stir in the shallots and onions. Cook at a steady simmer, stirring occasionally and adjusting the heat as needed, until the onions are tender and browned but the bacon is not crispy, about 15 minutes more. Remove from the heat. Drain the excess fat from the skillet.

2 Increase the heat to high and add the whiskey. Using a long match, carefully ignite the whiskey and let the flames burn down. (If the flames do not extinguish on their own after 30 seconds, tightly cover the skillet.) Stir in the honey and brown sugar. Simmer until the liquid is syrupy but the jam is not thick, about 8 minutes. Stir in the red pepper flakes. Remove from the heat and let cool to lukewarm, about 30 minutes.

3 In batches, pulse the mixture until it has a coarse, jam-like texture. Transfer to a bowl. (The jam can be covered and refrigerated for up to 5 days.)

4 To serve, position the broiler rack about 6 in/15 cm from the heat source and preheat the broiler on high. Lightly toast the baguette slices on both sides in the broiler, about 1 minute.

5 Spread the baguette slices with equal amounts of the bacon jam and top with the crumbled cheese. (Don't feel like you have to use all of the jam.) Return to the broiler and broil just until the jam is warmed, 15 to 30 seconds. Serve immediately.

MAKES 8 SERVINGS

At its most basic, guacamole is avocado mashed up with a few ingredients. But, for a dip that will have your guests asking for the recipe, make this version with a depth of flavor provided by a pepper salsa that is also served on the side as a bonus dip. Be sure to use ripe Hass avocados for the best flavor.

SPIKED GUACAMOLE WITH FIRE-ROASTED PEPPER SALSA

FIRE-ROASTED PEPPER SALSA

½ red bell pepper (cut lengthwise), cored, seeded, and flattened

½ green bell pepper (cut lengthwise), cored, seeded, and flattened

½ small yellow onion

1 small garlic clove, coarsely chopped

1 Tbsp chopped fresh cilantro

2 tsp green pepper sauce, such as Tabasco Hot Green Pepper Sauce, as needed

1 tsp sweet paprika

1 tsp fresh lime juice

Kosher salt

GUACAMOLE

2 ripe avocados, peeled, pitted, and cut into ¼-in/6-mm dice

1 ripe Roma (plum) tomato, seeded, and cut into ¼-in/6-mm dice

1 Tbsp Fire-Roasted Pepper Salsa (see above)

1 Tbsp fresh lime juice

1 tsp vegetable-herb seasoning, preferably Spike, as needed

1 tsp green jalapeño sauce

¼ tsp granulated onion

¼ tsp freshly ground white pepper

Kosher salt

Tortilla chips, preferably strips, for serving

1 **To make the salsa:** Position the broiler rack about 6 in/15 cm from the heat source and preheat the broiler on high.

2 Place the red and green peppers, skin side up, and the half onion on the broiler rack. Broil, occasionally turning the onion only, until the pepper skins are blackened and blistered and the onion exterior is charred and beginning to soften, about 6 minutes for the onion and 8 minutes for the peppers. Transfer the vegetables to a bowl as they are done, cover, and let stand for 10 minutes. Peel the peppers.

3 Coarsely chop the vegetables. Purée the peppers, onion, garlic, cilantro, green pepper sauce, paprika, and lime juice in a food processor. Season to taste with salt and additional green pepper sauce. (The salsa can be covered and refrigerated for up to 5 days.)

4 **To make the guacamole:** Mash all of the ingredients together with a large fork in a medium bowl until combined but still lumpy, seasoning to taste with the salt. (The guacamole can be covered with plastic wrap pressed directly onto the guacamole surface and refrigerated for up to 8 hours.)

5 Transfer the guacamole and the salsa to individual serving bowls. Sprinkle the guacamole with additional vegetable-herb seasoning, if desired. Serve with the tortilla chips.

MAKES 4 TO 6 SERVINGS

Texas caviar has nothing to do with fish eggs; it's just a fancy name for good ol' marinated black-eyed peas. This chunky mix was popularized at Neiman Marcus in Dallas in the 1950s and has migrated throughout the Lone Star State. This is a salad that thinks it's a salsa, and it's never better than when served with a longneck bottle of beer and a basket of tortilla chips.

TEXAS CAVIAR

2 ears fresh corn

1 red bell pepper

2 Tbsp cider vinegar

½ tsp sugar

1 garlic clove, crushed through a press

Kosher salt and freshly ground black pepper

2 Tbsp extra-virgin olive oil

One 15-oz/430-g can black-eyed peas, drained and rinsed

2 ripe Roma (plum) tomatoes, seeded and cut into ½-in/12-mm dice

⅓ cup/40 g finely chopped red onion

1 Tbsp minced seeded jalapeño chile

2 Tbsp chopped fresh cilantro

Tortilla chips, for serving

Lime wedges, for serving

1 Position the broiler rack about 8 in/20 cm from the heat source and preheat the broiler.

2 Place the corn and red pepper on the broiler rack and broil, turning the corn occasionally, until the corn kernels are toasted brown and the pepper skin is blackened and blistered, about 10 minutes. (Or grill in an outside grill over direct heat.) Remove the corn from the broiler if it is done before the pepper. Let stand for 10 minutes. Cut the corn kernels from the corn. Discard the skin, seeds, and core from the bell pepper and cut the pepper into ½-in/12-mm dice.

3 Whisk the vinegar, sugar, garlic, ½ tsp kosher salt, and ¼ tsp black pepper together in a medium bowl. Gradually whisk in the oil. Add the corn, red bell pepper, black-eyed peas, tomatoes, red onion, and jalapeño and mix well. Cover and refrigerate for at least 4 hours or up to 3 days. Just before serving, season with salt and pepper to taste and sprinkle with the cilantro. Serve the caviar with tortilla chips and lime wedges.

MAKES 8 SERVINGS

Tips for Making and Serving Cocktails

Some of the most famous cocktails in the history of mixed drinks are iconic libations from the Gulf Coast cultures—among them, the Mojito and Daiquiri from Cuba and the Sazerac from New Orleans, as well as the Mexican Margarita. We've scattered some of our most popular tipples throughout the book. Here are some tips for becoming the best mixologist in your circle of friends.

EQUIPMENT CHECKLIST

You will need a few bartending tools to make top-notch cocktails:

BOSTON COCKTAIL SHAKER: Preferred by professional bartenders, this two-part shaker has a glass bottom and a metal top of about the same size. Using it is fairly self-explanatory: Fill the bottom half with ice, add the cocktail ingredients, cover tightly with the metal top, and shake briskly a few times (most bartenders say for 10 seconds) to mix the ingredients. (Of course, some drinks should be stirred, not shaken—where have you heard that before? Shaking creates foam, and who wants a foamy martini?)

Mixing the drink in a Boston shaker does more than just combine the ingredients. During shaking (or stirring), the ice melts slightly, just enough to help unify and blend the disparate flavors. It does not water the drink down and actually makes the cocktail taste better. Note that the drink is rarely poured, ice and all, into a glass but, instead, is strained over fresh ice to maintain the chill.

Boston shakers are used in conjunction with a cocktail strainer to get the drink out of the glass. A shaker with a strainer built into the lid is called a cobbler shaker, and it works well, too. (Professional bartenders like the Boston model because it can be washed quickly and easily at a busy bar, but you won't have that problem at home, so use a cobbler shaker, if you so please.)

COCKTAIL STRAINER: A strainer is placed over the top of a shaker to hold back the ice for pouring. There are two kinds, and they work equally well. The Hawthorne strainer has a spring running around its perimeter so it fits snugly in the shaker. The julep strainer is simply a perforated metal lid, slightly curved to fit into the shaker. In either case, the strainer is held in place at the top of the shaker with your first two fingers as you wrap the rest of your hand around the shaker to hold it for pouring.

COCKTAIL SPOON: A long-handled spoon that can reach all the way into the bottom of a shaker to efficiently stir a drink. An iced tea spoon will work.

MUDDLER: You can't make a Mojito without a good muddler, which is a pestle used to mash up mint and other ingredients in the shaker so they can release their juices into the drink. You'll find metal, plastic, and wooden models.

JIGGER: In America, a jigger is a measurement of 1½ fl oz/45 ml, but it is also the name of a small measuring glass with the same volume. Cocktail ingredients need to be measured, just like any other ingredient. Jiggers come in a variety of sizes and designs and can be unmarked, so be sure that you know the exact volume of the one on your bar.

If you are making your cocktails in a country that uses another measuring system, such as British or metric, use your locality's jigger, which may be slightly larger than the U.S. one. Cocktails are also mixed according to increments, so for conversion purposes, it is easy to go by "parts" instead of ounces. For example, 1 fl oz/30 ml liquor with ½ fl oz/15 ml fruit juice can be translated as 1 part and ½ part. This way, you won't have to measure 7.5 ml to equal ¼ fl oz.

THE HOUSE COCKTAIL

In a perfect world, you would be able to serve any drink under the sun for your guests, from aquavit to a Zombie. But since you're probably not a mixologist, that might not be possible. It's your party, though, so you could designate a single drink as the house cocktail and offer an alternative drink or two along the lines of wine or beer (and of course, something nonalcoholic).

Many of the following cocktails lend themselves to being mixed and served in pitchers. At our restaurants, we also serve communal cocktails in small punch bowls for six to eight servings. Both solutions save the designated bartender a lot of effort during the course of an event. If making cocktails ahead, mix them up to store in the pitcher or punch bowl, but do not add ice until just before serving to avoid diluting the drinks.

KEEP IT FRESH

Many cocktails get their lip-smacking flavor from the proper balance of liquor with a sweet-and-sour component, and fresh fruit juices are an important part of the equation. Too many bars lean on instant sour mixes, but you can do better. We make our own sour mix from scratch with sweetened fresh juices (page 55). Fresh juices and other ingredients are also used to make tasty syrups for flavoring cocktails. These are usually based on simple syrup, which is no more than equal parts superfine sugar and water shaken together to dissolve the sugar.

Be sure you have an efficient juicer. A wooden reamer is good, but if you are juicing a lot of fruit, consider a metal lever-type squeezer or even an inexpensive electric model.

Named for one of writer Ernest Hemingway's favorite bars, this kissin' cousin of the Daiquiri deserves to be better known. Maraschino liqueur sets this cocktail apart. Imported from Italy, it is made from the same Marasca cherries as the best cocktail cherries (not the neon red American ones). Because it is an ingredient in many classic cocktails, maraschino is now considered an essential for a well-stocked bar.

HEMINGWAY LA FLORIDITA

SIMPLE SYRUP

½ cup/100 g superfine sugar

COCKTAIL

1½ fl oz/45 ml white rum, preferably Brugal

¾ fl oz/22.5 ml maraschino liqueur, preferably Luxardo

¾ fl oz/22.5 ml fresh lime juice

¾ fl oz/22.5 ml Simple Syrup, above

½ fl oz/15 ml fresh grapefruit juice

GARNISH: Grapefruit zest and Marasca cherry on a cocktail skewer

1 **To make the syrup:** Shake the sugar and ½ cup/120 ml water together in a covered jar until the sugar is dissolved. (Makes ½ cup/120 ml. The syrup can be refrigerated for up to 1 month.)

2 Fill a Martini glass with ice cubes and set aside to chill. Add the cocktail ingredients to an ice-filled cocktail shaker. Shake well.

3 Empty the ice from the glass. Strain the cocktail into the glass. Garnish with the skewer and serve.

MAKES 1 DRINK

As the art of mixology evolves, a seemingly endless parade of ingredients crop up and demand the home bartender's attention. This citrusy cocktail has a unique quality that comes from three spirits that may be new to you but are worth stocking: a wheat-based vodka, a vanilla-spice cordial, and a Key lime liqueur. Mixed together, they create a sweeter drink that is not your grandfather's martini.

KEY LIME MARTINI

Lime wedge, for the glass

3 Tbsp finely crushed graham crackers, for the glass

2 fl oz/60 ml Key lime cream liqueur, such as Ke Ke

1½ fl oz/45 ml wheat-based vodka, such as Van Gogh Blue

½ fl oz/15 ml vanilla-spice liqueur, such as Licor 43

½ fl oz/15 ml fresh lime juice

1 Fill a Martini glass with ice cubes and set aside to chill well. Empty the ice from the glass. Run the lime wedge around the rim of the glass, then discard the lime wedge. Holding the glass upside down, sprinkle the crumbs around the outside edge of the glass only. Discard the remaining crumbs.

2 Add the Key lime liqueur, vodka, vanilla liqueur, and lime juice to an ice-filled cocktail shaker. Stir well.

3 Strain the cocktail into the prepared glass and serve.

MAKES 1 DRINK

Pickling summer's bounty is a time-honored tradition in the South. Admittedly, okra can be an acquired taste, but pickled okra is an entirely different matter, as the vinegar tends to dissipate the vegetable's sticky texture, making it more agreeable to the palate. This is a super-easy recipe, meant for storing in the fridge so you don't have to bother with sterilizing the jar or hot-packing the pickles.

SPICY PICKLED OKRA

2 cups/480 ml cider vinegar

2 Tbsp sugar

2 teaspoons fine sea salt

2 garlic cloves, crushed under a knife and peeled

1 teaspoon yellow mustard seeds

¼ tsp red pepper flakes

12 oz/340 g okra (about 30)

SPECIAL EQUIPMENT: 1-qt/960-ml canning jar

1 Bring the vinegar, 1 cup/240 ml water, the sugar, salt, garlic, mustard seeds, and red pepper flakes to a boil in a medium nonreactive saucepan over high heat, stirring often to dissolve the sugar and salt.

2 Tightly pack the okra side by side into the jar, using the longest ones first, and laying the smaller ones on top. Pour enough hot vinegar brine into the jar to cover the okra, making sure to add all of the mixed spices and garlic. Discard any remaining brine. Close the jar with its lid and ring.

3 Let stand until the pickles reach room temperature, about 2 hours. Cover and refrigerate overnight. (The pickles can be refrigerated for up to 1 month.)

MAKES 1 QT/960 ML

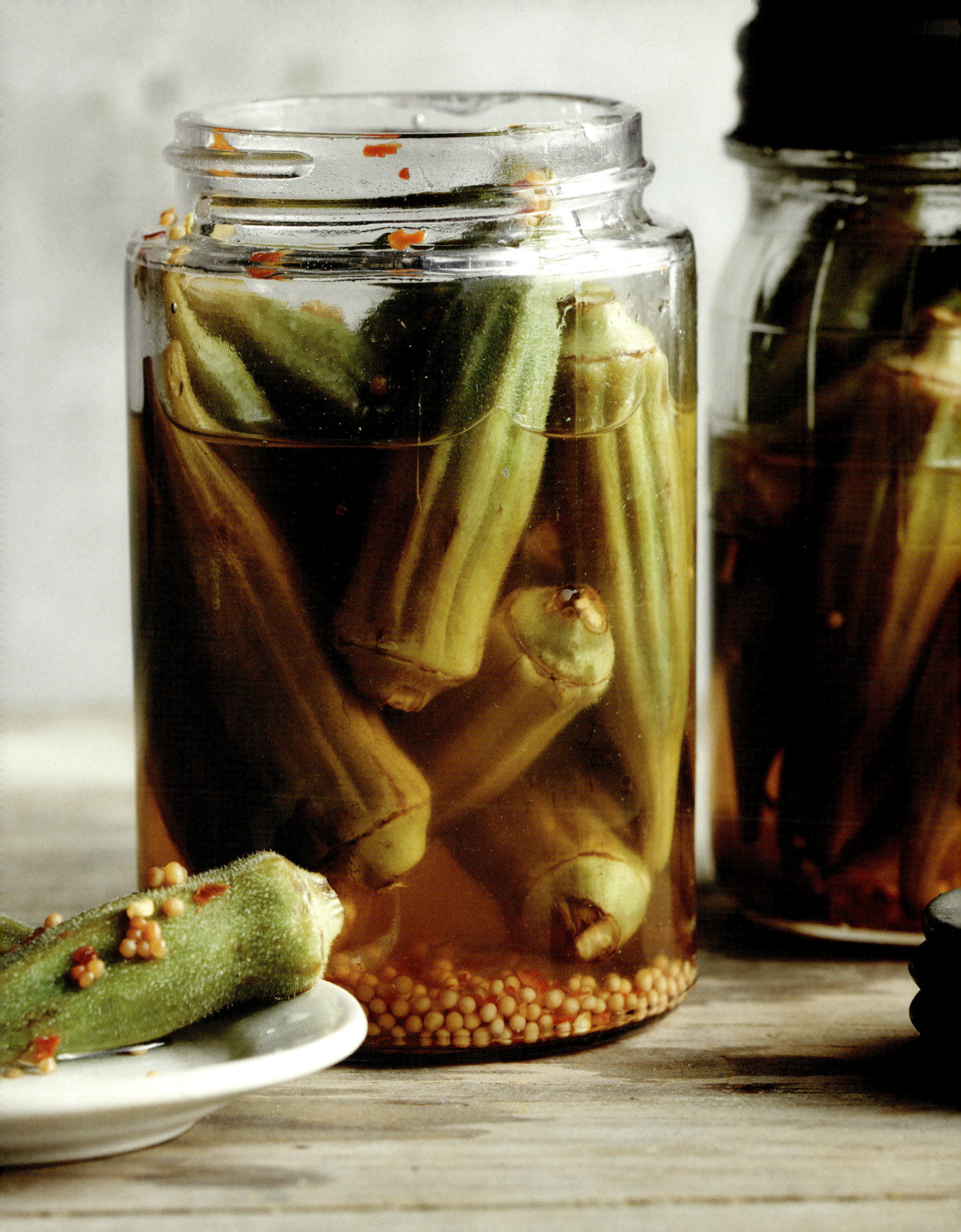

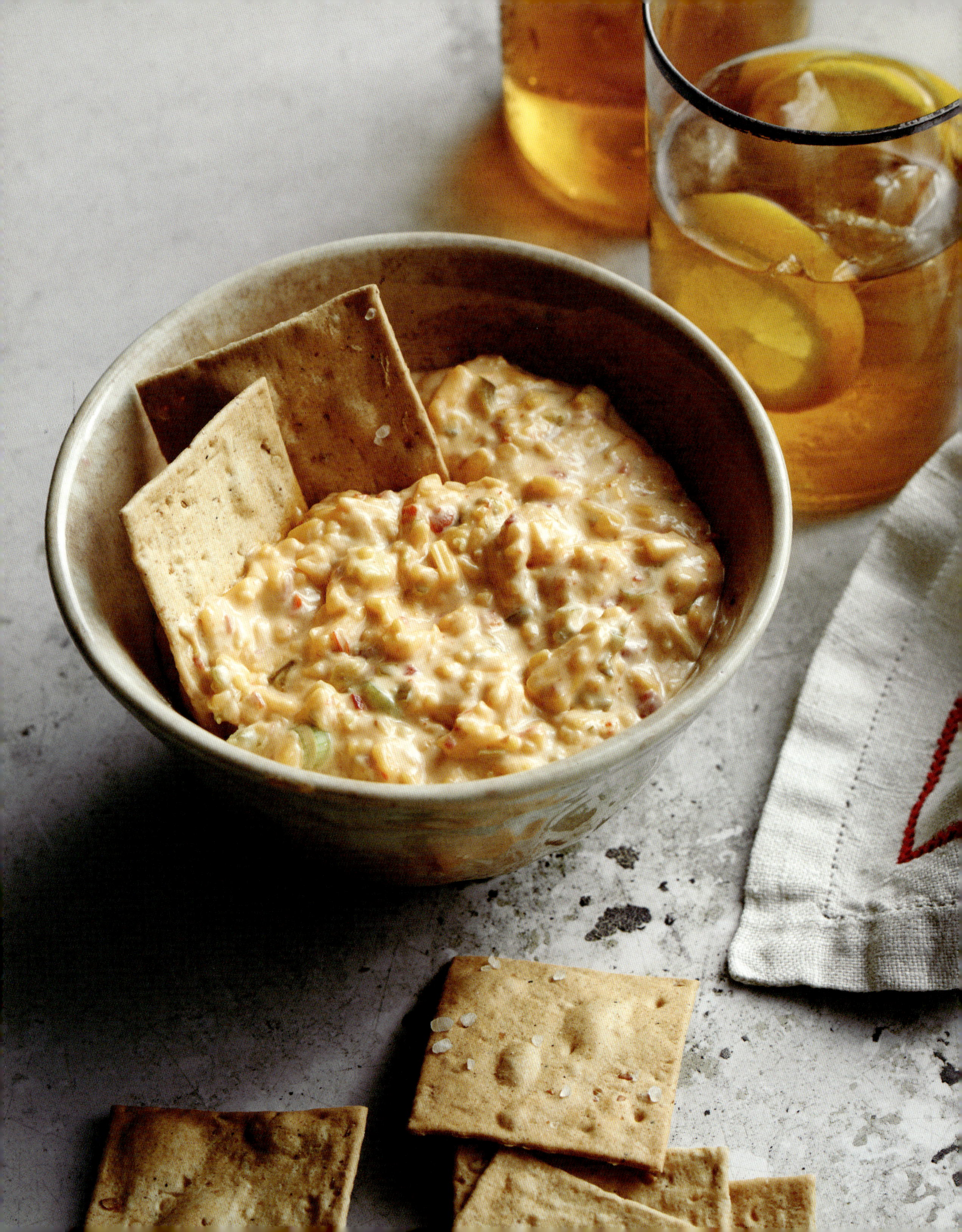

The sweet peppers used to make this dish are often called pimientos, but the classic Southern spread is known as "pimento" cheese (although we call it Zesty Pub Cheese at our restaurants). This version for the twenty-first century starts with Cheddar, mayonnaise, and jarred pimientos, then adds heat with two kinds of chiles. If you want pimento cheese the way that Grandma made it, leave out the chiles and lime juice.

ZESTY PIMENTO CHEESE (AKA ZESTY PUB CHEESE)

2 cups/225 g shredded sharp Cheddar cheese

½ cup/120 ml mayonnaise

1 tsp minced canned chipotle in adobo

1 tsp fresh lime juice

¼ tsp Worcestershire sauce

2 Tbsp finely chopped pickled jalapeño slices (for nachos), plus ½ tsp brine

2 Tbsp drained and finely chopped pimiento

1 Tbsp minced sliced green onion, white part only

Buttery snack crackers, such as Ritz, flatbread, or tortilla chips, for serving

1 Mix the cheese, mayonnaise, chipotle, lime juice, and Worcestershire sauce together in the bowl of a heavy-duty stand mixer fitted with the paddle attachment on low speed until the cheese is broken up and the mixture is well combined.

2 Add the jalapeños and their brine, the pimientos, and green onion and mix well, scraping down the sides of the bowl as needed. Transfer to a serving bowl, cover, and refrigerate to blend the flavors for at least 1 hour or up to 5 days.

3 Remove from the refrigerator and let stand for 30 minutes. Serve with crackers or tortilla chips.

MAKES 8 SERVINGS

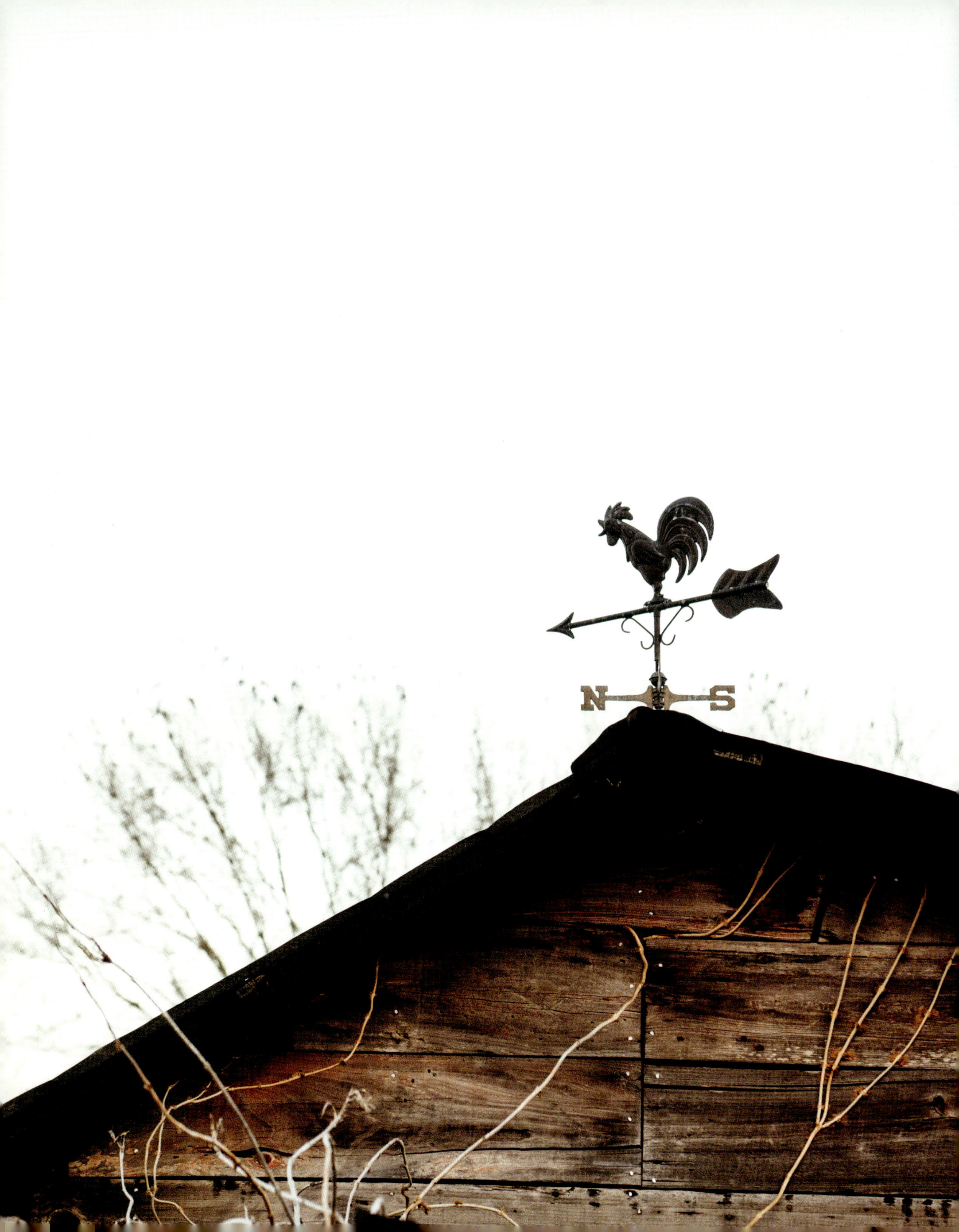
N
S

This savory pie is more versatile than actress Meryl Streep. Many Southern cooks serve it in thin slices before dinner with cocktails, but it can also be a lunch main course, a meatless supper, or a side dish to a simple grilled entrée. To give it a European spin, use basil in place of dill, Gruyère or mozzarella in place of Cheddar, and add a clove of chopped garlic. Just don't call it quiche!

SAVORY TOMATO AND CHEESE PIE

CRUST

Pastry Dough (page 196)

1 Tbsp Dijon mustard

FILLING

2 to 3 large, firm-ripe tomatoes, cored, about 1½ lb/680 g

½ tsp kosher salt

1 cup/249 ml mayonnaise

1 cup/225 g shredded sharp Cheddar cheese

2 green onions, white and green parts, finely chopped

2 tsp finely chopped fresh dill, or 1 tsp dried dill

¼ tsp red pepper sauce, such as Tabasco

⅛ tsp freshly ground black pepper

1 Position a rack in the bottom third of the oven and preheat the oven to 375°F/190°C. Heat a rimmed baking sheet in the oven.

2 Unwrap the dough. On a lightly floured work surface, roll the dough into a round about 13 in/33 cm in diameter and ⅛ in/3 mm thick. You should see flattened flakes of fat in the dough. Fit the dough into a 9-in/23-cm pie pan, preferably Pyrex. Trim the dough to a ½-in/12-mm overhang. Fold the edge of the dough under so it is flush with the edge of the pan and flute the edges. Prick the dough all over with a fork. Freeze or refrigerate the pie crust for 10 to 15 minutes.

3 Line the dough with a sheet of aluminum foil. Fill the foil with pie weights or dried beans. Place the pan on the hot baking sheet and bake until the dough looks set and is beginning to brown, about 15 minutes. Remove the foil and weights. Continue baking, pricking the dough with a fork if it bubbles up, until crisp and golden brown, 10 to 15 minutes more. Spread the mustard on the crust bottom with the back of a spoon. Return to the oven and bake until the mustard looks dry, about 5 minutes. Remove from the oven.

4 **Meanwhile, make the filling:** Using a serrated knife, cut the tomatoes crosswise into ½-in/12-mm slices. Poke out the seeds with your finger. In a colander, sprinkle the tomato slices with the salt and let drain in the sink for about 30 minutes. Do not rinse the tomatoes. Pat the tomatoes with paper towels. Transfer to fresh paper towels, cover with another layer of towels, and let them drain for a few minutes more. Coarsely chop the tomatoes into ¾-in/2-cm pieces.

5 Whisk the mayonnaise, Cheddar, green onions, dill, hot sauce, and black pepper together in a medium bowl. Layer the tomatoes in the pie shell. Spread the mayonnaise mixture on top. Bake until the top is golden brown, about 35 minutes. Let cool on a wire rack for at least 15 minutes. Serve warm or cooled to room temperature.

MAKES 6 TO 10 SERVINGS, DEPENDING ON USE

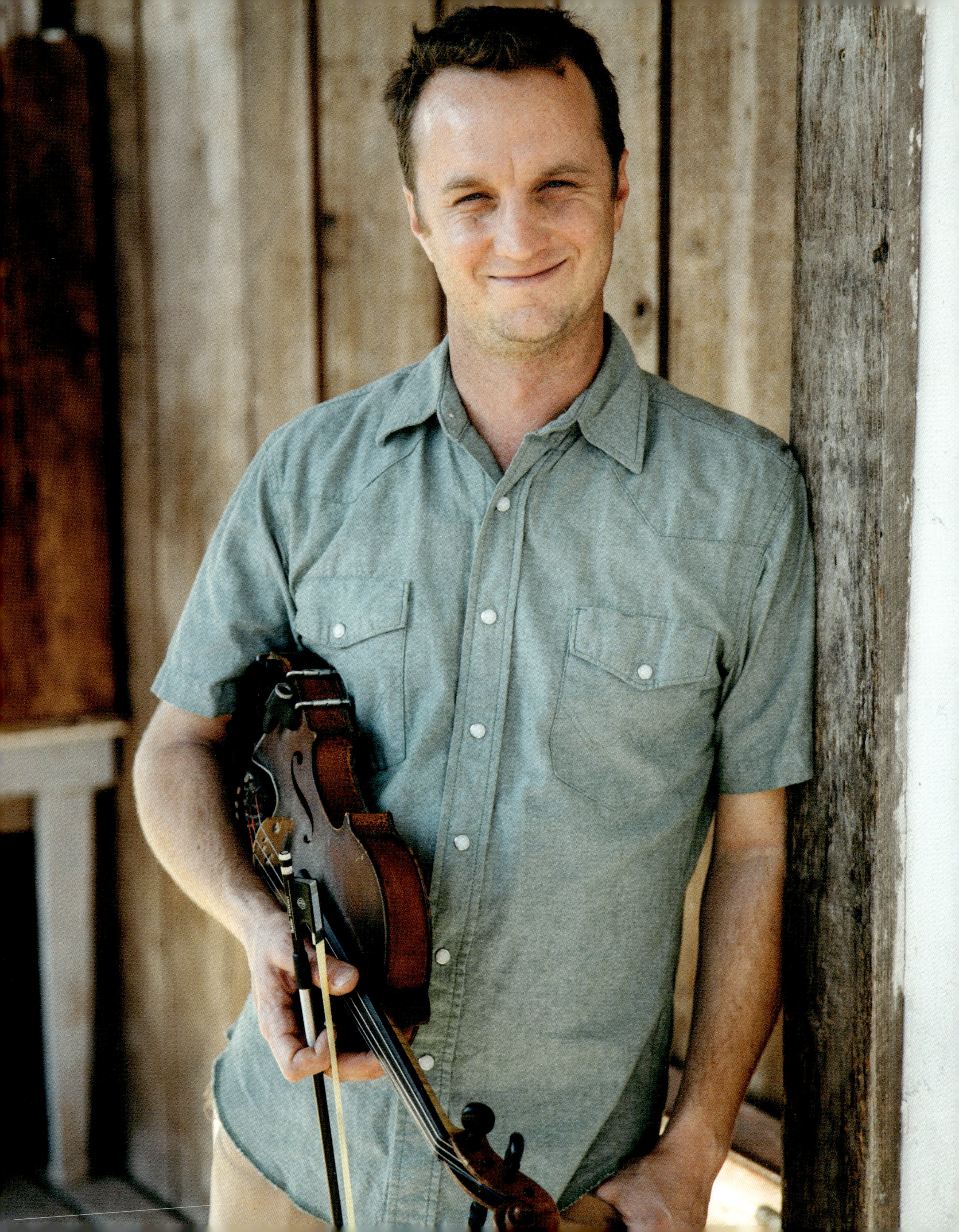

LOUIS MICHOT, SEED COLLECTOR

Louis Michot is a Cajun Renaissance man for the twenty-first century. His daytime (or nighttime) job is performing as the fiddler and vocalist with the Lost Bayou Ramblers, which includes his brother Andre on guitar and accordion. He is also involved with Bayou Teche Brewery, which creates beers that complement the famously spicy food of South Louisiana. But it was his long-time passion for sustainable agriculture that led Louis to form the Cultural Research Institute of Arcadia. "There is lots of research about Cajun music, language, architecture, and cooking," he says, "but it's just as important to know about the actual plants that fed the people."

The project grew from a chance sighting of unusual produce at a roadside stand. Soon, Louis was driving around the bayous talking with elders about forgotten edible and medicinal plants and collecting seeds. Some of these included *mamou* and *monglei*, both of which are used to relieve symptoms of the common cold. Another rare find is *casse-banane de Brésil*, a type of gourd cucumber that can be candied or used to make jam and grows on the region's oak trees. CRIA has since collected over fifty different kinds of seeds from local elders, recording their unique stories during the process.

The hurricanes and oil spills in recent times have underscored the fragility of the rural lifestyles of the Gulf Coast. As these disasters destroy farms, often bringing in saltwater that renders the land useless, the farmers have to move farther inland to make a living. About half of the population of Southern Louisiana has already had to move. "These people are homegrown experts in sustainable agriculture and have a lot to teach us about local knowledge and traditions," Louis points out. "If we don't save their stories now, they could be lost forever." And he wants to be sure that does not happen.

SALADS AND SOUPS

When warm weather hits the coast, a light meal is in order, and that's when our main-course salads truly shine. Also on the menu are simple first-course and side-dish salads as well as a choice of hot soups for when the sea winds blow and the temperature drops.

43
CHOPPED CHICKEN TACO SALAD WITH CHIPOTLE RANCH DRESSING

44
GRILLED CHICKEN AND MANGO SALAD

47
MUFFALETTA SALAD WITH OLIVE VINAIGRETTE

48
HORIATIKI GREEK SALAD WITH MARINATED GRILLED SHRIMP

50
BABY SPINACH WITH LIME-MUSTARD VINAIGRETTE AND SWEET AND SPICY PECANS

51
FRESH AMBROSIA WITH SOUR CREAM DRESSING

52
COLESLAW WITH POPPY SEED DRESSING

56
CHURCH SUPPER POTATO SALAD

57
SHRIMP AND SAUSAGE GUMBO WITH SLOW ROUX

58
TORTOLA TORTILLA SOUP

61
CRAB BISQUE

63
CUBAN BLACK BEAN SOUP WITH CHORIZO SOFRITO

A chopped salad, loaded with bits of tasty ingredients and tossed with a zesty dressing, is one of the world's great lunches. This one, with a zippy ranch dressing, is Tex-Mex style, but banish any thoughts of taco shells or ground meat. It is fresh, refreshing, and altogether worthy of serving to pals for a casual afternoon meal or a light supper.

CHOPPED CHICKEN TACO SALAD WITH CHIPOTLE RANCH DRESSING

DRESSING

¾ cup/180 ml buttermilk

2 green onions, chopped

3 Tbsp fresh lime juice

1 canned chipotle en adobo, minced

1 tsp adobo from canned chipotle

1 garlic clove, minced

1 cup/240 ml mayonnaise

Kosher salt and freshly ground black pepper

CHICKEN

3 skinless, boneless chicken breast halves, each about 6 oz/170 g

2 tsp chili powder

1 tsp kosher salt

¼ tsp granulated garlic

¼ tsp granulated onion

¼ tsp freshly ground black pepper

Extra-virgin olive oil

1 head iceberg lettuce, coarsely chopped

2 cups/340 g cherry or grape tomatoes, halved lengthwise

2 ripe Hass avocados, peeled, pitted, and cut into ½-in/12-mm cubes

One 15-oz/430 g can black beans, drained

2 green onions, thinly sliced

½ cup/30 g coarsely crushed tortilla chips

2 Tbsp coarsely chopped fresh cilantro

Lime wedges, for serving

1 To make the dressing: Process the buttermilk, green onions, lime juice, chipotle, adobo, and garlic in a blender or food processor until minced. Add the mayonnaise and process until combined. Season to taste with salt and pepper. Transfer to a bowl, cover, and refrigerate to blend the flavors for at least 1 hour or up to 1 day.

2 To prepare the chicken: One at a time, place a chicken breast half between two plastic bags. Using the flat side of a meat pounder or a rolling pin, pound the chicken until about ½ in/12 mm thick. Mix the chili powder, salt, granulated garlic, granulated onion, and black pepper together in a small bowl. Lightly coat the chicken with the oil and sprinkle with the chili powder mixture. Let stand at room temperature for 15 to 30 minutes.

3 Prepare an outdoor grill for direct cooking over medium heat (see page 19).

4 Brush the grill grate clean. Grill the chicken, with the lid closed as much as possible, until the undersides are seared with grill marks, about 4 minutes. Flip the chicken and continue cooking until the chicken feels firm when pressed and shows no sign of pink when pierced in the thickest part with the tip of a small, sharp knife, 4 to 6 minutes more. (The chicken can also be cooked in a nonstick skillet over medium-high heat.) Transfer the chicken to a carving board and let cool for about 15 minutes.

5 Using a large knife, chop the chicken into bite-size pieces. Toss the lettuce, tomatoes, avocados, beans, and green onions in a large bowl. Add about half of the dressing and toss again. Divide the salad among 4 shallow soup bowls. Top the salads with equal amounts of the chicken and sprinkle the tortilla chips and cilantro over the salads. Serve immediately, with lime wedges, and with the remaining dressing passed on the side.

MAKES 4 SERVINGS

This enticing salad mixes tropical and Mediterranean flavors for a winning combination. At the restaurants, we serve it with three kinds of nuts, although you can use one or two of your favorites. You might need to plan ahead so the mango has time to ripen at home at room temperature, as this fruit (like avocados and papayas) is usually sold slightly underripe.

GRILLED CHICKEN AND MANGO SALAD

MARINADE

1 cup/240 ml olive oil, plus more for brushing

¼ cup/60 ml fresh lemon juice

1 Tbsp mashed Roasted Garlic (page 213)

1 Tbsp coarsely chopped fresh rosemary

1 Tbsp coarsely chopped fresh flat-leaf parsley

1½ tsp coarsely cracked black pepper

¼ tsp red pepper flakes

4 skinless, boneless chicken breast halves, each about 6 oz/170 g

5 oz/140 g mixed baby salad greens

½ cup/55 g crumbled feta cheese

3 Tbsp dried blueberries or cherries

3 Tbsp slivered natural almonds, toasted (see below)

3 Tbsp toasted and coarsely crushed macadamia nuts (see below)

3 Tbsp purchased roasted salted pumpkin seeds

⅔ cup/165 ml Meyer Lemon Vinaigrette (page 211)

2 ripe mangoes, peeled, pitted, and cut into ½-in/12-mm slices

1 **To make the marinade:** Pulse all the ingredients together in a blender until combined.

2 One at a time, place a chicken breast half between two sheets of plastic wrap. Lightly pound the chicken with the flat side of a meat pounder or a rolling pin until the chicken is about ½ in/12 mm thick. Transfer the chicken to a 1-gl/3.8-L self-sealing plastic bag. Pour in the marinade. Close the bag and refrigerate, turning occasionally, for at least 2 hours or up to 12 hours.

3 Prepare an outdoor grill for direct cooking over medium heat (see page 19).

4 Remove the chicken from the marinade, shaking off the excess marinade. Lightly brush the chicken with oil. Put the chicken on the grill grate. Grill with the lid closed as much as possible, turning once, until the chicken feels firm when pressed, about 8 minutes. Transfer to a carving board and let cool for 3 minutes. Cut the chicken across the grain on a diagonal into slices about ½ in/12 mm thick.

5 Toss the greens, feta, blueberries, almonds, macadamia nuts, and pumpkin seeds together in a large bowl. Add the vinaigrette and toss again. Divide the salad among four dinner plates. Add equal amounts of the sliced chicken and mango to each and serve.

MAKES 4 SERVINGS

Toasting Nuts

Toasting nuts in the oven enhances their flavor. (Some cooks use a skillet, but this is not nearly as reliable as baking, and the nuts can burn in spots.) For a small amount of nuts, less than ½ cup/55 g, a toaster oven may be more efficient than a standard oven. Preheat the oven to 350°F/180°C. Spread the nuts on a small baking sheet or toaster oven tray and bake, stirring occasionally, until the nuts are lightly toasted, 8 to 11 minutes. Nuts with high oil content, such as macadamias, will take the least amount of time.

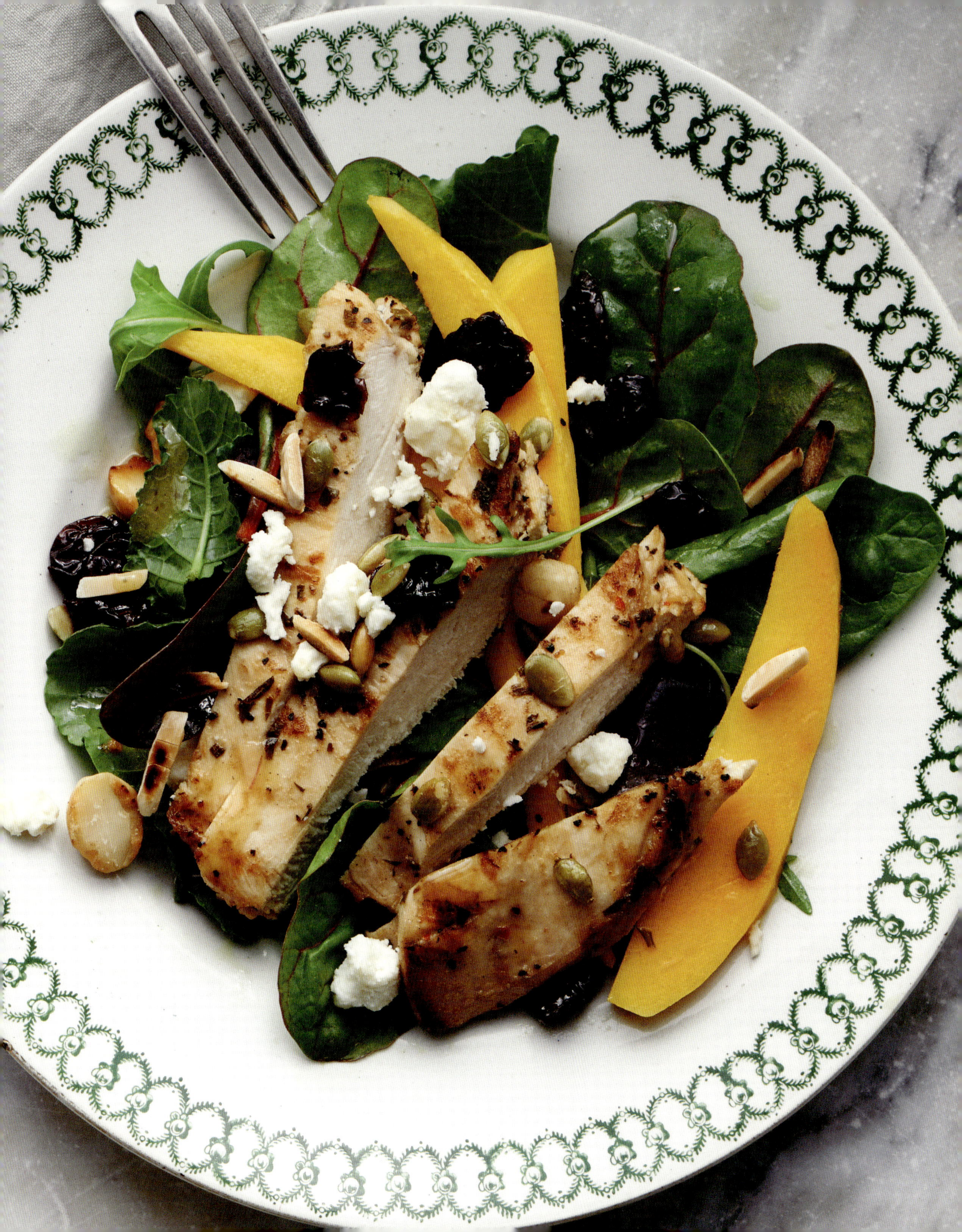

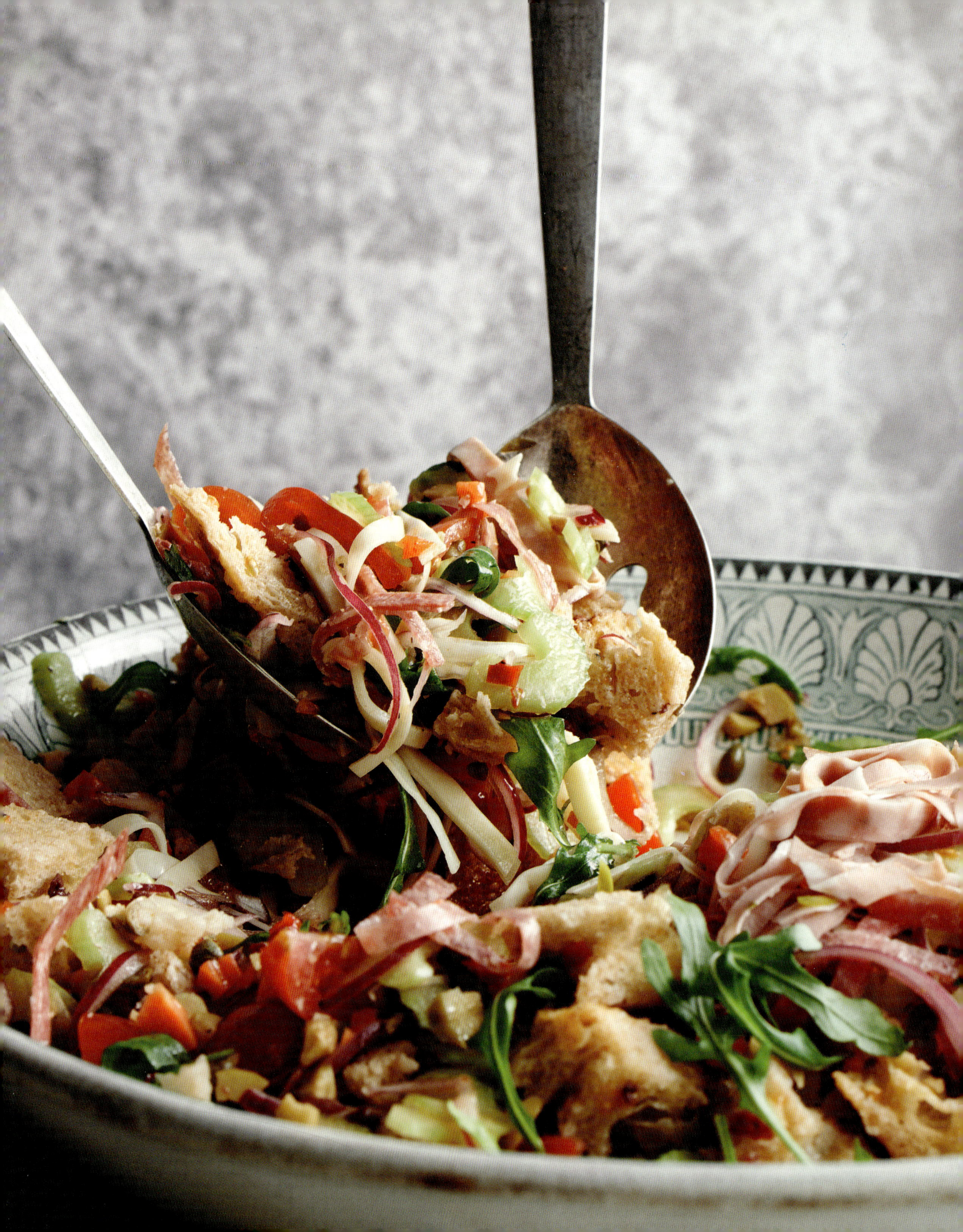

For about a hundred years, the Central Market in New Orleans has been selling the muffaletta sandwich, a large loaf filled with Italian cold cuts, cheese, and an olive salad. We've taken these same elements and turned them into a variation of panzanella, the Tuscan bread salad. This version is not exactly diet food, but it is still a lot lighter than the average hubcap-sized muffaletta.

MUFFALETTA SALAD WITH OLIVE VINAIGRETTE

VINAIGRETTE

2 Tbsp red wine vinegar

1 garlic clove, crushed through a press

Kosher salt and freshly ground black pepper

½ cup/120 ml extra-virgin olive oil

½ cup/75 g coarsely chopped pimiento-stuffed green olives

3 Tbsp drained nonpareil capers

8 oz/225 g (about half a large round loaf) day-old crusty bread

5 oz/140 g baby arugula

2 cups/350 g halved grape tomatoes

1 cup/150 g coarsely chopped drained giardinera (Italian pickled vegetables)

½ cup/75 g coarsely chopped pitted kalamata olives

4 celery stalks, thinly sliced

½ small red onion, thinly sliced

4 oz/115 g sliced Genoa salami or cappicola

4 oz/115 g sliced mild provolone cheese or mozzarella

4 oz/115 g sliced mortadella or boiled ham

1 To make the vinaigrette: Whisk the vinegar, garlic, ½ teaspoon salt, and ½ teaspoon pepper in a medium bowl to dissolve the salt. Gradually whisk in the oil. Stir in the olives and capers.

2 Tear the bread into pieces about 1 in/2.5 cm square. You should have about 4 cups/960 ml. Transfer to a large bowl and add the arugula, tomatoes, pickled vegetables, olives, celery, and red onion and toss. Add the vinaigrette and toss well. Let the salad stand for about 5 minutes so the bread can absorb some of the dressing.

3 Cut the salami, provolone, and mortadella into 1-in/2.5-cm strips. Scatter the strips over the salad and serve immediately.

MAKES 4 TO 6 SERVINGS

The original Greek salad, horiatiki, is a chunky mix of tomatoes, cucumber, onion, olives, and feta. In some communities, bell peppers are included, but this version has a fresh flavor without any spicy heat. The vegetables give off juices as the salad stands, so dress it at the last minute. In Tampa, there are restaurants that serve this with a scoop of potato salad, so do the same if you're feeling Floridian.

HORIATIKI GREEK SALAD WITH MARINATED GRILLED SHRIMP

SHRIMP

2 Tbsp fresh lemon juice

2 Tbsp extra-virgin olive oil

1 tsp dried oregano

1 garlic clove, minced

½ tsp kosher salt

¼ tsp red pepper flakes

20 extra-jumbo (16 to 20 count) shrimp, peeled with tail segment attached and deveined

SALAD

3 Israeli or Kirby cucumbers, about 12 oz/340 g total, cut into ¾-in/2-cm dice

4 ripe Roma (plum) tomatoes, about 12 oz/340 g total, seeded and cut into ¾-in/2-cm dice

½ small red onion, finely chopped

½ cup/75 g pitted kalamata olives

2 Tbsp red wine vinegar

1 garlic clove, minced

Kosher salt and freshly ground black pepper

½ cup/120 ml extra-virgin olive oil

6 oz/170 g feta cheese, cut into 4 slabs

Dried oregano, for serving

SPECIAL EQUIPMENT: 4 long bamboo skewers, soaked in water for at least 30 minutes

1 To marinate the shrimp: Whisk the lemon juice, olive oil, oregano, garlic, salt, and red pepper flakes together in a medium bowl. Pour into a 1-gl/3.8-L self-sealing plastic bag and add the shrimp. Close the bag and refrigerate, turning occasionally, for at least 15 minutes or up to 30 minutes but no longer.

2 Meanwhile, prepare the salad: Toss the cucumbers, tomatoes, red onion, and olives together in a large bowl. Whisk the vinegar, garlic, ¼ teaspoon salt, and ¼ teaspoon pepper together in a small bowl. Whisk in the ½ cup/120 ml oil and set the salad and dressing aside.

3 Prepare an outdoor grill for two-zone cooking with medium heat (see page 19). (Or position a broiler rack about 6 in/15 cm from the source of heat and preheat the broiler on high.)

4 One at a time, holding the shrimp in its natural "C" shape, thread 5 shrimp onto each drained skewer. Brush the grill grate clean. Place the shrimp on the grill. Slip a long strip of aluminum foil under the exposed "handles" of the skewers to protect them from the heat. Cook, with the lid closed as much as possible, turning once, until the shrimp are seared on both sides and turn opaque, 4 to 6 minutes. Remove from the grill.

5 Toss the salad and dressing together and season to taste with salt and pepper. Divide the Greek salad among 4 shallow bowls. Top each with a slice of feta and sprinkle the feta lightly with oregano. Add a shrimp skewer to each and serve immediately.

MAKES 4 SERVINGS

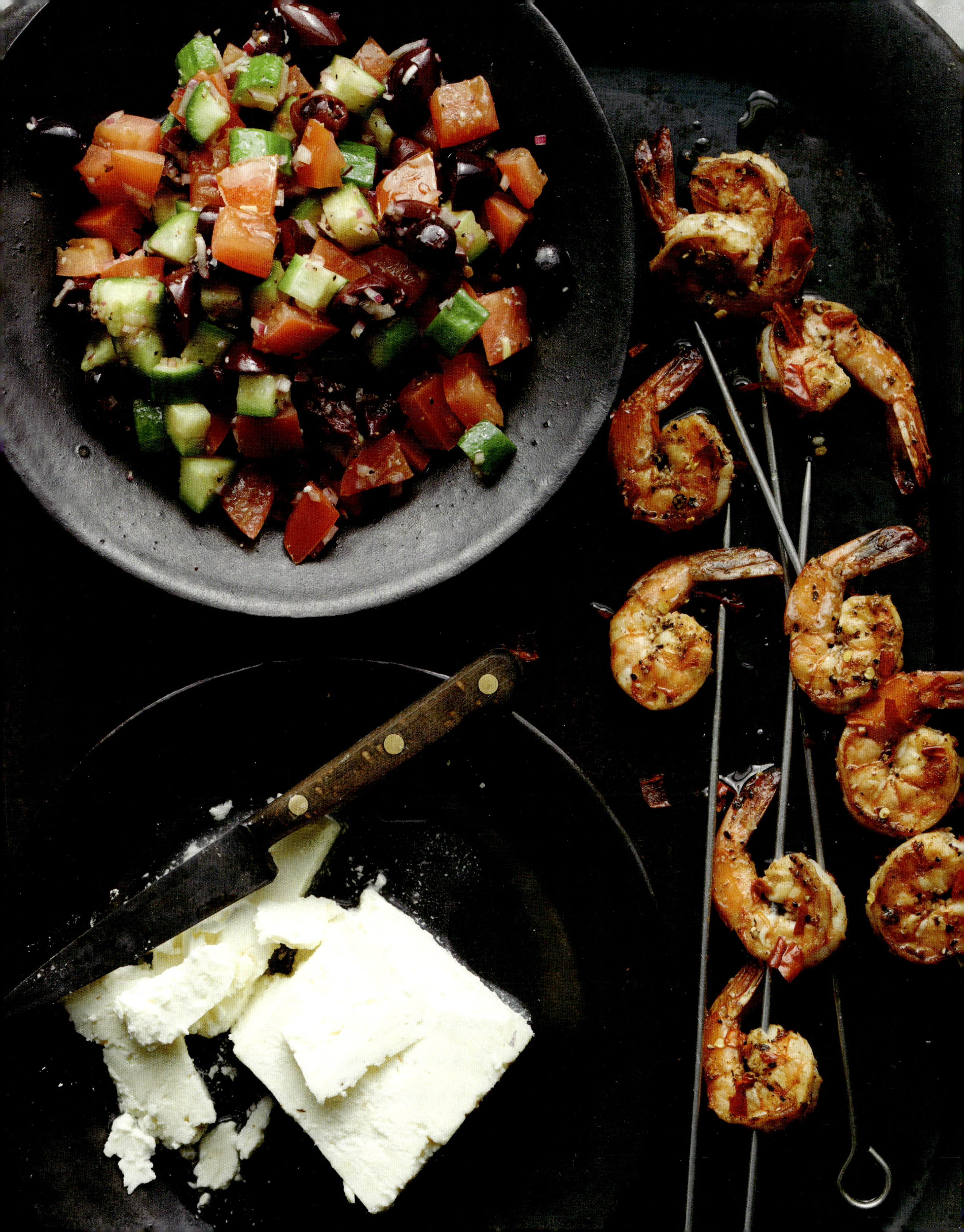

This simple salad uses a couple of easy tricks that allow the cook to dial it either up or down. The dressing is all-purpose and can be used on just about any greens, although baby spinach loves mustard. The sweet onions take about an hour for a quick pickle, so use raw rings if you run out of time. As for the pecans, this recipe makes a lot, so you can nibble some while making the salad.

BABY SPINACH WITH LIME-MUSTARD VINAIGRETTE AND SWEET AND SPICY PECANS

PICKLED ONIONS

¾ cup/180 ml cider vinegar

1½ tsp sugar

¾ tsp kosher salt

⅛ tsp red pepper flakes

1 sweet onion, cut into thin slices and separated into rings

PECANS

1 tsp vegetable oil

1 cup/110 g pecans

2 tsp confectioners' sugar

1 tsp Cajun Seasoning (page 213) or commercial Cajun seasoning

¼ tsp kosher salt

VINAIGRETTE

⅔ cup/165 ml olive oil

2 Tbsp fresh lime juice

2 tsp Creole mustard, such as Zatarain's or Tabasco Spicy Brown, or use Dijon mustard

½ tsp sugar

¼ tsp kosher salt

¼ tsp freshly ground black pepper

5 oz/140 g baby spinach

½ cup/55 g crumbled goat cheese (optional)

1 To make the onions: Bring the vinegar, ½ cup/120 ml water, the sugar, salt, and red pepper flakes to a boil over high heat in a small saucepan. Put the onion rings in a small heatproof bowl and pour in the vinegar mixture. Let cool completely. (The onions can be covered and refrigerated for up to 5 days.)

2 To make the pecans: Heat the oil in a medium nonstick skillet over medium heat. Add the pecans and cook, stirring often, until they begin to toast, about 1 minute. Mix the confectioners' sugar and Cajun seasoning together and sprinkle over the pecans. (Do not inhale the fumes, as they are irritating.) Cook, stirring almost constantly, until the pecans are coated and glazed, about 1 minute more. Season to taste with the salt. Transfer to a plate and let cool. Coarsely chop the pecans. (The pecans can be covered and stored at room temperature for up to 3 days.)

3 To make the vinaigrette: Process all of the ingredients together in a blender until thickened, about 15 seconds.

4 Toss the baby spinach with the vinaigrette. Drain the pickled onions. Divide the salad among 4 salad bowls. Top with the pecans (you may not use all of them), pickled onion rings, and goat cheese, if using, and serve immediately.

MAKES 4 SERVINGS

Ambrosia is the star of many Southern buffets, but it is usually made with canned fruit and marshmallows. This updated version with fresh fruit is truly the food of the gods, with the intermingling flavors creating a truly exceptional salad. Strawberries, blackberries, or pitted cherries can stand in for the raspberries. A sweet sour cream dressing is served on the side for those who wish to gild the lily.

FRESH AMBROSIA WITH SOUR CREAM DRESSING

DRESSING

1 cup/240 ml whole-fat sour cream

2 Tbsp confectioners' sugar

2 Tbsp golden rum or orange-flavored liqueur (optional)

AMBROSIA

6 large navel oranges

1 ripe pineapple (see Note)

One 6-oz/170 g container fresh raspberries (1⅓ cups)

1 cup/115 g shredded dried coconut

1 To make the dressing: Whisk the sour cream, confectioners' sugar, and rum, if using, together in a small bowl. Cover with plastic wrap and refrigerate to blend the flavors for at least 1 hour or up to 8 hours.

2 To make the ambrosia: Using a serrated knife, cut off the top and bottom of each orange. Following the curve of each orange, cut off the thick skin, including the white pith, where it meets the orange flesh. Working over a bowl, cut between the membranes to remove the segments, letting them drop into the bowl.

3 Cut off the top of the pineapple, including the leafy crown. Cut the thick rind from the pineapple where it meets the flesh. Remove the dark eyes in the flesh. Quarter the pineapple lengthwise and cut the hard core from each quarter. Cut each quarter lengthwise again, then into bite-size pieces.

4 Combine the oranges and pineapple chunks in a large, preferably glass bowl. Cover with plastic wrap and refrigerate until chilled, at least 1 hour or up to 8 hours.

5 Just before serving, gently mix in the raspberries and coconut. Serve chilled, with the dressing on the side.

MAKES 8 SERVINGS

NOTE: If you wish, purchase a peeled and cored fresh pineapple, skip the preparation instructions, and cut the flesh into bite-size chunks.

Coleslaw lovers generally fall into two camps, divided by the choice of dressing: sweet and creamy or clear and tart. This vinaigrette-based version is especially good when the other dishes on your menu are rich. The poppy seed dressing and shredded green apple are often ingredients in the coleslaw found in many Texan communities of German heritage.

COLESLAW WITH POPPY SEED DRESSING

1 small head green cabbage, cored and shredded, about 6 cups/450 g

2 carrots, peeled and shredded

1 Granny Smith apple, scrubbed, cored, and shredded

2 green onions, white and green parts, finely chopped

¾ cup/180 ml vegetable oil

3 Tbsp sherry or cider vinegar

2 Tbsp poppy seeds

1 Tbsp honey

Kosher salt and freshly ground black pepper

1 Thoroughly combine the cabbage, carrots, apples, and green onions in a large bowl (the apple tends to clump, so mix it in well).

2 Process the oil, vinegar, poppy seeds, honey, ½ tsp salt, and ¼ tsp pepper together in a blender until thickened and combined, about 5 seconds. Do not overprocess, as the poppy seeds should be lightly crushed, not pulverized into a paste.

3 Pour the dressing over the cabbage mixture and mix well. Cover and refrigerate for at least 1 hour or up to 2 days. Season to taste with salt and pepper. Serve chilled.

MAKES 6 TO 8 SERVINGS

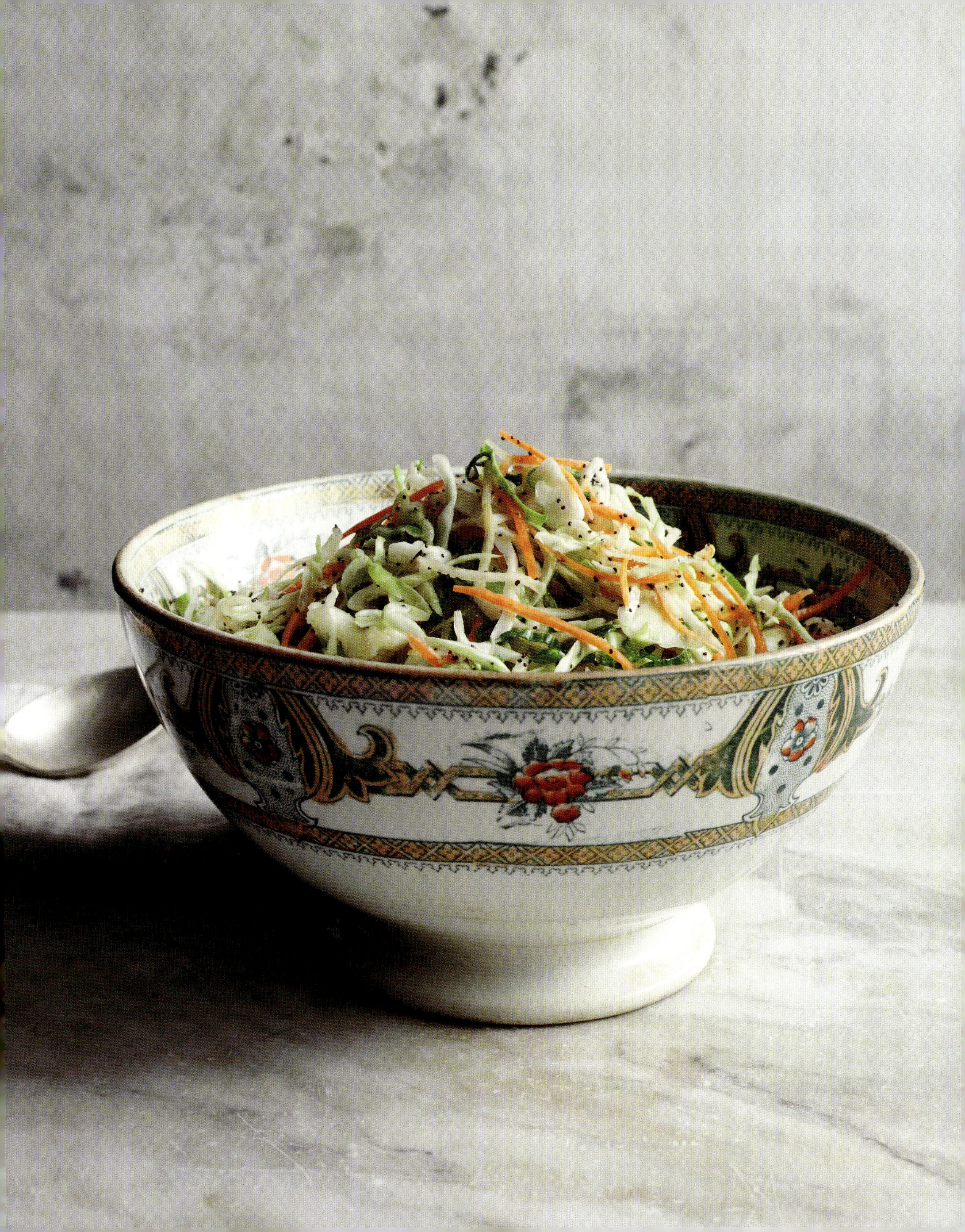

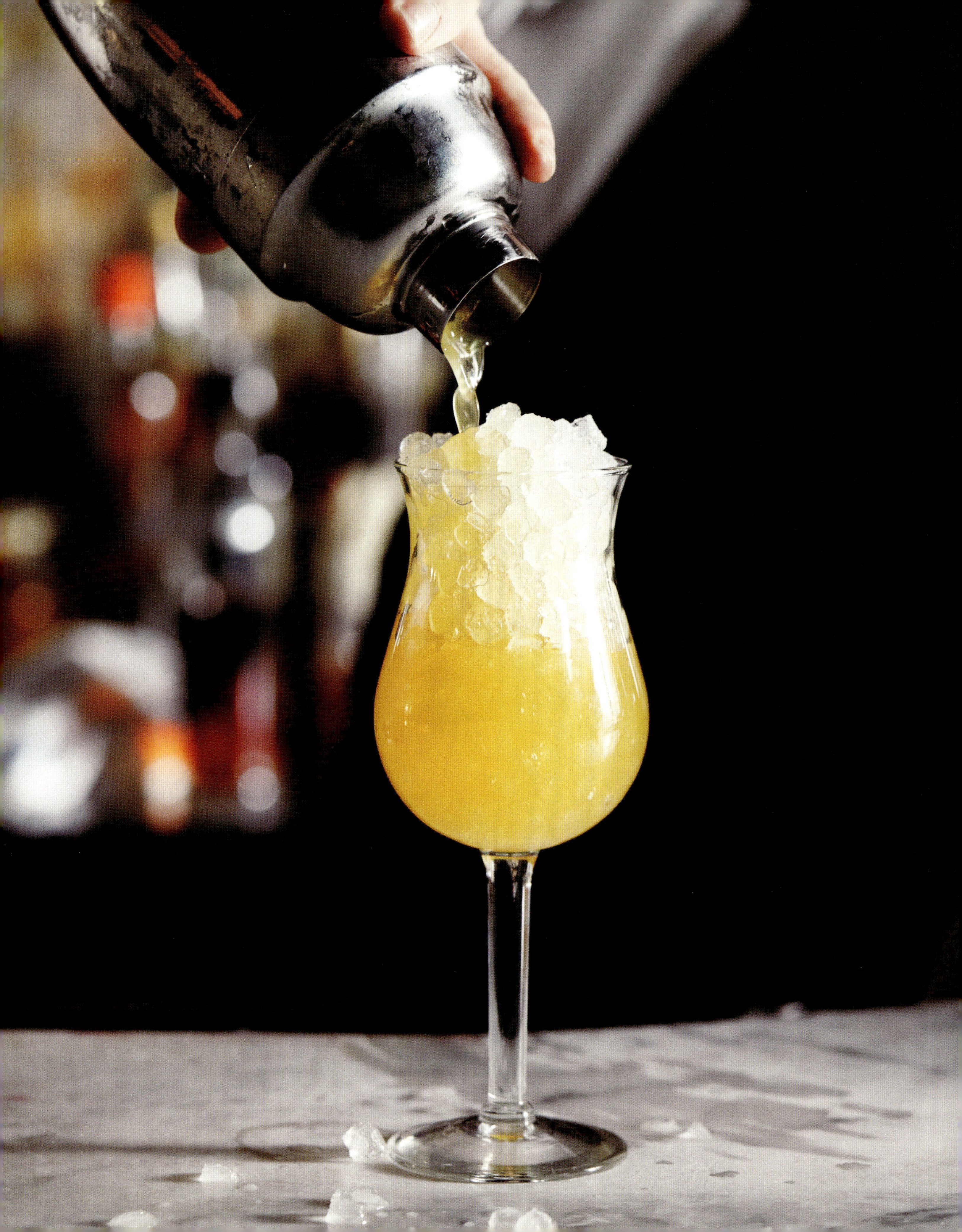

There are people who would consider it a cardinal sin to visit New Orleans and not drink a Hurricane—or two. No one can quite agree on the exact ingredients in this infamous drink, although you can skip the instant mix for sale in every tourist store on Bourbon Street. Here's our version, which is as good as it gets. Serve it in a tall, curvy hurricane glass for an authentic touch.

HURRICANE

COCKTAIL

2½ fl oz/75 ml pineapple juice

1 fl oz/30 ml white rum, preferably Cruzan

1 fl oz/30 ml spiced amber rum, preferably Cruzan 9

1 fl oz/30 ml From-Scratch Sour Mix (see below)

½ fl oz/15 ml apricot brandy

GARNISH: Pineapple wedge and Marasca cherry on a cocktail skewer

1 Add the cocktail ingredients to an ice-filled shaker. Shake well.

2 Fill a Hurricane glass or a tall Collins glass with ice. Strain the cocktail into the glass. Garnish with the pineapple wedge and cherry and serve.

MAKES 1 DRINK

There are many stories about how the Margarita got its name. But *margarita* means "daisy" in Spanish, and the Daisy is an old American cocktail that has similar ingredients to the Margarita, except that it's made with gin or brandy instead of tequila. Note that using a cheap instant sour mix is the easiest way to mess up this classic, so we give our recipe for a great homemade version.

MARGARITA

FROM-SCRATCH SOUR MIX

½ cup/120 ml fresh orange juice

1 Tbsp/15 ml fresh lime juice

1 Tbsp/15 ml fresh lemon juice

¼ cup/50 g superfine sugar

COCKTAIL

1 lime wedge, for the glass

Kosher salt, for the glass

2 fl oz/60 ml white tequila, such as Sauza Conmemorativo

2 fl oz/60 ml From-Scratch Sour Mix, above

1 fl oz/30 ml Cointreau

½ fl oz/15 ml fresh lime juice

½ fl oz/15 ml Grand Marnier

1 To make the sour mix: Shake the ingredients with ½ cup/120 ml water in a covered jar until the sugar is dissolved. (Makes about ¾ cup/180 ml. The mix can be refrigerated for up to 1 week.)

2 Run the lime wedge around the lip of a double Old-Fashioned glass. Holding the glass upside down, sprinkle the salt around the outside edge of the glass only (if the salt gets in the glass, the cocktail will be too salty). Reserve the lime wedge. Fill the glass with ice.

3 Add the tequila, sour mix, Cointreau, and lime juice to an ice-filled cocktail shaker. Shake well. Strain into the prepared glass and pour the Grand Marnier on top. Garnish with the reserved lime wedge.

MAKES 1 DRINK

A top-notch potato salad will have guests lining up for seconds. There are many choices to be made: tender baking potatoes or firm boiling potatoes? Vinegar or pickle brine? Slightly sweet, or savory with plenty of mustard? We present our version as a surefire crowd-pleaser, but with plenty of opportunity for adding your own personal touches.

CHURCH SUPPER POTATO SALAD

8 large baking potatoes, such as russets, scrubbed, about 2½ lb/1.2 kg total

3 Tbsp brine from pickles, below

4 large eggs

4 celery stalks, cut into ½-in/12-mm dice

4 green onions, white and green parts, finely chopped

½ cup/90 g chopped (½-in/12-mm) pimiento or roasted red bell pepper

⅓ cup/50 g chopped (½-in/12-mm) dill or sweet pickles

2 Tbsp finely chopped fresh flat-leaf parsley

1 cup/240 ml mayonnaise

1 Tbsp spicy brown or yellow mustard

Kosher salt and freshly ground black pepper

Sweet paprika, for garnish

1 Put the potatoes in a large saucepan and add cold salted water to cover by 1 in/2.5 cm. Cover and bring to a boil over high heat. Reduce the heat to medium and set the lid ajar. Cook at a brisk simmer until the potatoes are tender when pierced with the tip of a sharp knife, 20 to 30 minutes. Drain in a colander, rinse under cold running water, and let cool until easy to handle. Peel the potatoes and cut into ¾-inch/2-cm slices. Transfer to a large bowl and sprinkle with the pickle brine.

2 Meanwhile, cook the eggs: Put the eggs in a small saucepan and add cold water to cover by 1 in/2.5 cm. Bring to a boil over high heat. Remove from the heat and tightly cover the saucepan. Let the eggs stand in the water for 15 minutes. Drain the eggs and transfer them to a bowl of ice water. Let stand until chilled, about 5 minutes. Peel the eggs. Chop 2 eggs. Cover and refrigerate the remaining eggs.

3 Add the chopped eggs, celery, green onions, bell pepper, pickles, and parsley to the potatoes. Whisk the mayonnaise and mustard together in a small bowl. Add to the potato mixture and mix. Season to taste with salt and pepper. Cover with plastic wrap and refrigerate until chilled, at least 2 or up to 8 hours.

4 Cut the reserved eggs into ¼-in/6-mm rounds. Top the salad with the sliced eggs and sprinkle with the paprika. Serve chilled.

MAKES 8 SERVINGS

When gumbo is made correctly, one spicy slurp should inspire you to want to pick up an accordion and play some zydeco. There are two must-haves in this deep, dark soup-stew. One is okra (after all, gumbo means "okra" in African Bantu dialect), whose juices act as a thickener. And you'll need to make a proper, slowly browned roux—a job that takes about the same amount of time needed to drink a nice, cold beer.

SHRIMP AND SAUSAGE GUMBO WITH SLOW ROUX

ROUX

6 bacon slices, cut into 1-in/2.5-cm lengths

¾ cup/180 ml vegetable oil

1 cup/140 g all-purpose flour

1 large yellow onion, chopped

3 large celery stalks, cut into ½-in/12-mm dice

1 green bell pepper, cut into ½-in/12-mm dice

4 garlic cloves, minced

1 tsp sweet paprika

½ tsp dried thyme

Kosher salt and freshly ground black pepper

⅛ tsp cayenne pepper

1½ qt/1.4 L canned low-sodium chicken broth

1 Tbsp Worcestershire sauce

1 tsp red pepper sauce, such as Tabasco, plus more for serving

2 bay leaves

12 oz/340 g andouille, spicy kielbasa, or other smoked sausage, cut into ¼-in/6-mm rounds

9 oz/255 g okra, tops and tails trimmed, cut into ¼-in/6-mm rounds (see Note)

3 Tbsp finely chopped fresh flat-leaf parsley

1 lb/455 g small (35 to 41 count) shrimp, peeled and deveined

Basic Rice (page 209)

2 green onions, thinly sliced

1 To make the roux: Cook the bacon in a large, heavy soup pot over medium heat, stirring occasionally, until browned, 6 to 8 minutes. Using a slotted spoon, transfer the bacon to paper towels to drain. Refrigerate until ready to serve.

2 Add the oil to the fat in the pot. Whisk in the flour to make a thin roux. Cook over medium heat, whisking almost constantly, until the roux is light brown and slightly smoking, about 20 minutes.

3 Add the onion, celery, and bell pepper to the roux in the pot. Cook, stirring often, until the onion is translucent, 6 to 8 minutes. (The roux may continue to color during this period.) Stir in the garlic, paprika, thyme, 1 tsp salt, ½ tsp black pepper, and the cayenne and mix well. Gradually whisk in the broth and 2 cups/480 ml water. Stir in the Worcestershire sauce and the 1 tsp hot sauce. Add the bay leaves. Bring to a boil over high heat. Reduce the heat to low. Simmer, stirring occasionally, to blend the flavors, about 1 hour.

4 Meanwhile, cook the andouille over medium heat, stirring occasionally, until browned, about 8 minutes. Add the sausage, okra, and parsley to the gumbo and cook until the okra is quite tender, about 30 minutes. Stir in the shrimp and cook until the shrimp is opaque, about 5 minutes more. Coarsely chop the bacon and stir half of it into the gumbo. Reserve the remaining bacon for serving. Season to taste with salt.

5 For each serving, scoop about ½-cup/80-g rice into a large soup bowl. (If you wish, pack the rice into an oiled ½-cup/120-ml custard cup and unmold the rice into the bowl.) Ladle in the gumbo and sprinkle with the green onions and reserved bacon. Serve hot, with the hot sauce passed on the side.

MAKES 8 SERVINGS

NOTE: This recipe omits filé powder, ground sassafras leaves, which is used as a thickener and flavoring in some versions. We don't use it because it can get stringy when gumbo is cooked too long, which is easy to do when reheating leftovers.

Every cuisine has its special chicken soup, a recipe that cooks turn to for curing a cold or warming the insides on a chilly day. Tortilla soup is the chicken soup of Mexico. Often, it is merely a spicy thin broth with a garnish of fried tortillas, but our version is lightly thickened and topped with fresh corn salsa. Be sure to make the roasted garlic on page 213 before starting.

TORTOLA TORTILLA SOUP

GRILLED CORN SALSA

1 Tbsp fresh lime juice

1 Tbsp extra-virgin olive oil

Kosher salt and freshly ground black pepper

1 cup/175 g grilled corn kernels (from 2 ears corn; see page 31)

1 Tbsp finely chopped fresh cilantro

SOUP

6 cups/1.4 L canned reduced-sodium chicken broth

1 lb/455 g chicken thighs

3 Tbsp unsalted butter

3 Tbsp olive oil

1 yellow onion, chopped

½ cup/80 g chopped green bell pepper

1 Tbsp mashed Roasted Garlic (page 213)

3½ corn tortillas, coarsely chopped (3 oz/85 g)

⅓ cup/45 g all-purpose flour

1 tsp kosher salt

1½ tsp chili powder

1 tsp ground cumin

⅛ tsp freshly ground black pepper

⅛ tsp cayenne pepper

½ cup/120 ml Lime Sour Cream (page 154), for serving

2 Tbsp finely chopped fresh cilantro, for serving

1 **To make the corn salsa:** Whisk the lime juice, oil, ⅛ tsp salt, and a large pinch of pepper together in a medium bowl. Add the corn and cilantro and mix well. Let stand to blend the flavors while making the soup.

2 **To make the soup:** Combine the broth and chicken in a medium saucepan. Add 2 cups/240 ml water and bring to a boil over high heat, skimming off any foam that rises to the surface. Reduce the heat to low. Simmer until the chicken shows no sign of pink when pierced at the bone, about 45 minutes. Strain through a sieve, reserving 6 cups/1.4 L of the broth.

3 Let the chicken cool until easy to handle. Cut the meat into ½-in/12-mm pieces, discarding the skin and bones.

4 Melt the butter with the oil in a large saucepan over medium heat. Add the onion, bell pepper, and roasted garlic and cook, stirring occasionally, until the vegetables are beginning to brown, about 5 minutes.

5 Process the tortilla strips in a food processor until finely ground. Add the flour and salt and pulse until combined. Stir into the vegetable mixture and mix well. Reduce the heat to medium-low and cook, stirring occasionally, until the flour mixture is lightly toasted to a medium-brown color, 12 to 15 minutes. Stir in the chili powder, cumin, black pepper, and cayenne.

6 Gradually whisk in the broth and bring to a boil over high heat. Return the heat to medium-low. Cook at a very low simmer, stirring often to avoid scorching, until the soup is lightly thickened to a consistency similar to heavy cream, about 40 minutes. Remove from the heat. Using an immersion blender, process the soup until smooth. (Or process in batches in a standing blender, with the lid ajar.) Return to the saucepan, add the chicken, and heat over low heat until the chicken is hot, about 3 minutes.

7 Transfer the cream to a plastic food-service squeeze bottle. (Or put it in a small self-sealing plastic bag and snip off one corner of the bag to make an opening ¼ in/6 mm wide.) Ladle the soup into 6 soup bowls. Top each with a squiggle of cream from the bottle, about 2 Tbsp of the salsa, and a sprinkling of cilantro. Serve hot.

MAKES 6 SERVINGS

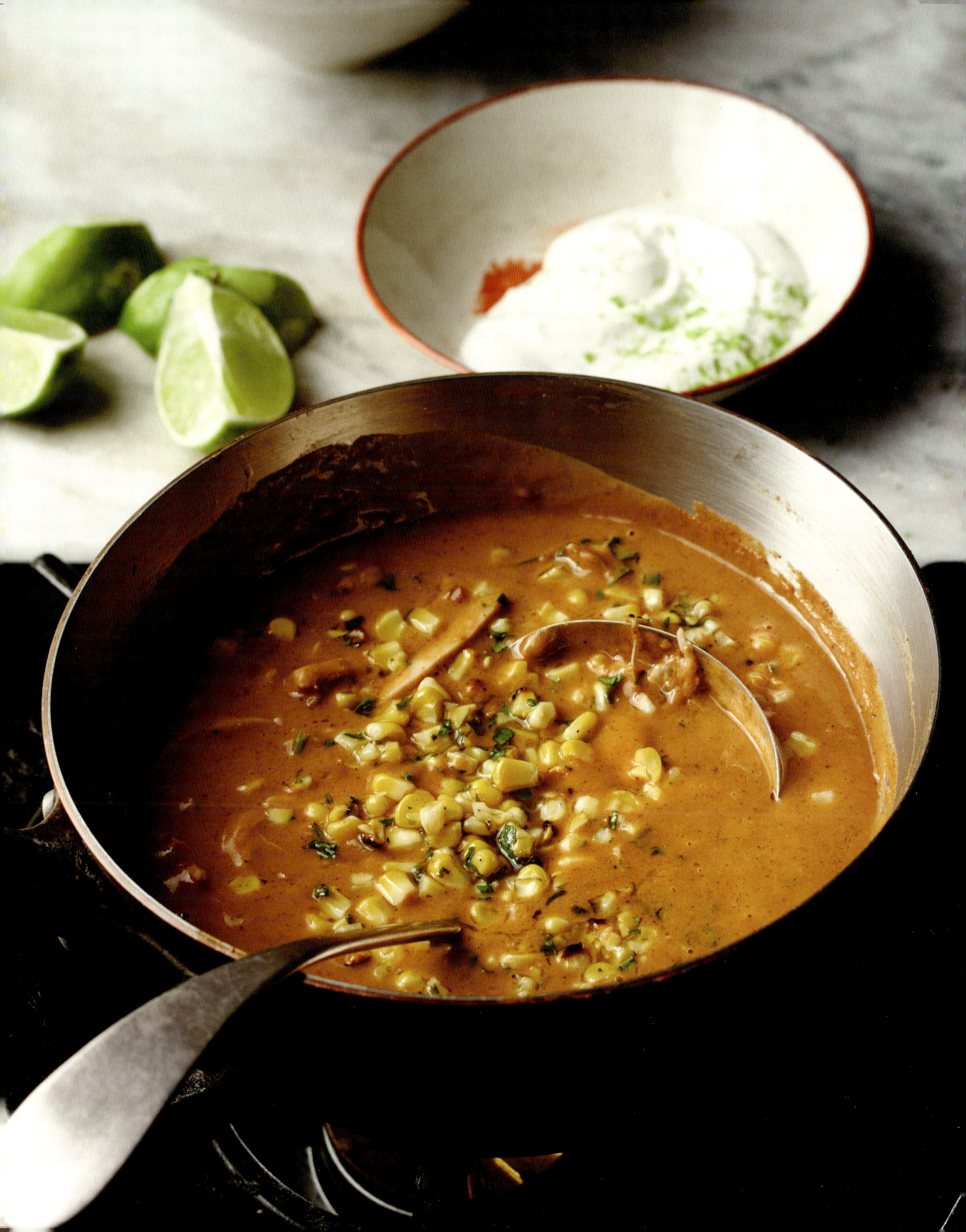

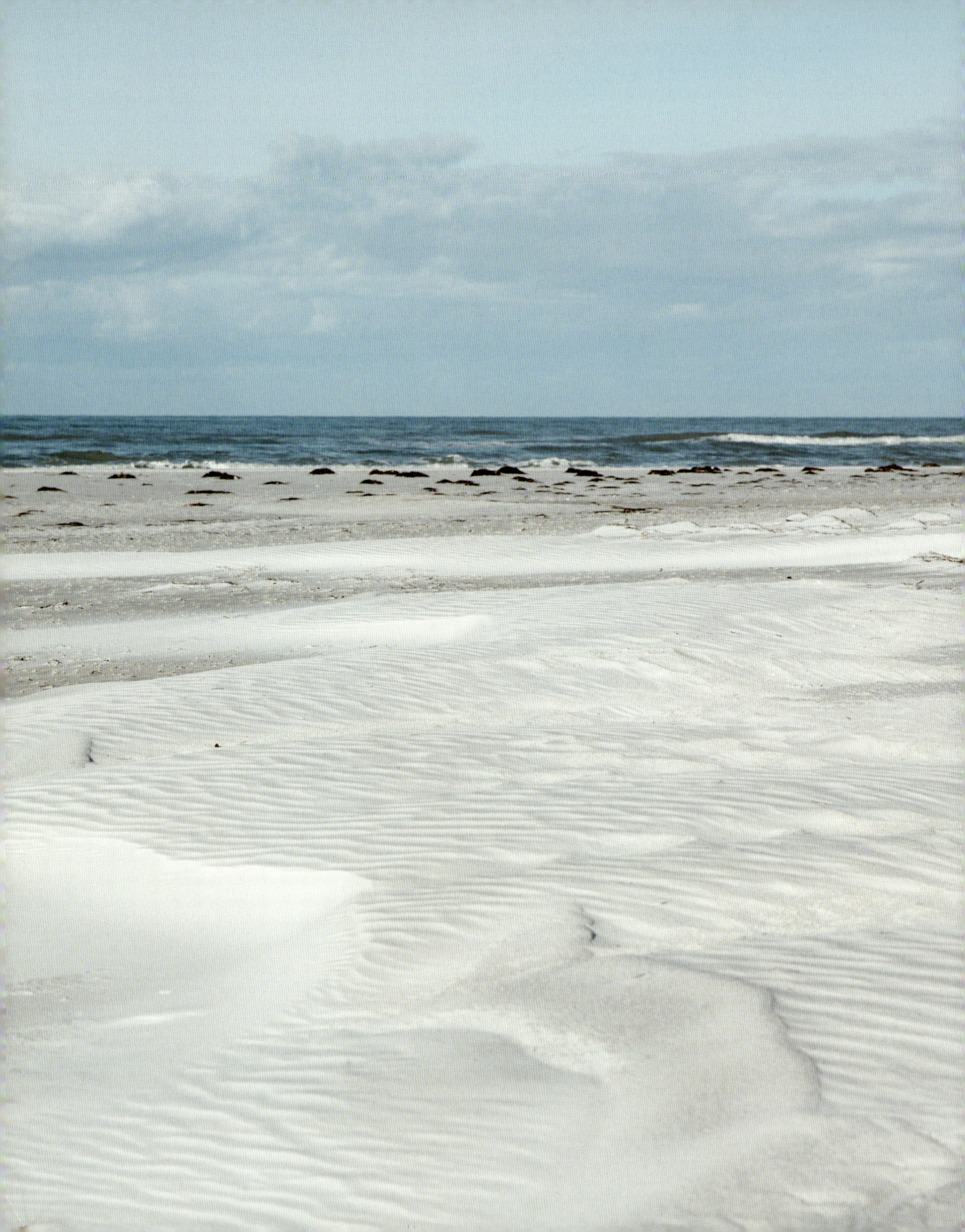

Since the day the first Tommy Bahama Restaurant opened its doors in Naples, Florida, we've served buckets of this luscious soup at our eateries around the globe. Here's the recipe, with every indulgent ounce of cream intact. Remember, you don't eat crab bisque every day, and if you did, it should always be this good! Because it's a main flavoring in this soup, please use a good imported Spanish sherry.

CRAB BISQUE

BASE

4 Tbsp/55 g unsalted butter

¼ cup/35 g all-purpose flour

4 cups/960 ml heavy cream, heated

BISQUE

2 Tbsp unsalted butter

1 large celery stalk, finely chopped

2 carrots, peeled and finely chopped

½ cup/70 g finely chopped red onion

2 Tbsp finely chopped shallots

6 garlic cloves, finely chopped

1 tsp minced fresh thyme

1 cup/240 ml dry (fino) sherry

1 cup/240 ml fish stock or bottled clam juice

2 cups/480 ml heavy cream

½ tsp red pepper sauce, such as Tabasco

SERVING

¼ cup/60 ml dry (fino) sherry

4 Tbsp/55 g cold unsalted butter, thinly sliced

1 lb/455 g lump crabmeat, picked over for cartilage

Kosher salt and freshly ground black pepper

¾ cup/40 g coarsely crushed herbed croutons

1 green onion, white and green parts, thinly sliced on the diagonal

1 To make the cream base: Melt the butter in a medium saucepan over medium heat. Whisk in the flour and let bubble without browning for 1 minute. Gradually whisk in the cream. Cook, whisking often, until the mixture is simmering and lightly thickened, about 5 minutes. Remove from the heat.

2 To make the bisque: Melt the butter in a large saucepan over medium heat. Add the celery, carrots, red onion, shallot, garlic, and thyme, and cook, stirring occasionally, until the onion is softened, about 3 minutes. Add the sherry, bring to a boil, and cook until reduced by half, about 5 minutes. Add the fish stock and bring to a boil over high heat. Reduce the heat to low and simmer until the vegetables are tender, about 20 minutes. Strain the mixture through a fine-mesh sieve over a bowl, pressing hard on the solids with the back of a wooden spoon to extract the juices. Return the stock to the pot.

3 Whisk in the cream base. Add the 2 cups/480 ml heavy cream and the pepper sauce and bring to a simmer over medium heat, whisking often. Reduce the heat to medium-low and simmer, whisking often, until the bisque has lightly thickened, about 20 minutes. (The bisque can be cooled, covered, and refrigerated for up to 1 day. Reheat gently before serving.)

4 To serve: Whisk in the sherry. Gradually whisk in the sliced butter, letting the bisque absorb the first addition before adding another. Stir in the crabmeat and cook until it is heated through, about 2 minutes. Season to taste with salt and pepper.

5 Divide the soup among 8 bowls. Top each with the croutons and a sprinkle of green onions. Serve hot.

MAKES 8 SERVINGS

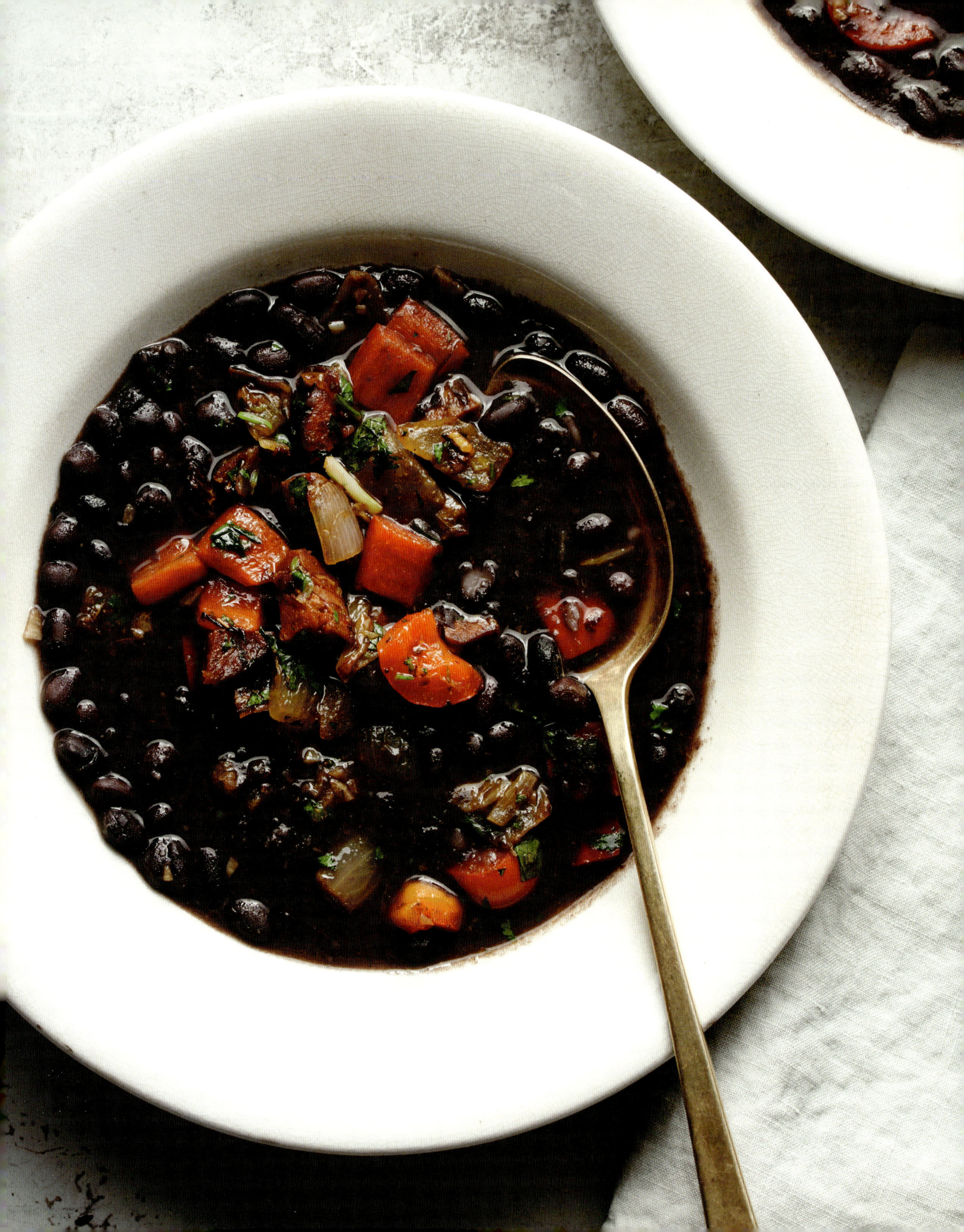

In the Caribbean, black bean soup is usually vegetarian, as the vegetables deliver plenty of flavor on their own. But we can't leave a good thing alone, so we've added some chorizo to the sofrito vegetable mixture that tops off the soup (just leave it out for a meatless version). This soup takes time to develop flavor, so don't rush it. It's even better reheated after a day's refrigeration.

CUBAN BLACK BEAN SOUP WITH CHORIZO SOFRITO

SOUP

- 1 lb/455 g dried black beans, picked over for stones, rinsed well, and drained
- 1 yellow onion, quartered
- ½ green bell pepper, cored, seeded, and cut into 3 or 4 large chunks
- 6 garlic cloves, crushed under a knife and peeled
- 2 tsp ground cumin
- 2 tsp dried oregano
- 2 bay leaves
- Kosher salt
- 2 Tbsp cider vinegar
- Freshly ground black pepper

SOFRITO

- 3 Tbsp olive oil
- 8 oz/225 g smoked chorizo links, cut into ½-in/12-mm dice
- 1 large yellow onion, cut into ½-in/12-mm dice
- 1 large red bell pepper, cored, seeded, and cut into ½-in/12-mm dice
- 6 *ajís dulces* chiles, seeded and minced (see Note)
- 3 garlic cloves, minced
- ½ tsp ground cumin
- ½ tsp dried oregano
- ½ tsp kosher salt
- 3 Tbsp finely chopped fresh cilantro

1 To make the soup: Put the black beans in a soup pot and add cold water to cover by 1 in/2.5 cm. Bring to a boil over high heat and cook for 1 minute. Remove from the heat and cover. Let stand for 1 hour. Do not drain the beans—the dark liquid will help them maintain their black color.

2 Add the onion, bell pepper, garlic, cumin, oregano, bay leaves, and 1 tsp kosher salt to the pot. Pour additional water into the pot to cover the ingredients by 1 in/2.5 cm. Bring to a boil over high heat. Reduce the heat to low and simmer, adding hot water as needed to keep the beans well covered, until they are tender, about 2 hours. Discard the bay leaves.

3 Transfer the vegetable chunks with about 2 cups/480 ml of the cooking liquid to a blender. With the blender lid ajar to allow steam to escape, purée the mixture. Stir the purée back into the pot. Adjust the soup consistency with more purée or water, as needed. Stir in the cider vinegar and season to taste with salt and pepper. Keep the soup hot.

4 While the soup is simmering, make the sofrito: Heat 1 Tbsp of the oil in a large skillet over medium heat. Add the chorizo and cook, stirring often (it burns easily), until browned, about 5 minutes. Using a slotted spoon, transfer the chorizo to paper towels to drain. (If making vegetarian soup, skip the preceding step.)

5 Add the remaining 2 Tbsp oil to the skillet and heat over medium heat. Add the onion, bell pepper, chiles, garlic, cumin, oregano, and salt. Cook, stirring often, until the sofrito is tender but not browned, about 15 minutes. Remove from the heat and stir in the cilantro. Stir the reserved chorizo into the sofrito.

6 Stir about half of the sofrito into the soup. Spoon the soup into bowls and garnish each serving with a spoonful of the remaining sofrito.

MAKES 8 SERVINGS

BLACK BEAN SOUP WITH SHERRY: This Americanized version of the soup isn't authentic, but it is excellent. Make the soup above, omitting the chorizo. Stir ⅓ cup/80 ml dry sherry into the soup during the last 15 minutes of simmering. Stir all of the sofrito into the soup. Top each serving with a dollop of sour cream and a thin lemon slice. Makes 8 servings.

NOTE: *Ají dulce* (also called *cachucha*) is a mild chile used in Puerto Rican and Cuban cooking. Small, round, and green (changing to red, yellow, or orange when ripe), it is easily confused with fiery habanero and Scotch bonnet chiles, so take care when purchasing at Latino markets. If desired, substitute ½ Cubanelle or green bell pepper, cored, seeded, and cut into ½-in/12-mm dice, for the *ajís dulces* in this recipe.

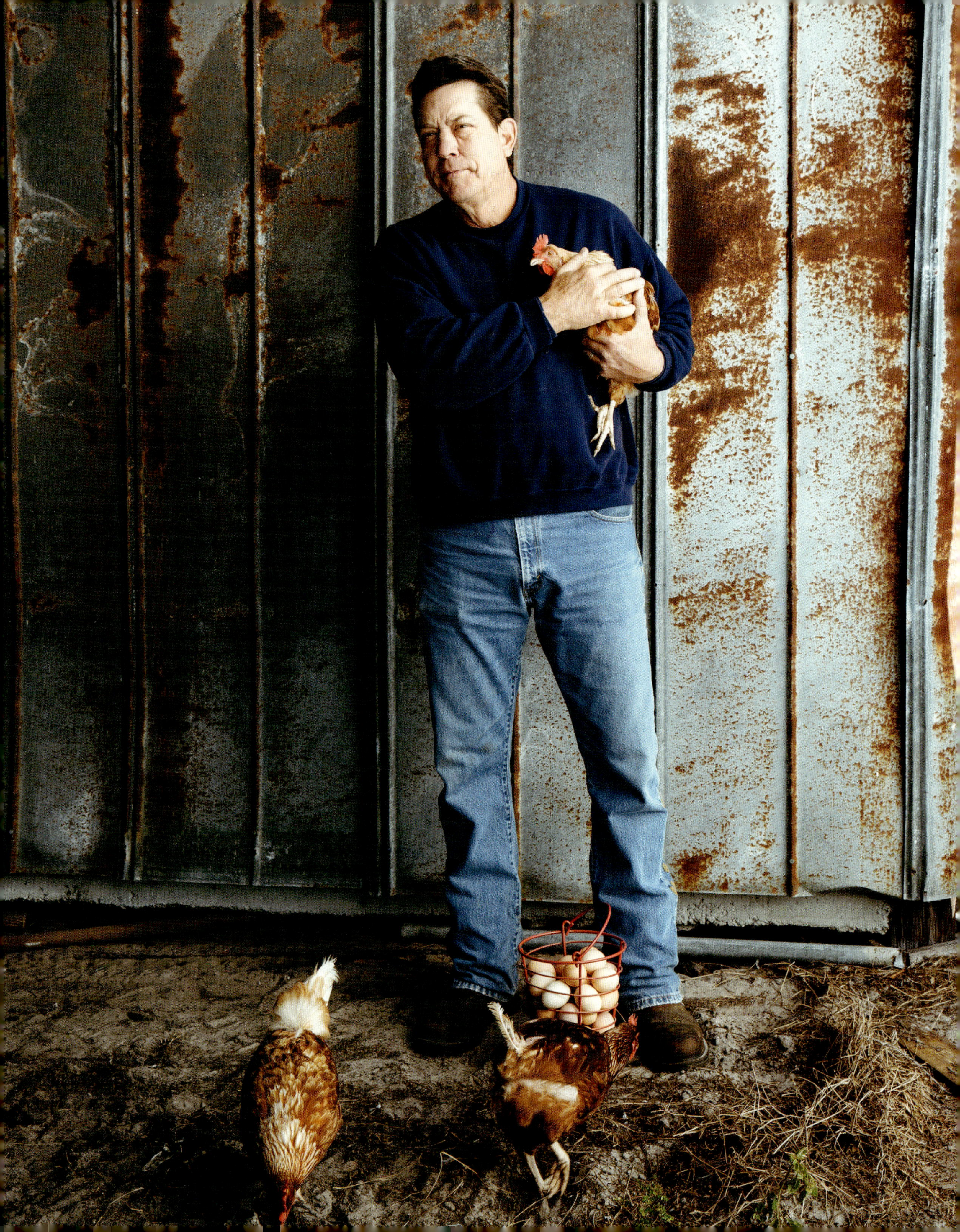

LEONARD HORAK, CHICKEN FARMER

Leonard Horak's eyes shine as he hands farm-fresh eggs to his customer. For Leonard, the term *farm fresh* is not a marketing ploy. In fact, just hours before this exchange, he and his wife, Arlene, gathered the eggs from the nests of their Sex Linked chickens (chickens raised to be red or black so as to easily distinguish the gender). Although the market will operate into the afternoon, it is more than likely that Leonard will run out of the approximately eighty-five dozen eggs he has to sell before closing. "It's frustrating," he says, "but we can only raise so many chickens at once and keep quality control. We do all of the work on the farm, and I know the care that goes into my product. I won't have it any other way."

Three days a week, Leonard travels to farmers' markets in the Tampa region, about one hour from the city of Duette. The Horaks' Circle 6 Farm & Ranch makes up five hundred acres and is part of a larger farm owned by Arlene's family, in its fifth generation of ownership. The smaller operation concentrates on the hands-on raising of chickens (for both eggs and meat) and cattle.

Leonard came to farming later in life, after several white-collar jobs: "If the farmers' markets had been as strong twenty years ago, I would have become a farmer earlier." What makes Circle 6 unique is the direct contact with the customer. There is no middleman—Leonard is always face-to-face with his clientele. "If there are ever problems, I would know about them. Luckily, I only hear compliments—except when I run out of eggs. The people are what makes my job a joy. Our demographic runs from twenty to seventy, but they have one thing in common: they all want better, cleaner food. And we can provide it. But I'll never get so big that I can't accommodate the natural way to grow food."

CHICKEN

Truly a fine feathered friend to the cook, here is chicken served up in many delicious guises. The Southern states contribute such dishes as crispy fried chicken and creamy fricassee, while a mole-grilled bird and arroz con pollo represent Tex-Mex cuisine.

67
ROAST CHICKEN ASADO WITH ROOT VEGETABLES

68
HICKORY BBQ CHICKEN WITH SWEET AND STICKY ROOT BEER SAUCE

71
FRIED CHICKEN WITH ICED TEA BRINE

72
CHICKEN BREASTS WITH JERK MARINADE

74
CHEESE-STUFFED CHICKEN BREASTS WITH ROASTED RED PEPPER CREAM

78
TANDOORI-STYLE CHICKEN

79
CHICKEN FRICASSEE WITH SPRING VEGETABLES AND CHIVE DUMPLINGS

80
ARROZ CON POLLO Y CHORIZO

83
GRILLED CHICKEN WINGS WITH MOLE RUB

Mojo is a tart marinade/sauce used all over the Caribbean to add zest to meats, poultry, and seafood. Its main ingredient, sour oranges, can be challenging to find, but this alternative combination of regular oranges and lime juice works well. Spatchcocking (butterflying) the chicken dramatically reduces the roasting time and exposes more of the skin to the oven heat to create golden brown, tasty skin.

ROAST CHICKEN ASADO WITH ROOT VEGETABLES

MOJO

¼ cup/35 g finely chopped yellow onion

4 garlic cloves, coarsely chopped

⅓ cup/75 ml fresh orange juice

3 Tbsp fresh lime juice

3 Tbsp extra-virgin olive oil

2 tsp dried oregano

2 tsp dried cumin

1½ tsp kosher salt

½ tsp coarsely ground black peppercorns

One 5-lb/2.3-kg whole chicken, giblets reserved for another use

2 large baking potatoes, such as russets, peeled and each cut lengthwise into eighths

2 large carrots, peeled, halved lengthwise, and cut into 2-in/5-cm lengths

2 Tbsp extra-virgin olive oil

Kosher salt and freshly ground black pepper

2 Tbsp coarsely chopped fresh cilantro or flat-leaf parsley, for garnish

1 To make the mojo: Process all of the ingredients in a blender to make a thick paste.

2 Using kitchen shears or a large knife, cut down both sides of the backbone of the chicken to remove it, reserving the backbone for another use (such as stock). Place the chicken, skin side up, on a carving board. Press hard on the breastbone to crack it and flatten the chicken.

3 Put the chicken and mojo in a 1-gl/3.8-L self-sealing plastic bag. Massage the chicken through the bag to rub in the marinade. Close the bag and refrigerate, turning occasionally, for at least 2 hours or up to 8 hours. Let the chicken stand at room temperature for 30 minutes before roasting.

4 Position a rack in the center of the oven and preheat the oven to 425°F/220°C.

5 Remove the chicken from the mojo, keeping the clinging marinade intact. Discard the remaining marinade. Spread the chicken, skin side up, in an 18-by-13-in/46-by-33-cm sided baking sheet. Roast for 30 minutes. Toss the potatoes and carrots with the oil in a large bowl. Remove the baking sheet from the oven. Spread the potatoes and carrots around the chicken. Return to the oven and continue roasting until an instant-read thermometer inserted in the thickest part of the breast reaches 165°F/73°C, about 30 minutes more.

6 Transfer the chicken to a carving board and tent loosely with aluminum foil to keep warm. Using a metal pancake turner, scrape up and turn the vegetables in the pan and spread them out. Continue roasting until the potatoes are tender and browned, 5 to 10 minutes more.

7 Season the vegetables with salt and pepper and transfer to a large platter. Using the shears or large knife, chop the chicken into serving pieces. Place over the vegetables and drizzle any carving juices on top. Sprinkle with the cilantro and serve.

MAKES 4 TO 6 SERVINGS

There's more to making great barbecued chicken than meets the eye. A combination of flavorings—homemade sauce, a brightly seasoned rub, and smoke from wood chips—make this a bird that will give you a reputation as the top grill master in the neighborhood. This is Southern-style BBQ, with a sauce that's sweetened with root beer and molasses and accented with sharp vinegar.

HICKORY BBQ CHICKEN WITH SWEET AND STICKY ROOT BEER SAUCE

SAUCE

1 Tbsp unsalted butter

1 yellow onion, finely chopped

1 garlic clove, minced

1 cup/240 ml plus ½ cup/120 ml root beer (not diet)

1 cup/240 ml ketchup

⅓ cup/75 ml molasses (not blackstrap)

⅓ cup/75 ml cider vinegar

2 Tbsp thick steak sauce, preferably A-1

1 tsp red pepper sauce, such as Tabasco

RUB AND CHICKEN

1 Tbsp light brown sugar

1½ tsp kosher salt

2 tsp sweet paprika

1 tsp granulated garlic

1 tsp granulated onion

1 tsp freshly ground black pepper

¼ tsp cayenne pepper

1 chicken, about 5 lb/2.3 kg, cut into 2 wings, 2 breast halves, 2 drumsticks, 2 thighs, and 1 back

Vegetable oil, for brushing

2 large handfuls hickory wood chips, soaked in cold water for 30 minutes

1 To make the sauce: Melt the butter in a medium saucepan over medium heat. Add the onion and cover. Cook until the onion is translucent, about 5 minutes. Reduce the heat to medium-low and cook, uncovered, stirring occasionally, until the onion is caramelized, about 15 minutes. Stir in the garlic and cook until it is fragrant, about 1 minute. Add 1 cup/240 ml of the root beer, bring to a boil over high heat, and cook until the root beer is reduced to about 3 Tbsp, about 10 minutes.

2 Add the remaining ½ cup/120 ml root beer with the ketchup, the molasses, vinegar, steak sauce, and hot sauce and stir well. Bring to a boil and reduce the heat to medium-low. Simmer, stirring often, until the sauce is thickened and reduced to about 2½ cups/600 ml, 20 to 30 minutes. Remove from the heat and let cool completely. (The sauce can be covered and refrigerated for up to 1 week.)

3 To prepare the chicken: Mix the brown sugar, salt, paprika, granulated garlic, granulated onion, black pepper, and cayenne together in a small bowl, crumbling the brown sugar well with your fingers. On a large rimmed baking sheet, brush the chicken all over with the oil, then season with the spice rub. Let the chicken stand at room temperature for 15 to 30 minutes.

4 Prepare an outdoor grill for indirect cooking over medium-high heat (see page 19).

5 Drain and add half of the wood chips directly to the burning coals or to the smoker box of a gas grill, following the manufacturer's instructions. When the chips are smoking, brush the grill grate clean. Place the chicken on the grill, skin side down. Cook, with the lid closed as much as possible, flipping the chicken occasionally and adding the remaining drained chips after 20 minutes, until an instant-read thermometer inserted into the thickest part of the breast reads 165°F/73°C, 45 to 55 minutes. During the last 10 minutes, brush the chicken occasionally with the sauce to glaze it.

6 Transfer the chicken to a serving platter and let stand at room temperature for 3 to 5 minutes. Using a cleaver or large knife, cut each breast portion in half crosswise to make 4 pieces total. Serve immediately with the remaining sauce. (The leftover sauce can be covered and refrigerated for up to 1 month.)

MAKES 4 TO 6 SERVINGS

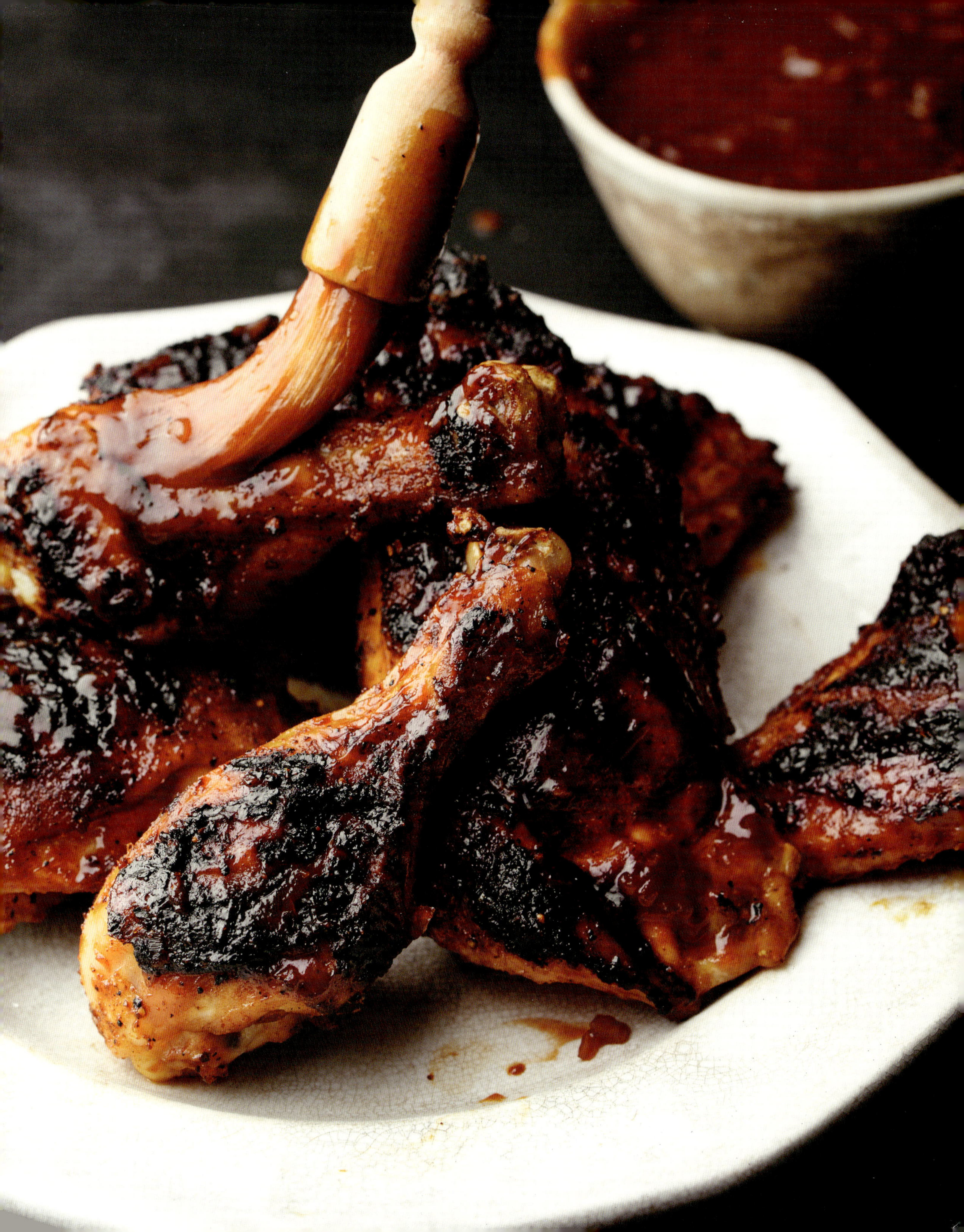

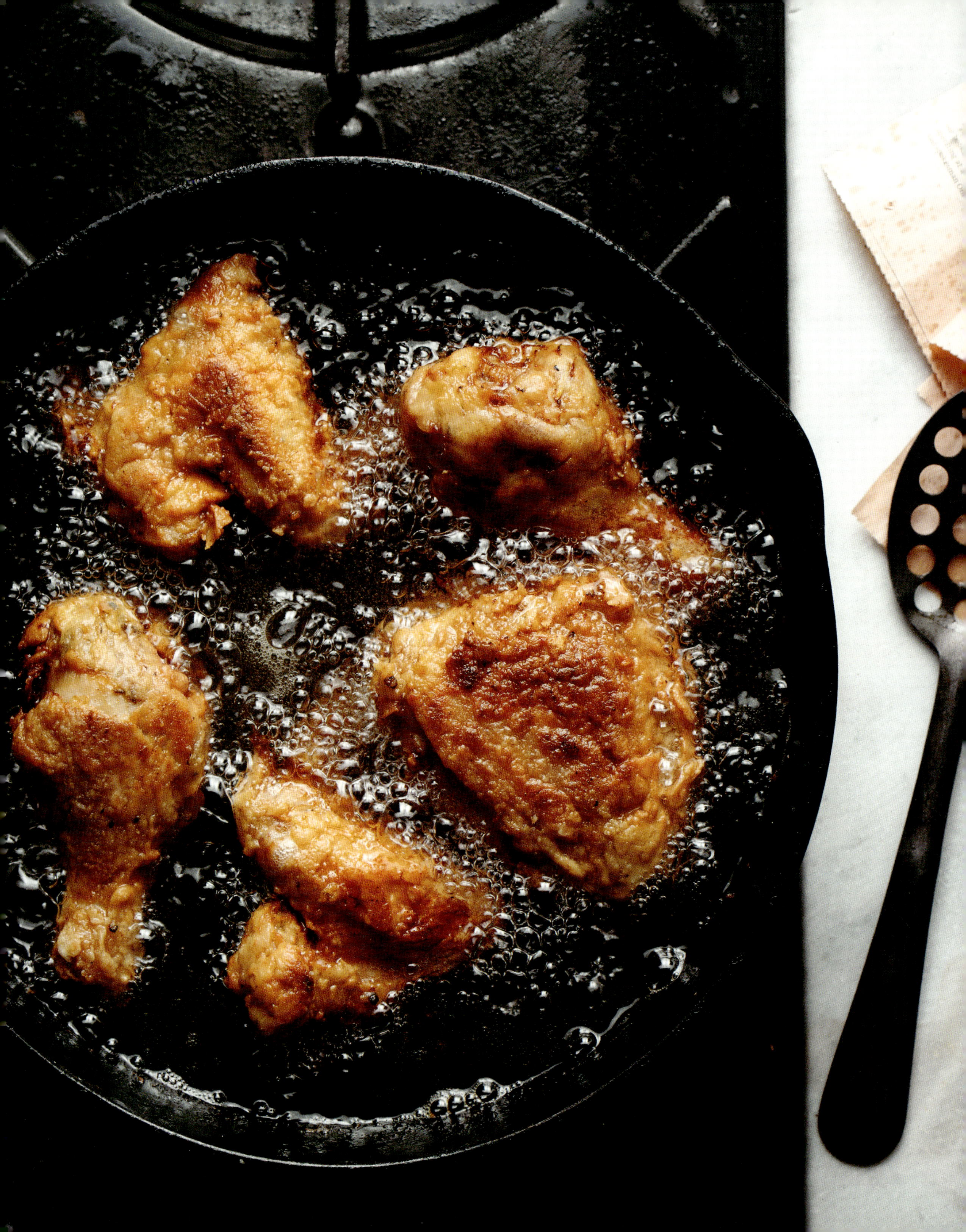

Great fried chicken is the proof of a good Southern cook. This is our favorite version, with a moisture-enhancing soak in a sweet iced tea brine, and lots of details in the recipe to ensure success. Be sure to buy a small chicken, as the large ones take too long to cook through, leading to burned bird. Get ready to enjoy some of the crispiest, juiciest fried chicken you've ever sunk your teeth into.

FRIED CHICKEN WITH ICED TEA BRINE

BRINE

⅓ cup/75 g fine sea salt

½ cup/100 g packed light brown sugar

6 orange pekoe tea bags

6 garlic cloves, crushed under a knife and peeled

1 tsp dried thyme

1 tsp dried rosemary

1 tsp black peppercorns

2 bay leaves

4 cups/960 ml ice water

1 chicken, about 3½ lb/1.6 kg, cut into 2 wings, 2 breast halves, 2 drumsticks, 2 thighs, and 1 back

1 cup /140 g unbleached all-purpose flour

1 tsp baking powder

½ teaspoon granulated garlic

½ tsp granulated onion

½ tsp kosher salt

½ tsp freshly ground black pepper

1 cup/240 ml buttermilk

1 tsp red pepper sauce, such as Tabasco

Vegetable oil, for deep-frying

1 Combine 4 cups/960 ml tap water with the salt and sugar in a large nonreactive saucepan and bring to a boil over high heat, stirring to dissolve the salt. Remove from the heat. Add the tea bags and let stand for 3 to 5 minutes. Using a slotted spoon, remove the tea bags, pressing hard on the bags with the back of a large spoon before discarding. Add the garlic, thyme, rosemary, peppercorns, and bay leaves. Let cool. Stir in the ice water.

2 Put the chicken in a large bowl and pour in the brine. Cover and refrigerate for at least 3 or up to 5 hours. The chicken will not improve with extra brining time.

3 Whisk the flour, baking powder, granulated garlic, granulated onion, salt, and pepper together in a large bowl. Whisk the buttermilk and hot sauce together in another large bowl. Line a large baking sheet with waxed or parchment paper. Remove the chicken, discard the brine, and pat the chicken dry with paper towels. One piece at a time, dip the chicken in the buttermilk mixture, letting the excess buttermilk drip back into the bowl. Roll the chicken in the flour mixture to coat and transfer to the baking sheet. Let the chicken stand for 15 to 30 minutes to set the coating.

4 Position a rack in the center of the oven and preheat the oven to 200°F/95°C.

5 Place a wire rack on a second large baking sheet. Pour 1 in/2.5 cm oil into a very large, heavy skillet, preferably cast iron, and heat over high heat until the oil is shimmering but not smoking. Carefully add the thighs, drumsticks, and wings to the oil and cover the skillet. Cook, adjusting the heat so the oil is bubbling steadily but not furiously, until the underside is beginning to brown, about 7 minutes. Turn the chicken and cook, uncovered, until the other side is browned and an instant-read thermometer inserted in the thickest part of the thigh but not touching bone reads 165°F/73°C, about 7 minutes more. Transfer the chicken to the wire rack and keep warm in the oven while repeating with the breast halves and back.

6 Let the chicken stand at room temperature for 5 minutes. Using a cleaver or large, heavy knife, cut each breast portion in half crosswise to make 4 pieces total. Serve the chicken warm.

MAKES 4 SERVINGS

Jerk is an incredibly delicious Jamaican conglomeration of many spices and other seasonings—never trust a jerk recipe that contains just a few ingredients. The word probably comes from the Peruvian term that evolved into jerky, also a meat dish cooked over fire. Here's the way we make jerk chicken at our restaurants, with an outdoor grilling alternative.

CHICKEN BREASTS WITH JERK MARINADE

MARINADE

1½ teaspoons whole allspice

6 green onions, white and green parts, coarsely chopped

¼ cup/30 g peeled and coarsely chopped fresh ginger

¼ cup/60 ml fresh lime juice

¼ cup/60 ml malt or cider vinegar

¼ cup/60 ml Japanese soy sauce

8 garlic cloves, coarsely chopped

2 tsp seeded and minced jalapeño chiles

1 tsp seeded and minced habanero or Scotch bonnet chile

1 Tbsp olive oil

1 Tbsp light brown sugar

2 tsp molasses (not blackstrap)

1 tsp coarsely chopped fresh thyme

¾ tsp dry mustard

¾ tsp Dry Jerk Seasoning (page 213) or commercial jerk seasoning

½ tsp freshly ground black pepper

⅛ tsp ground cinnamon

⅛ tsp freshly grated nutmeg

⅛ tsp kosher salt

6 chicken breast halves with skin and bone, about 10 oz/280 g each

1 Tbsp Dry Jerk Seasoning (page 213) or commercial jerk seasoning

½ cup/120 ml reduced-sodium chicken broth

1 **To make the marinade:** Process the allspice in a blender until finely ground. Add the green onions, ginger, lime juice, vinegar, soy sauce, garlic, jalapeños, and habanero and process until the green onions are minced. Add the oil, brown sugar, molasses, thyme, mustard, jerk seasoning, black pepper, cinnamon, nutmeg, and salt and process until well combined.

2 Place the chicken in a jumbo 2-gl/7.5 L self-sealing plastic bag and pour in the marinade. Close the bag and refrigerate, occasionally turning the bag, for at least 4 hours or up to 1 day.

3 Position a rack in the top third of the oven and preheat the oven to 450°F/230°C.

4 Remove the chicken from the marinade, shaking off the excess; reserve ½ cup/120 ml of the marinade. Season the chicken with the dry jerk seasoning.

5 Heat a large nonstick skillet over medium-high heat. In batches, add the chicken, skin side down, to the skillet and cook until the underside is well browned, about 3 minutes. Transfer the chicken, skin side up, to an 18-by-13-in/46-by-33-cm sided baking sheet. Add the reserved marinade to the skillet and bring to a boil. Spoon the marinade over the chicken and pour the broth around the chicken. Cook until an instant-read thermometer inserted in the thickest part of a breast half registers 165°F/73°C, 35 to 45 minutes.

6 Transfer each chicken breast to a dinner plate and top each with a spoonful of the pan juices. Serve immediately.

MAKES 6 SERVINGS

Grilled Jerk Chicken

Soak 2 large handfuls of apple or cherry wood chips in water to cover for at least 30 minutes; drain. Prepare an outdoor grill for indirect cooking over medium-high heat (see page 19). Remove the chicken from the marinade; shake off the excess marinade and discard the remaining marinade. Scatter the chips over the coals or put in the smoker box of a gas grill. Grill the chicken, skin side down, with the lid closed, over indirect medium-high heat, turning occasionally, until an instant-read thermometer inserted into the thickest part of the breast but not touching bone reads 165°F/73°C, about 45 minutes.

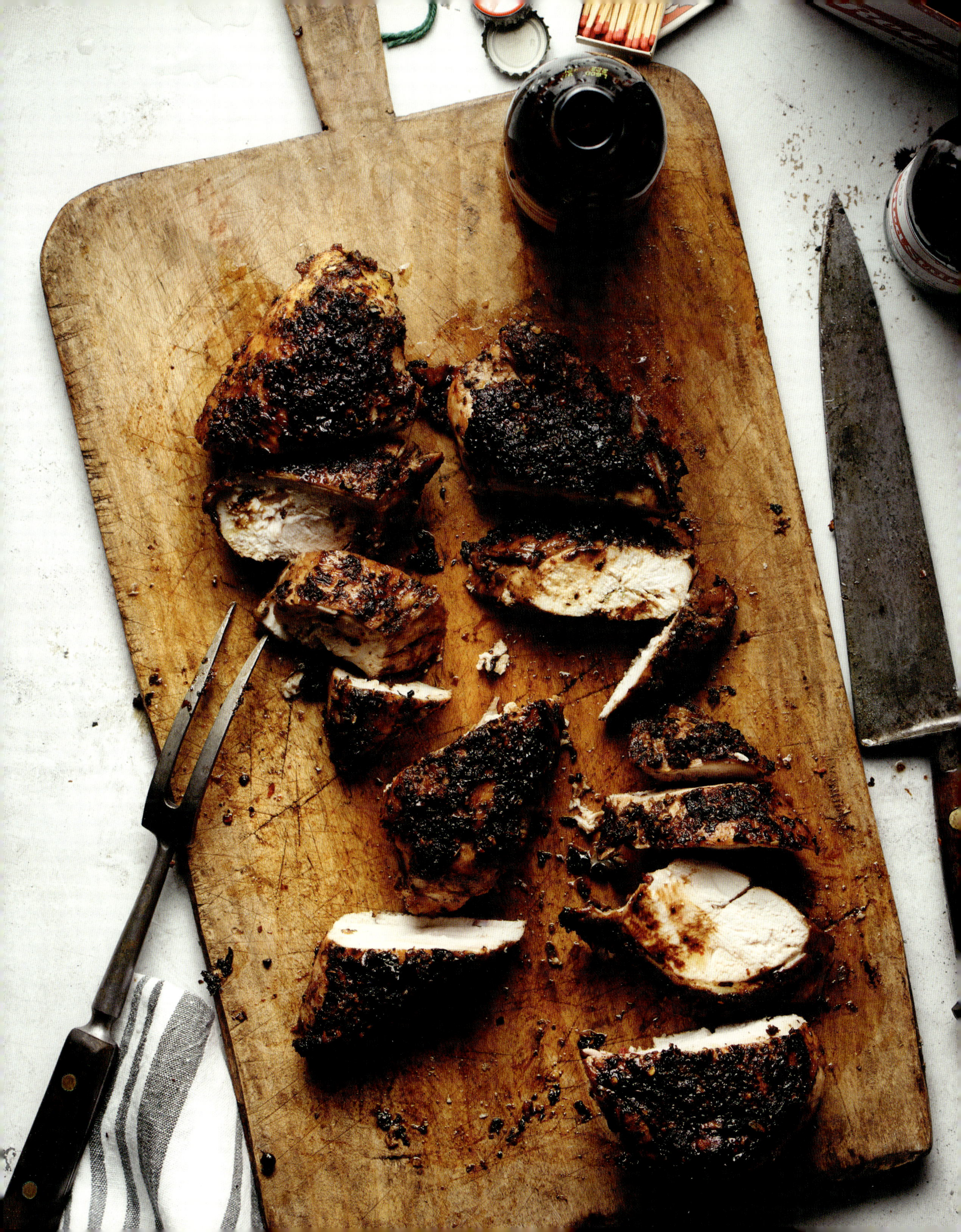

Tourism plays a big part in the Gulf Coast experience, and where there are tourists, there are restaurants. While this excellent dish is not an authentic example of any particular cuisine, it is a fine model of what might be called "resort food." It is also a great choice for a dinner party at home, as the components can be made well ahead, and the chicken just needs a few minutes of attention before serving.

CHEESE-STUFFED CHICKEN BREASTS WITH ROASTED RED PEPPER CREAM

SAUCE

1 Tbsp olive oil

1 red bell pepper, roasted (see below), peeled, seeded, and coarsely chopped

3 Tbsp finely chopped shallots

1 Tbsp mashed Roasted Garlic (page 213)

⅛ tsp dried thyme

2 Tbsp dry sherry

1 Tbsp unsalted butter

1 Tbsp all-purpose flour

½ cup/120 ml reduced-sodium chicken broth

½ cup/120 ml heavy cream

Kosher salt and freshly ground black pepper

CHICKEN

6 skinless, boneless chicken breast halves, about 7oz/200 g each

1 tsp kosher salt

½ tsp freshly ground black pepper

6 oz/170 g spreadable garlic-and-herb flavored cheese, such as Alouette

1 large red bell pepper, roasted (see below), peeled, seeded, and cut into strips about 2 in/5 cm long

1 cup/70 g panko (Japanese bread crumbs)

¾ cup/90 g freshly grated Parmigiano-Reggiano or Grana Padano cheese

3 Tbsp minced fresh flat-leaf parsley, squeezed dry in a towel

2 Tbsp minced fresh basil

½ cup/70 g all-purpose flour

¾ cup/180 ml half-and-half

¼ cup/60 ml olive oil

1 **To make the sauce:** Heat the oil in a medium saucepan over medium heat. Add the roasted bell pepper, shallot, roasted garlic, and thyme and cook, stirring occasionally, until the shallot softens, about 3 minutes. Add the sherry, increase the heat to high, and cook until the liquid is almost completely evaporated, about 2 minutes. Stir in the butter and let it melt. Sprinkle in the flour and mix to coat the vegetable mixture. Add the broth and cream, mix well, and bring to a simmer. Reduce the heat to medium-low and simmer until the sauce has thickened slightly, about 10 minutes. Using an immersion blender, process the sauce until smooth. (Or purée in batches in a blender or food processor.) Season to taste with salt and pepper. (The sauce can be cooled, covered, and refrigerated for up to 1 day. Reheat gently before using.)

Roasting Peppers and Chiles

Most bell peppers and chiles have a bitter skin that should be removed. Roasting blackens the skin and separates it from the flesh, making it easier to peel. Position the broiler rack about 8 in/20 cm from the heat source. Place the peppers or chiles on the rack and broil, turning them occasionally, until the skin is blackened and blistered, 10 to 12 minutes. Transfer to a large bowl, cover with plastic wrap, and let stand for 15 minutes before peeling. You can substitute jarred roasted red peppers, drained, rinsed, and patted dry, for freshly roasted bell peppers.

2 One at a time, place a chicken breast half between two plastic bags. Using the flat side of a meat pounder or a rolling pin, pound the chicken until ¼ in/6 mm thick. Season the chicken with the salt and pepper. Place a chicken breast with a long side facing you on the work surface. Add about 2 Tbsp of the spreadable cheese and one-sixth of the bell pepper strips in the center of the cheese. Fold in the short sides of the chicken and roll it up from the bottom to form a neat packet to enclose the stuffing. Be sure the cheese is completely covered. (The chicken can be covered and refrigerated for up to 6 hours.)

3 Mix the panko, grated cheese, parsley, and basil in a shallow dish. Place the flour in a second dish and the half-and-half in a third dish. Roll each chicken half in the flour to coat, shaking off the excess flour. Dip in the half-and-half, then coat with the panko mixture. Transfer to a platter and let stand for 15 minutes to set the coating.

4 Position a rack in the center of the oven and preheat the oven to 350°F/180°C. Line a large rimmed baking sheet with parchment paper or a silicone baking mat.

5 Heat the oil in a large skillet over medium-high heat until shimmering but not smoking. In batches, without crowding, add the chicken and cook, turning occasionally, until lightly browned on all sides, about 3 minutes. Transfer to the baking sheet. Bake until the chicken is golden brown and cooked through, about 15 minutes.

6 To serve, divide the sauce evenly among six dinner plates, spooning the sauce into the center of the each plate. Top each with a chicken breast half and serve hot.

MAKES 6 SERVINGS

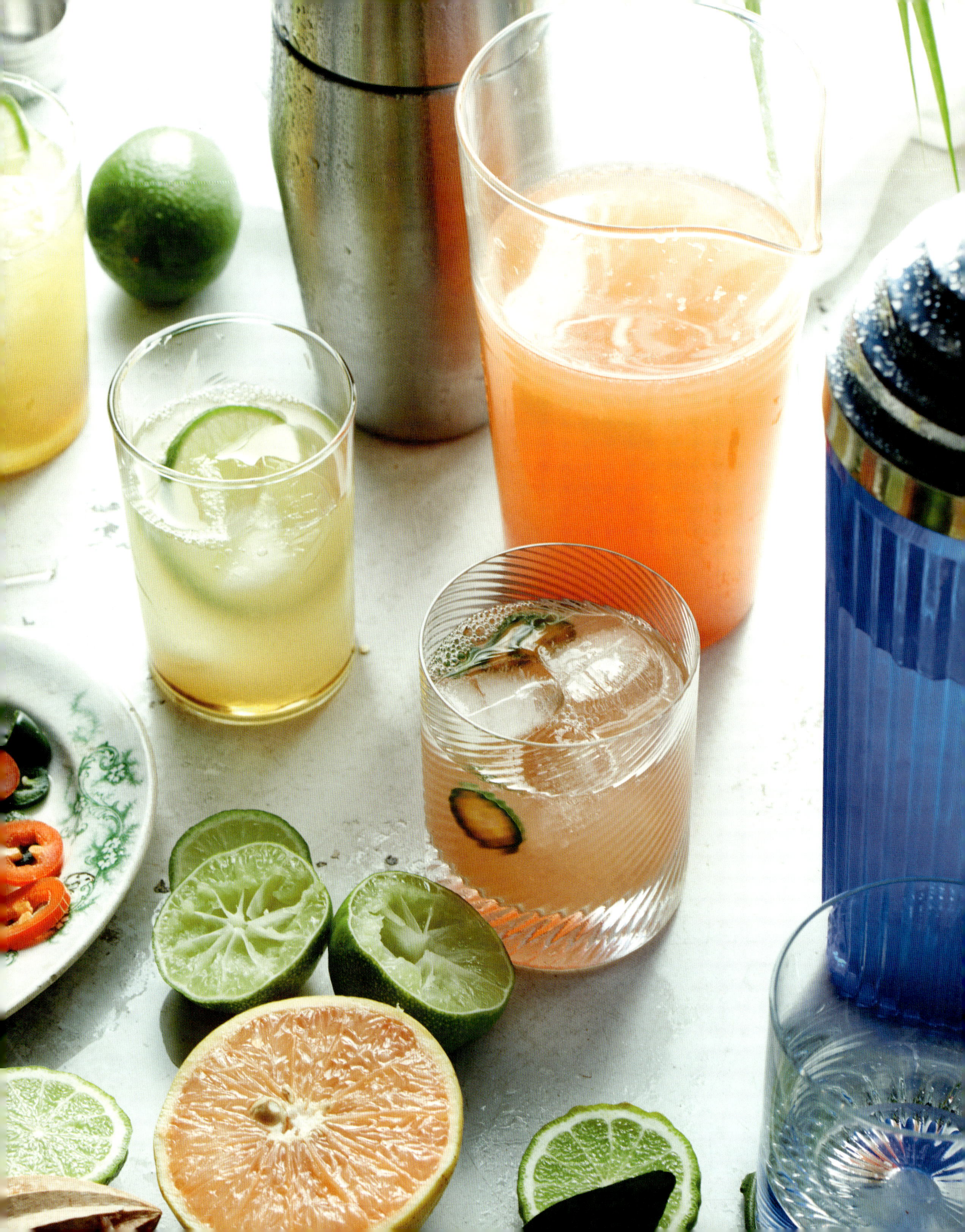

The origin of the Daiquiri can be traced to its namesake, a village in Cuba, where an American mining engineer, Jennings Cox, mixed up a batch in a punch bowl in the late 1800s. His visitors brought the recipe back to the States, where it gained a foothold before and after Prohibition. Like the La Floridita (page 33), this is another Hemingway fave, which he drank by the bucket at El Floridita Bar in Cuba.

DAIQUIRI

COCKTAIL

2 fl oz/60 ml premium rum, such as Ron Zacapa Centenario

¾ fl oz/22.5 ml fresh lime juice

½ fl oz/15 ml maple syrup

Dash of Angostura bitters

GARNISH: 1 lime slice

1 Add the cocktail ingredients to an ice-filled cocktail shaker. Stir well.

2 Fill a double Old-Fashioned glass with ice. Strain the cocktail into the glass. Garnish with the lime slice.

MAKES 1 DRINK

It was a brave person who drank the first jalapeño-spiked cocktail. But with the right balance of hot, sour, and sweet, this libation is as addictive as a big bowl of tortilla chips. The recipe calls for jalapeño tequila, but if you can't find it, make your own by steeping 1 Tbsp chopped jalapeño (include the seeds) with 1 cup/240 ml plain tequila overnight in a covered jar; strain, and refrigerate for up to 1 month.

LEAP OF FAITH

COCKTAIL

2 fl oz/60 ml fresh grapefruit juice

1½ fl oz/45 ml jalapeño-flavored tequila, such as Tanteo Jalapeño

½ fl oz/15 ml fresh lime juice

½ fl oz/15 ml agave nectar

GARNISH: 1 jalapeño slice

1 Add the cocktail ingredients to an ice-filled cocktail shaker. Shake well.

2 Fill a double Old-Fashioned glass with ice. Strain the cocktail into the glass. Float the jalapeño slice on top and serve.

MAKES 1 DRINK

Every cuisine that feeds into the melting pot of Gulf Coast cooking has some kind of chicken and rice dish. Our recipe takes a little from each one to make a hearty meal with a bit of spiciness. For a more paella-like dish, substitute ¼ tsp crumbled saffron threads for the paprika. Do use a starchy medium-grain rice, as its slight stickiness makes it much easier to serve from the pot.

ARROZ CON POLLO Y CHORIZO

3 Tbsp olive oil

12 oz/340 g Spanish-style smoked chorizo links, cut into ½-in/12-mm rounds

4 chicken thighs, each about 8 oz/225 g

1 tsp kosher salt

½ tsp freshly ground black pepper

1 yellow onion, chopped

1 red bell pepper, seeded and cut into ½-in/12-mm dice

2 garlic cloves, minced

1 tsp dried oregano

1 tsp sweet paprika

1 bay leaf

1½ cups/300 g medium-grain rice, such as Valencia, Bomba, or Arborio (see Note)

2 cups/480 ml canned reduced-sodium chicken broth

1 cup/240 ml lager beer

1 Tbsp tomato paste

1 cup/135 g thawed frozen green or pigeon peas

1 Heat 1 Tbsp of the oil in a large, heavy Dutch oven over medium heat. Add the chorizo and cook, stirring often, until it is lightly browned, about 5 minutes. Using a slotted spoon, transfer the chorizo to a plate, leaving the fat in the pot.

2 Season the chicken with the salt and black pepper. Add to the Dutch oven, skin side down, and cook until browned on the bottom, about 5 minutes. Turn and brown the other side, about 5 minutes more. (The chicken should cook partially and not just brown during this step, so keep the heat at medium.) Transfer the chicken to the plate with the chorizo.

3 Add the remaining 2 Tbsp oil to the Dutch oven and heat the oil. Add the onion, bell pepper, and garlic and cook, stirring occasionally, until the onion is translucent, about 4 minutes. Stir in the oregano, paprika, and bay leaf. Add the rice and stir well.

4 Pour in the broth, beer, ½ cup/120 ml water, and the tomato paste and increase the heat to high. Stir to dissolve the tomato paste, scraping up any browned bits in the bottom of the pot. Return the chicken and chorizo to the pot.

5 Reduce the heat to medium-low and cover tightly. Simmer, without stirring, until the rice is tender and has absorbed almost all of the liquid and the chicken shows no sign of pink when pierced at the bone, 25 to 30 minutes. During the last 5 minutes, add the peas but do not stir them in. Remove from the oven and let stand, covered, for 5 minutes. Discard the bay leaf. Serve hot.

MAKES 4 SERVINGS

NOTE: While the listed varieties are imported, domestic medium-grain rice is sold at Latino markets and in the rice aisle of many supermarkets. Goya is a good brand.

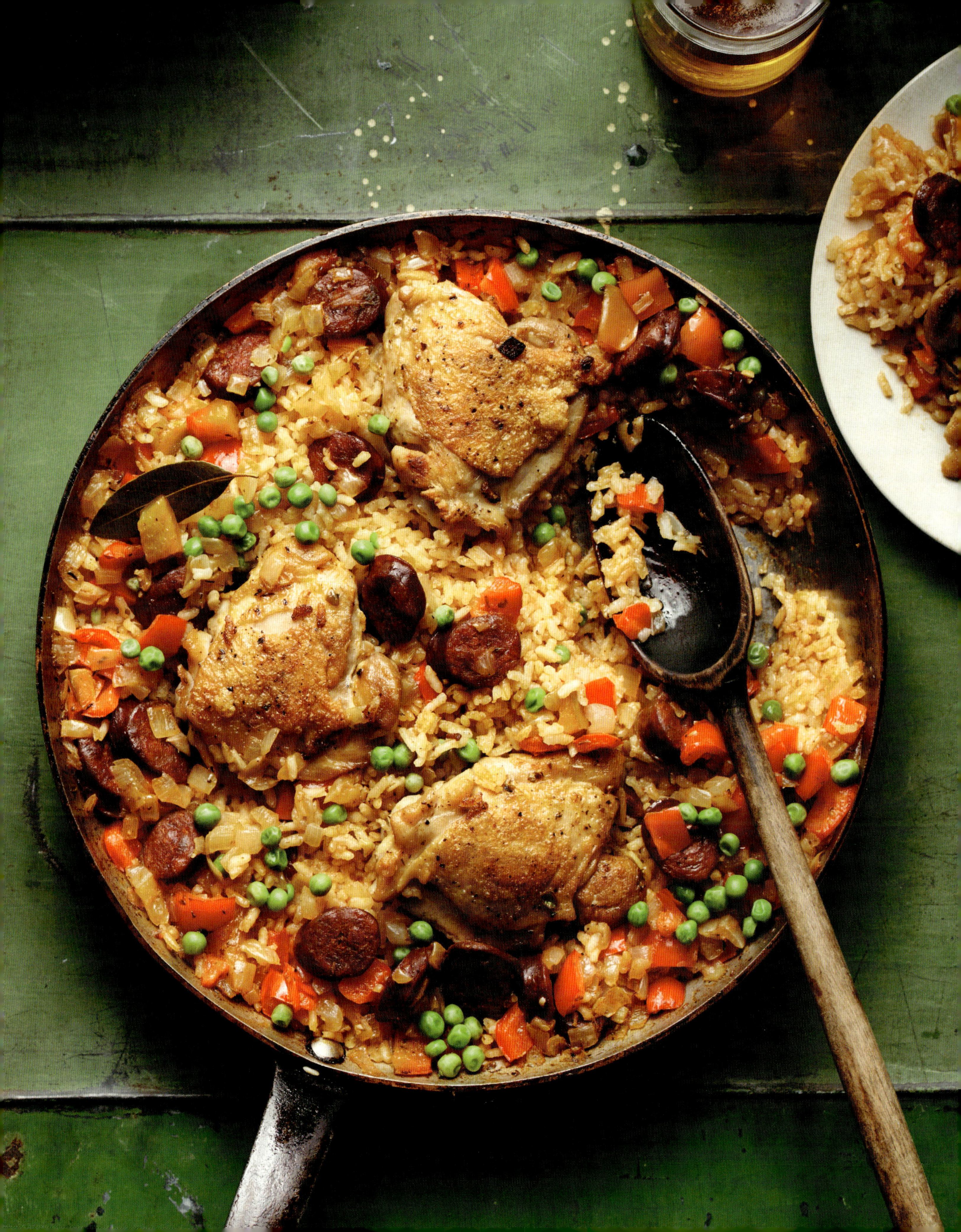

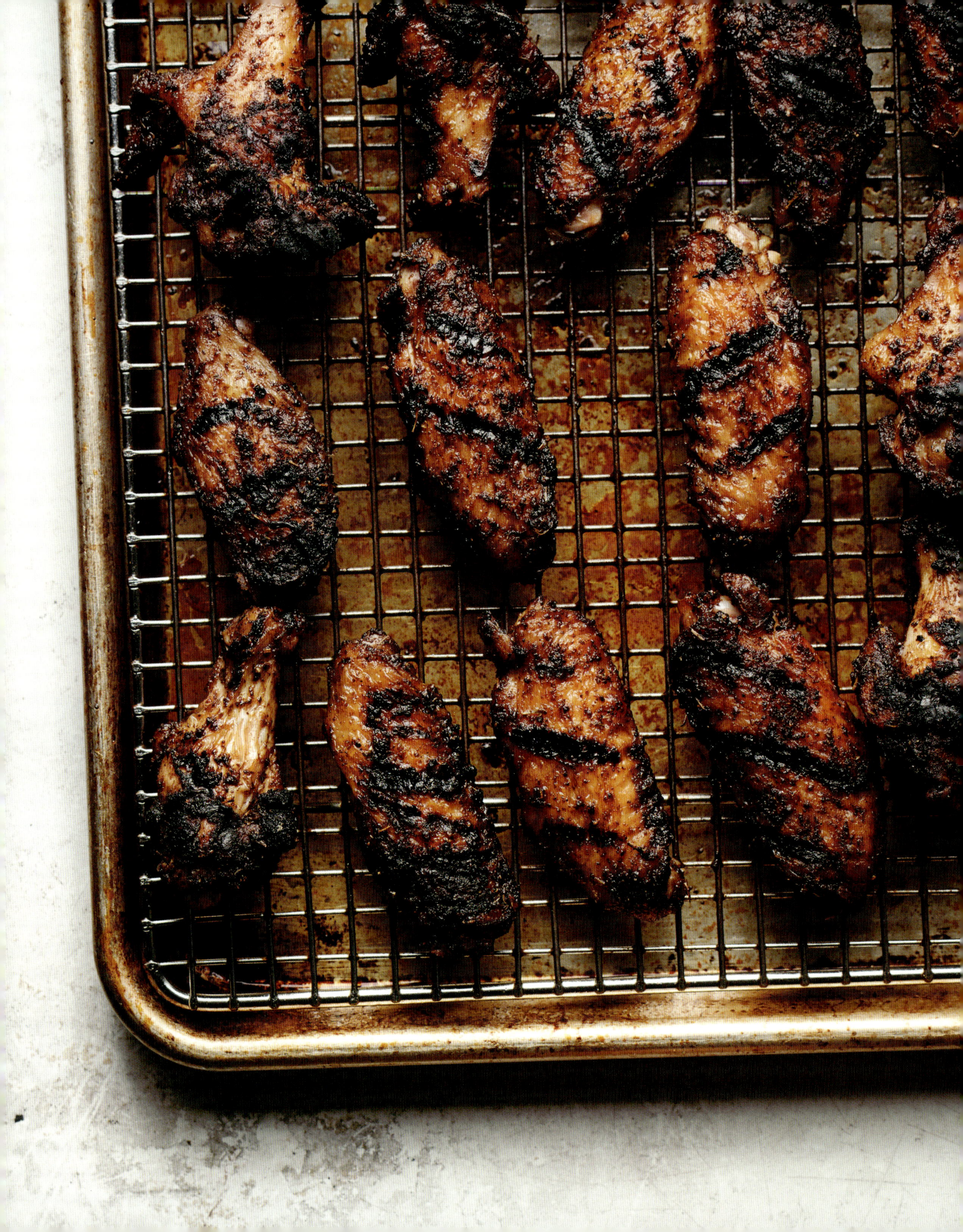

One of the most complex (and delicious) sauces in Mexican cuisine, mole can be reduced to its basic ingredients to make a quick and tasty rub for chicken. Chicken wings are especially good for grilling because they are moister than breasts and take less watching to avoid drying out. For an easy side, serve another eat-with-your-hands dish, such as corn on the cob, accompanied with Jalapeño-Lime Butter (page 211).

GRILLED CHICKEN WINGS WITH MOLE RUB

RUB

1 Tbsp pure ground ancho chile

1 Tbsp light brown sugar

1½ tsp kosher salt

1½ tsp unsweetened cocoa powder, preferably Dutch process

1½ tsp dried oregano, preferably Mexican

1½ tsp ground cumin

½ tsp granulated onion

½ tsp granulated garlic

½ tsp freshly ground black pepper

CHICKEN

5 lb/2.3 kg chicken wings, cut between joints and tips discarded

Olive oil, for brushing

2 large handfuls mesquite wood chips, soaked in cold water for 30 minutes and drained

1 Tbsp sesame seeds, preferably toasted (see Note)

1 **To make the rub:** Whisk all of the ingredients together in a small bowl.

2 **To prepare the chicken:** Toss the wings in a large bowl with the oil. Sprinkle with the rub and toss again. Let stand at room temperature for 15 to 30 minutes.

3 Prepare an outdoor grill for indirect cooking over medium-high heat (see page 19).

4 Drain the wood chips and add half of them to the burning coals or the smoker box of a gas grill, following the manufacturer's instructions. When the chips are smoking, brush the grill grate clean. Grill the chicken over indirect heat with the lid closed, adding the remaining chips after 20 minutes, turning them halfway through cooking, until the wings are browned and show no sign of pink when pierced at the bone with the tip of a small, sharp knife, about 45 minutes. Transfer to a platter.

5 Sprinkle the sesame seeds over the chicken and serve.

MAKES 4 SERVINGS

NOTE: To toast the sesame seeds, heat a small skillet over medium heat. Add the sesame seeds and cook, stirring occasionally, until lightly browned and fragrant, about 1 minute. Immediately transfer to a plate to cool.

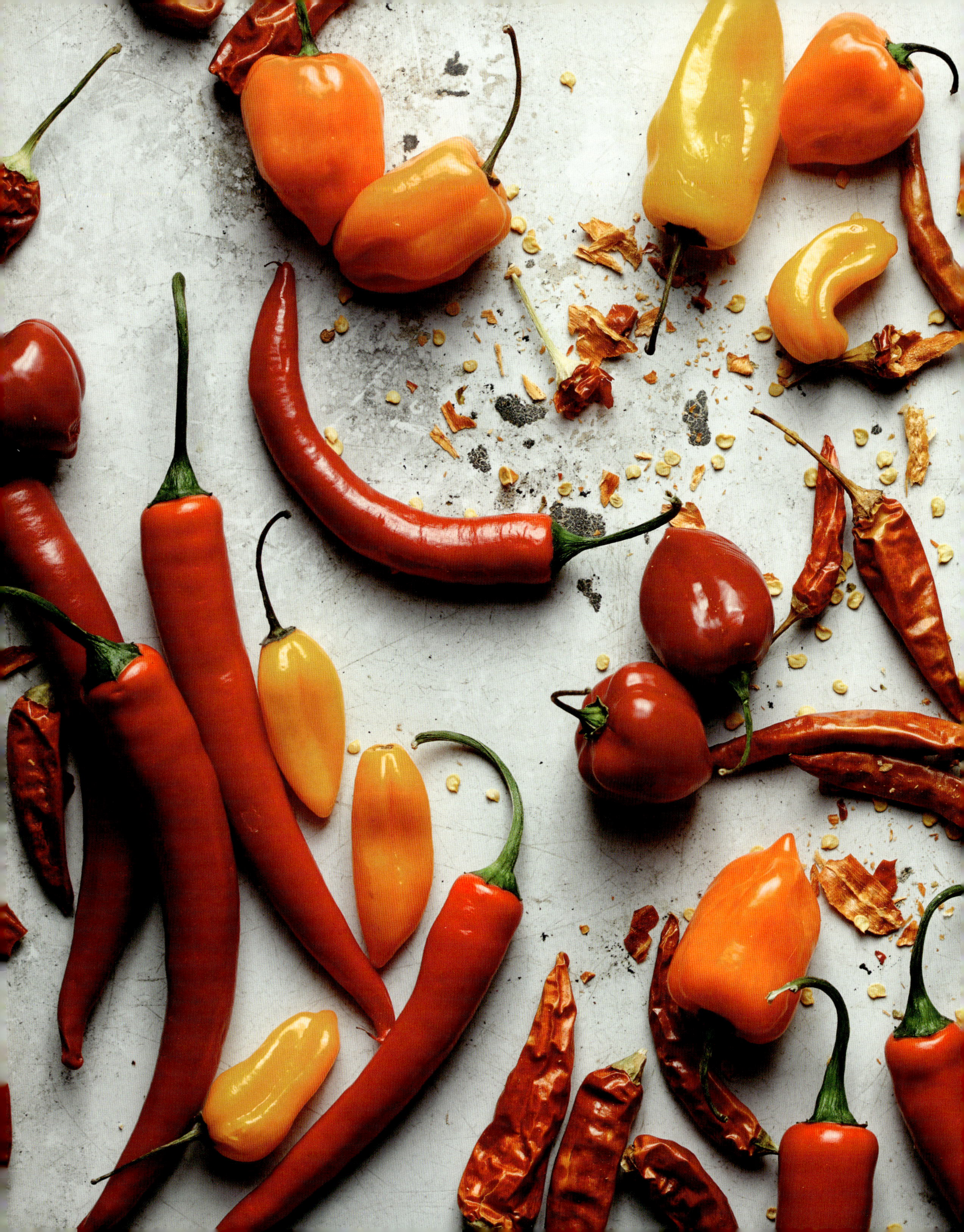

It is not too strong a statement to say that chiles—otherwise known as hot peppers—are the common thread running through the most important Gulf Coast cuisines. Remove the fiery Scotch bonnet from Jamaican cooking, or the *ají dulce* from a Puerto Rican kitchen, and cooks would be at a loss. Tex-Mex food uses both fresh (jalapeños, poblanos, serranos, and more) and dried (ancho and guajillo, among many others) chiles for their immediately identifiable flavors. Spices made from dried chiles, such as cayenne and paprika, are essential to Cajun dishes. Take away chiles? You may as well take away a cook's knife!

On virtually every Southern table, you will find a bottle of hot sauce, perfect for spicing up mildly seasoned comfort food. To many cooks, hot sauce boils down to a "holy trinity" of Tabasco, Frank's RedHot, and Crystal sauces, all originally made in Louisiana or from chiles grown in the state.

They're all red, in a bottle, and hot, so their differences are surprising. Tabasco (which has become a catchall word for any hot red sauce) is the only one made from Tabasco chiles, which hail from Mexico and were brought to Louisiana by Tabasco's founder in the mid-1800s. This variety has two unique attributes: the small fruit grows upright and is juicy, rather than dry, on the inside. While the sauce itself is made on Avery Island, near New Orleans, the plants are imported from warmer climates outside of the States. Once made, Tabasco is aged in oak barrels that formerly held bourbon.

Frank's RedHot Original Cayenne Pepper Sauce and Crystal Hot Sauce are both made with cayenne peppers, although Frank's is made in Missouri. The truth is in the tasting. According to the Scoville System for rating peppers, the common red fresh Tabasco chile registers 2,500 to 5,000 units (depending on the ripeness of the chiles when processed), which is only relatively hot by most people's standards. Frank's comes in a very mild 750 units, which is one reason why it is often the preferred hot sauce for Buffalo chicken wings. While Crystal Hot Sauce does not give its numbers, it is about as spicy as Frank's RedHot Original Cayenne Pepper Sauce. If you are a true "hothead," look to imported hot sauces to ratchet up the heat level, as it is not hard to find Mexican sauces with 8,000 Scoville units or more.

FIERY CHILES

RED MEAT

Some Southerners will tell you that pork is the king of the kitchen, but Texans sure love their beef, while Caribbean and Greek cooks have fondness for lamb. (Many Greeks migrated to Tampa to work in the fishing and sponge industries there, adding their cuisine to the Gulf Coast mix.) They are all represented here in dishes suitable for occasions from company dinners to backyard cookouts.

87
CREOLE SURF AND TURF WITH SPICY MUSTARD SAUCE

88
SMOKED AND BAKED TEXAS BRISKET

90
THE ULTIMATE TEXAS CHILI

91
ROPA VIEJA

94
JAMAICAN BEEF PATTIES

96
PICADILLO-STUFFED ACORN SQUASH

99
BABY BACK RIBS WITH BLACKBERRY BRANDY BBQ SAUCE

100
PUERTO RICAN PORK ROAST

102
JERK PORK TENDERLOIN WITH PINEAPPLE-RUM SAUCE

105
BOURBON-BRINED PORK CHOPS WITH PEACH GLAZE AND CORN-BACON HASH

107
JAMAICAN CURRY LAMB

110
GREEK LAMB SOUVLAKI WITH VEGETABLE KEBABS AND TZATZIKI

The grand culinary institutions of New Orleans (such as Arnaud's, Galatoire's, and Antoine's, which have more than three hundred years of history among them) have continuously served elegant Creole cuisine, a mélange of local ingredients and flavors with French influences. This steak-and-shrimp recipe is inspired by the timeless fare served at these classic restaurants.

CREOLE SURF AND TURF WITH SPICY MUSTARD SAUCE

STEAK

4 filet mignon steaks, each about 8 oz/225 g and 1½ in/4 cm thick

Vegetable oil, for brushing

1 tsp sweet paprika

1 tsp kosher salt

½ tsp dried thyme

½ tsp dried basil

½ tsp granulated garlic

½ tsp granulated onion

½ tsp freshly ground black pepper

⅛ tsp cayenne pepper

SHRIMP

12 extra-jumbo (16 to 20 count) shrimp, peeled with tail segment attached

Kosher salt and freshly ground black pepper

2 Tbsp unsalted butter

2 Tbsp minced shallots

¼ cup/60 ml dry white wine, such as Pinot Grigio

1 Tbsp Cognac or brandy

1 cup/240 ml heavy cream

1 Tbsp Creole mustard, such as Zatarain's or Tabasco Spicy Brown Mustard, or use Dijon mustard

Finely cut fresh chives, for garnish

1 To prepare the steaks: Lightly brush the steaks on both sides with oil. Mix the paprika, salt, thyme, basil, granulated garlic, granulated onion, black pepper, and cayenne together in a small bowl. Season the steaks all over with the paprika mixture. Let stand at room temperature for 15 to 30 minutes.

2 Prepare an outdoor grill for two-zone cooking with high heat (see page 19). Position a rack in the center of the oven and preheat the oven to its lowest setting, about 150°F/65°C.

3 To cook the shrimp: Season the shrimp with ¼ tsp salt and ¼ tsp pepper. Melt 1 Tbsp of the butter in a large skillet over medium-high heat. Add the shrimp to the skillet and cook, turning once, just until they turn opaque, 2½ to 3 minutes. Do not overcook the shrimp. Transfer the shrimp to a heatproof plate. Tent with aluminum foil and transfer to the oven to keep warm.

4 Add the shallots and the remaining 1 Tbsp butter to the skillet and stir over medium-high heat until the shallots soften, about 1 minute. Add the wine and Cognac and bring to a boil, scraping up the browned bits in the bottom of the pan with a wooden spoon. Cook until it reduces to 2 Tbsp, about 3 minutes. Stir in the cream and mustard, bring to a boil, and cook, stirring occasionally, until reduced by one-third, about 3 minutes. Season to taste with salt and pepper. Remove from the heat and cover with the lid ajar to keep warm.

5 Grill the steaks over the direct-high-heat side of the grill, with the lid closed, until the underside is browned and seared with grill marks, about 4 minutes. Turn and grill to brown the other side, about 4 minutes. Move the steaks to the indirect-heat side and continue cooking, covered, until an instant-read thermometer inserted horizontally into the center of a steak reads 125°F/52°C for medium-rare, about 4 minutes more. Transfer to a platter, tent with aluminum foil, and let stand for 3 to 5 minutes.

6 To serve, divide the steaks among 4 dinner plates and drizzle with any collected juices. Top each steak with 3 shrimp, with the tails standing up as much as possible. Quickly reheat the sauce over high heat for about 30 seconds and spoon equal amounts of the sauce over the shrimp and steak. Sprinkle with the chives and serve immediately.

MAKES 4 SERVINGS

A beautifully smoked brisket is a labor of love, and takes plenty of time. Our version uses a standard outdoor grill (yes, you can use a gas grill), not a specialized smoker, and switches to the oven to reduce the overall cooking time. You may have to order the beef—a whole untrimmed cut—from the butcher, although brisket is often available from wholesale clubs. It's traditional to serve soft white bread on the side with this.

SMOKED AND BAKED TEXAS BRISKET

RUB

3 Tbsp chili powder

1 Tbsp kosher salt

2 tsp ground cumin

2 tsp dry mustard

2 tsp granulated garlic

2 tsp granulated onion

2 tsp freshly ground black pepper

½ tsp cayenne pepper

BASTE

½ cup/120 ml lager beer

1 Tbsp Worcestershire sauce

1 beef brisket, about 9 lb/4 kg

3 large handfuls mesquite wood chips, soaked in water for at least 30 minutes

All-American BBQ Sauce (page 211), for serving

1 To make the rub: Whisk all of the ingredients together in a medium bowl.

2 To make the baste: Shake both ingredients together in a plastic spray bottle. Trim the excess fat from the brisket, leaving a layer about ¼ in/6 mm thick. Season the beef all over with the rub. Let stand at room temperature for 1 hour.

3 Prepare an outdoor grill for indirect cooking over low heat (see page 19). Scatter a handful of drained wood chips over the coals or in the smoker box.

4 Place the brisket on the cool area of the grill. Close the grill and cook for 45 minutes. Add another handful of drained wood chips to the grill (and 12 briquettes to the coals of a charcoal grill to maintain the heat; you may need to leave the lid ajar for a few minutes to allow enough oxygen into the grill for the briquettes to begin to turn gray around the edges). Spray well with the baste. Repeat after 45 minutes. Continue cooking, spraying about every 45 minutes, until the brisket has smoked for 3 hours and 45 minutes.

5 Meanwhile, position a rack in the center of the oven and preheat the oven to 350°F/180°C. Transfer the brisket to a large roasting pan and cover tightly with aluminum foil. Bake until the brisket is very tender when pierced with a knife and an instant-read thermometer inserted into the center of the meat reads 200°F/100°C, 1 to 1½ hours more. Uncover the brisket during the last 30 minutes of baking.

6 Remove the brisket from the oven and let it stand, covered, for 30 minutes.

7 Transfer the beef to a carving board. Carefully pour any pan juices into a medium bowl. Let stand for 5 minutes, then skim off any fat that rises to the surface. Using a thin, sharp knife, cut the beef across the grain into thin slices. Place the slices on a platter and drizzle with some of the juices. Serve hot, with the sauce.

MAKES 10 TO 12 SERVINGS

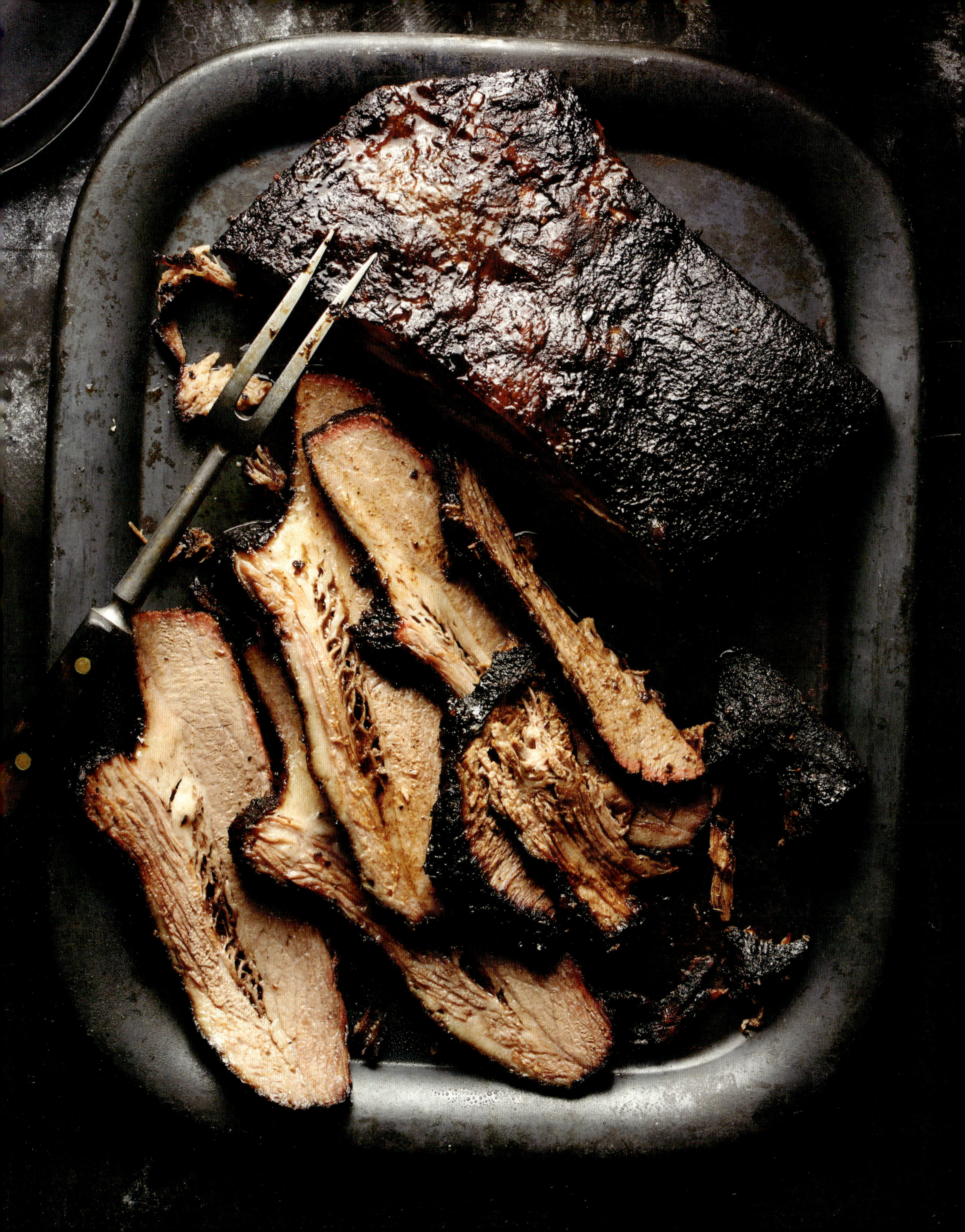

What makes us so confident that this is the ultimate Texas chili? First of all, it is made with hand-cut chunks of beef chuck—save your ground meat for burgers. Some folks use a chili purée, but we like easy-to-use chili powder. We pass on tomatoes, except a little tomato paste for color. The big question is "Beans or no beans?" We leave them out, in true Texas style, but add them if you want.

THE ULTIMATE TEXAS CHILI

5 bacon slices, coarsely chopped

Vegetable oil, as needed

3½ lb/1.6 kg beef chuck, cut into 1-in/2.5-cm pieces

Kosher salt and freshly ground black pepper

1 large yellow onion, finely chopped

1 green bell pepper, cored, seeded, and chopped

1 red bell pepper, cored, seeded, and chopped

1 jalapeño chile, seeded and minced

6 garlic cloves, finely chopped

3 Tbsp chili powder, preferably Gebhardt (see Note)

2 tsp smoked paprika (pimentón)

2 tsp ground cumin

2 tsp dried oregano

2 Tbsp tomato paste

One 12-oz/360-ml bottle lager beer

1 bay leaf

1 Tbsp yellow cornmeal, or as needed

Sour cream, for serving

Shredded mild Cheddar cheese, for serving

Chopped fresh cilantro, for serving

1 Position a rack in the center of the oven and preheat the oven to 325°F/165°C.

2 Cook the bacon in a medium skillet over medium heat, stirring occasionally, until browned, about 5 minutes. Using a slotted spoon, transfer the bacon to paper towels to drain. Pour the rendered bacon fat into a glass measuring cup. Add enough oil to the cup, if needed, to measure ¼ cup/60 ml.

3 Heat 2 Tbsp of the bacon fat mixture in a large Dutch oven over medium-high heat. Season the beef with 2 tsp salt and 1 tsp pepper. In batches, without crowding, add the beef to the pot and cook, stirring occasionally, until browned, adding oil as needed, about 5 minutes. Transfer the beef to a plate.

4 Add the remaining 2 Tbsp bacon fat mixture to the pot and heat over medium heat. Add the onion, green and red bell peppers, jalapeño, and garlic and cover. Cook, stirring occasionally, until the vegetables are tender, about 5 minutes. Return the beef and any juices to the pot. Stir in the chili powder, smoked paprika, cumin, and oregano and cook, uncovered, until the spices begin to toast, about 1 minute. Stir in the tomato paste, followed by the beer and bay leaf. Bring to a boil over high heat.

5 Cover and bake until the beef is tender, about 2 hours. Remove from the oven and let stand for 5 minutes. Skim any fat from the surface. Season to taste with salt and pepper. (If desired, thicken the cooking juices with cornmeal: bring the chili to a boil over medium heat. Stir in 1 Tbsp cornmeal at a time, letting the liquid come to a full boil before checking its thickness. Add more cornmeal as needed. Reduce the heat to low and simmer until the cornmeal loses its raw taste, about 5 minutes.) Discard the bay leaf.

6 Coarsely chop the reserved bacon. Serve the chili in bowls, with the bacon, sour cream, cheese, and cilantro passed on the side.

MAKES 4 TO 6 SERVINGS

NOTE: Gebhardt Chili Powder is made from an old recipe developed in San Antonio. It is sold in the Southwest and online.

CHILI WITH BEANS: Add 2 rinsed and drained 15-oz/430-g cans of black or pinto beans to the chili during the last 10 minutes of cooking. Makes 6 to 8 servings.

Cuban cooks call this braised beef stew *ropa vieja* ("old clothes" in Spanish) because the beef in the dish is cooked until very tender and then pulled into raggedy shreds. Olives and capers add a touch of bitterness to offset the rich meatiness of the beef. It is almost unthinkable to serve this dish without rice and black/green beans of some kind, like our Yellow Rice and Peas (page 173).

ROPA VIEJA

BRAISED BEEF

1 beef chuck roast, about 3 lb/1.4 kg

1½ tsp kosher salt

1 tsp freshly ground black pepper

2 Tbsp olive oil

1 large yellow onion, coarsely chopped

6 garlic cloves, coarsely chopped

3½ cups/840 ml reduced-sodium beef broth

2 bay leaves

SAUCE

2 Tbsp olive oil

1 large yellow onion, cut into ½-in/12-mm half-moons

1 large red bell pepper, cored, seeded, and cut into ½-in/12-mm strips

1 large green bell pepper, cored, seeded, and cut into ½-inch/12-mm strips

4 garlic cloves, minced

½ cup/120 ml dry sherry

¼ cup/55 g tomato paste

1 tsp dried oregano

½ tsp dried cumin

½ cup/75 g sliced pimiento-stuffed olives

3 Tbsp drained and rinsed nonpareil capers

Kosher salt and freshly ground black pepper

1 To braise the beef: Position a rack in the center of the oven and preheat the oven to 350°F/180°C.

2 Season the beef with the salt and pepper. Heat 1 Tbsp of the oil in a Dutch oven or flameproof casserole over medium-high heat. Add to the pot and cook, turning once, until the beef is browned, about 10 minutes. Transfer to a plate.

3 Add the remaining 1 Tbsp oil to the pot and heat. Add the onion and garlic and cook, stirring occasionally, until the onion softens, about 3 minutes. Add the broth and bay leaves. Bring to a boil, scraping up the browned bits in the bottom of the pot with a wooden spoon. Return the beef to the pot and add enough water to almost cover it. Bring to a boil.

4 Cover and bake until the meat is very tender and can be easily pulled apart into shreds, about 2 hours. Transfer the pot roast to a platter and let cool. Strain the cooking liquid through a medium-mesh sieve. Measure 2 cups/480 ml of the liquid into a large bowl and set aside. (Reserve any remaining liquid to use another time as beef broth.) Wash and dry the pot.

5 To make the sauce: Heat the oil in the Dutch oven over medium-high heat. Add the onion, red and green bell peppers, and garlic and cook, stirring occasionally, until the vegetables soften, about 5 minutes. Add the sherry, bring to a boil, and cook until reduced by half, about 5 minutes. Add the tomato paste to the reserved broth and whisk to dissolve the paste. Pour the broth mixture into the pot and add the oregano and cumin. Bring to a boil and cook until the mixture is reduced by half, about 15 minutes.

6 Use two forks to shred the beef into bite-size pieces. Stir the beef, olives, and capers into the sauce and reduce the heat to medium. Cook, stirring often, to blend the flavors, about 10 minutes. Season to taste with salt and pepper. Serve immediately.

MAKES 6 SERVINGS

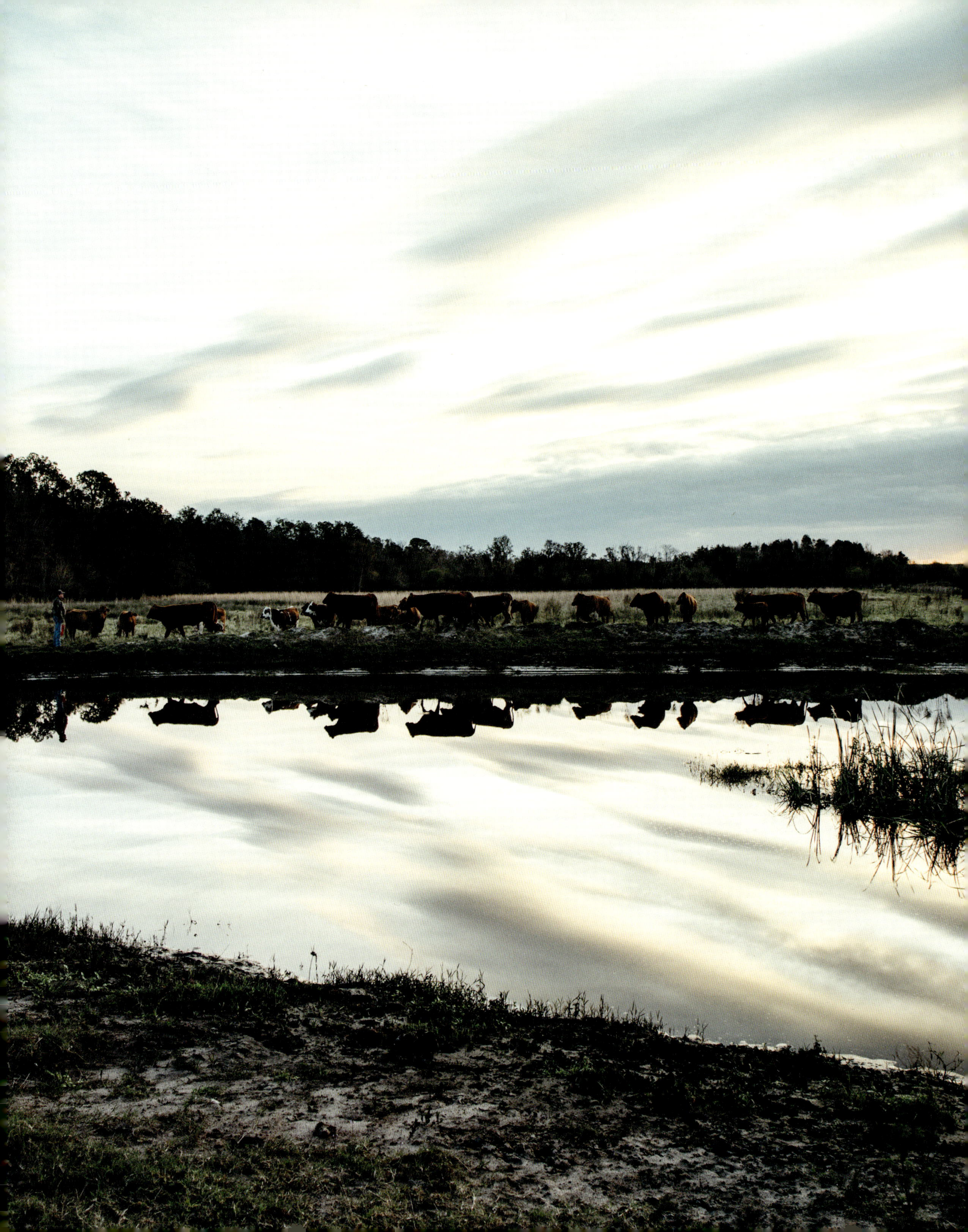

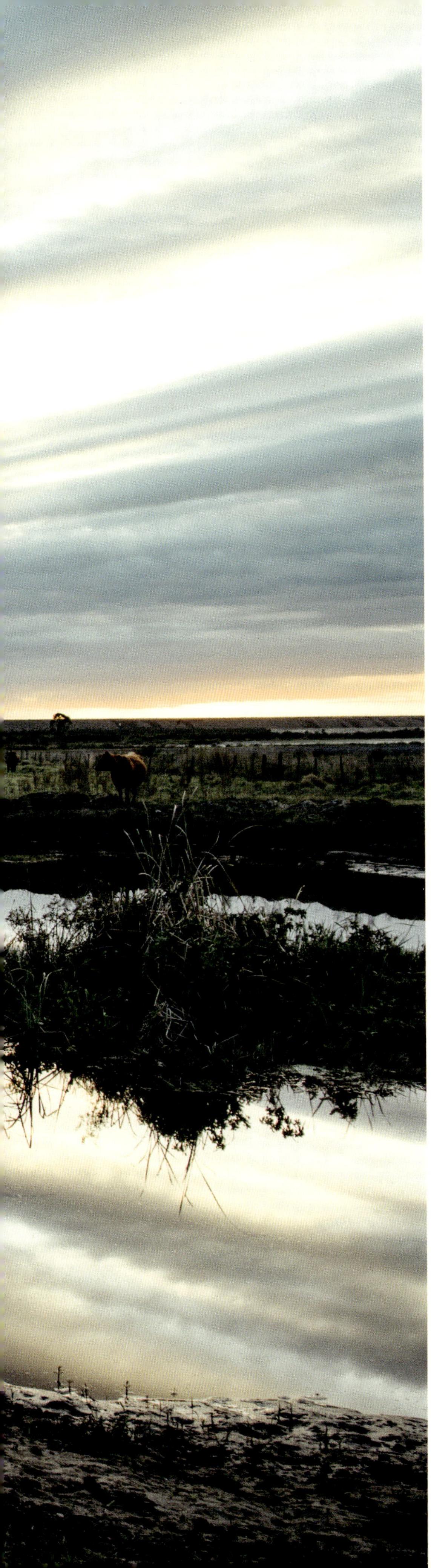

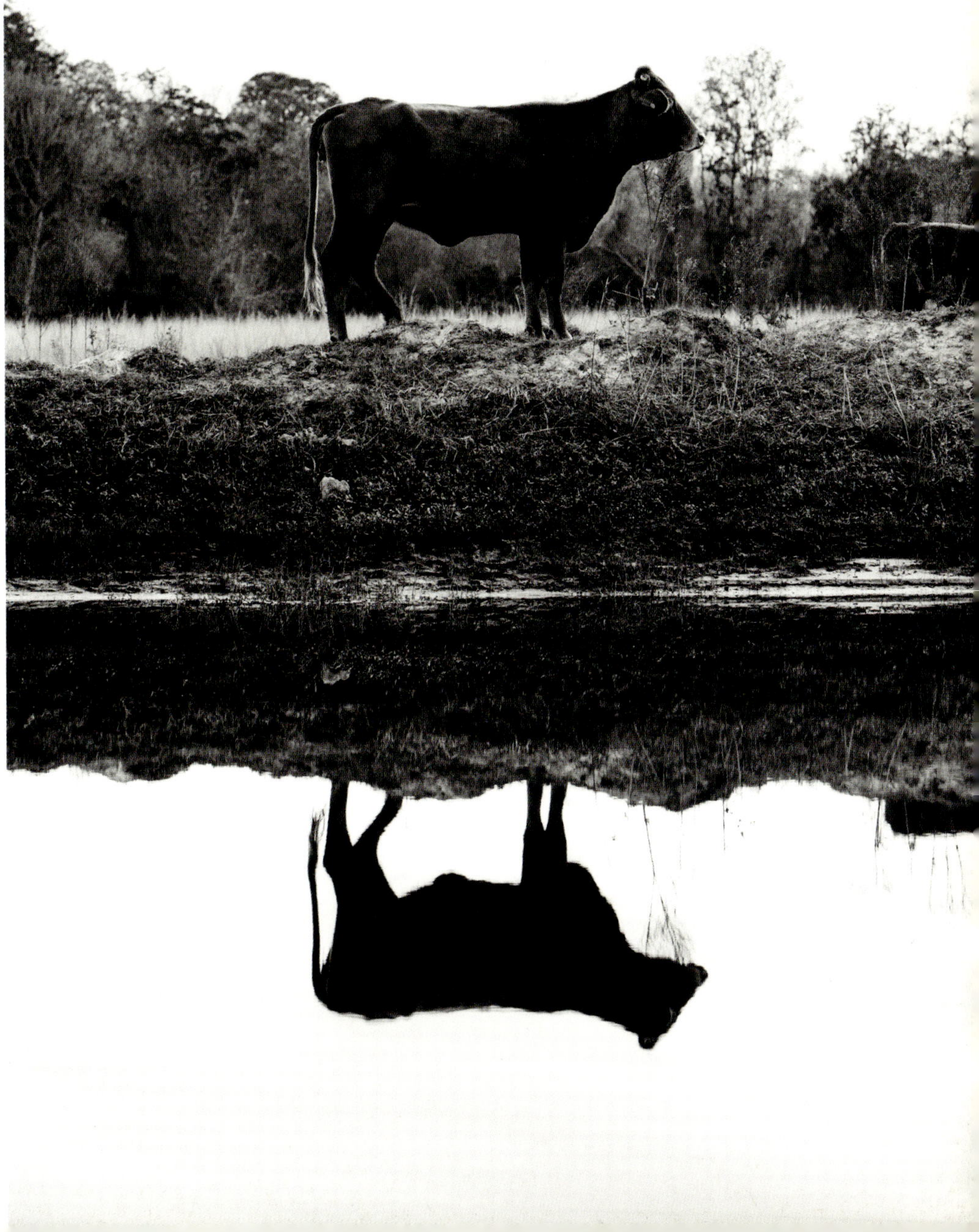

These hand-held savory pastries are sold wherever Jamaicans have settled. A Caribbean version of the Cornish pasty, they are flavored with Indian and African spices, and the crust gets its golden yellow color from the fat skimmed from a pot of curried goat (although we use curry powder here). Serve them with a big green salad and perhaps a chilled beer.

JAMAICAN BEEF PATTIES

DOUGH

3 cups/420 g unbleached all-purpose flour, plus more for rolling dough

2 tsp Jamaican curry powder (see Note) or ground turmeric

¾ tsp baking powder

1¼ tsp fine salt

6 Tbsp/85 g cold unsalted butter, cut into ½-in/12-mm cubes

6 Tbsp/85 g cold vegetable shortening, cut into ½-in/12-mm cubes

½ cup/120 ml ice water

FILLING

1 Tbsp vegetable oil

1 small yellow onion, finely chopped

1 tsp seeded and minced Scotch bonnet or habanero chile

2 garlic cloves, minced

1½ tsp curry powder, preferably Jamaican curry

½ tsp dried thyme

1 lb/455 g ground round beef (85 percent lean)

Kosher salt and freshly ground black pepper

½ cup/120 ml hot water

1 Tbsp tomato paste

1 cup/55 g fresh bread crumbs

2 green onions, white and green parts, minced

1 large egg, beaten until foamy

1 To make the dough: Pulse the 3 cups/420 g flour, the curry powder, baking powder, and salt in a food processor to combine them. Add the butter and shortening and pulse a few times until the mixture looks like coarse meal with some pea-sized pieces. Transfer the dough to a bowl. Gradually stir in enough of the ice water until the dough clumps together. Gather the dough into a ball. Divide in half and shape each portion into a thick disk. Wrap in plastic and refrigerate until chilled, at least 2 hours or up to 1 day.

2 To make the filling: Heat the oil in a large skillet over medium heat. Add the onion, chile, and garlic and cook, stirring occasionally, until they soften, about 3 minutes. Stir in the curry powder and thyme. Add the ground beef, 1 tsp salt, and ½ tsp pepper and increase the heat to medium-high. Cook, stirring often and breaking up the meat with the spoon, until it loses its raw color, 8 to 10 minutes. Drain off any excess fat from the skillet. Whisk the hot water and tomato paste together, dissolve the paste, and stir into the ground beef mixture. Stir in the bread crumbs and reduce the heat to medium-low. Simmer, stirring often, until the filling thickens, about 3 minutes. Stir in the green onions. Season to taste with salt and pepper. Transfer the filling to a bowl and let cool completely. (The filling can be covered and refrigerated for up to 1 day.)

3 Divide the dough into 12 equal pieces and roll them into balls. One at a time, roll the dough into a round about ⅛ in/3 mm thick. Using a 6-in/15-cm saucer as a template, cut a round from the dough, discarding the trimmings. Transfer to a plate, separating the rounds with waxed or parchment paper. Cover loosely with plastic wrap and refrigerate for 10 to 20 minutes.

4 Position racks in the center and top third of the oven and preheat the oven to 350°F/180°C.

5 For each patty, place a chilled round on a work surface. Brush the edges with beaten egg. Place 1 heaping Tbsp of the cooled filling on the bottom half of the round about ½ in/12 mm from the edge. Fold in half and seal the open edges with the tines of a fork. Pierce the top of the patty once with the fork. Place the assembled patties on two large rimmed baking sheets. Refrigerate until the dough is chilled, at least 10 minutes or up to 2 hours.

6 Bake, switching the positions of the racks halfway through baking from top to bottom and front to back, until the patties are golden brown, about 25 minutes. Let cool on the baking sheets for 10 minutes. Serve warm or at room temperature.

MAKES 12 PATTIES; SERVES 6 TO 8

NOTE: Jamaican curry powder may not contain cardamom, a frequent component in the Indian-style spice blend. Look for Jamaican curry powder at Latino markets, or just use the familiar supermarket brands.

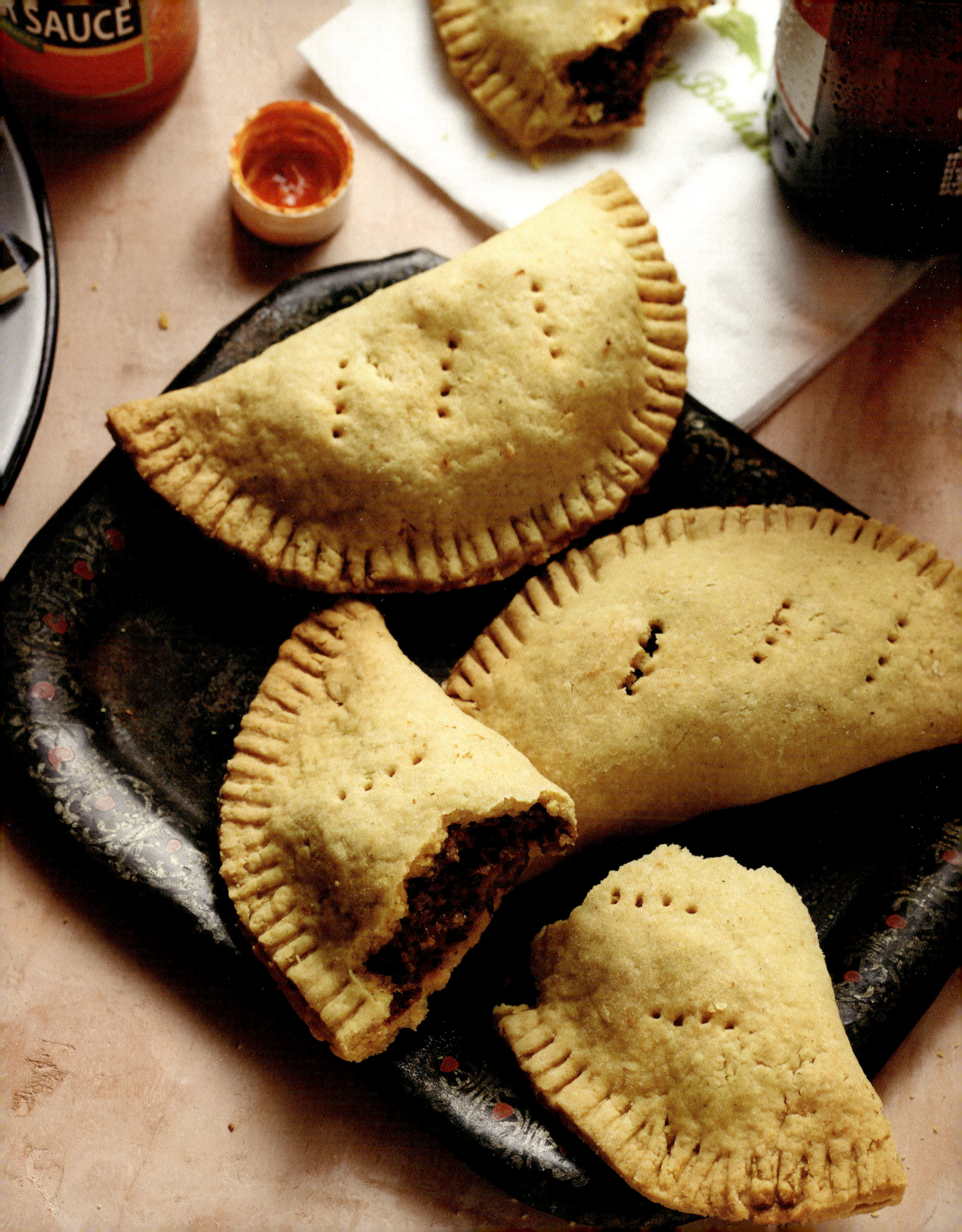
SAUCE

Every Cuban family has a recipe for picadillo, a braised hash of ground meat seasoned with green olives, raisins, and a pinch of cinnamon. Often used as a filling for empanadas or tacos, it makes a great sandwich in a roll (think of it as a "sloppy José"). It can also be served on a bed of lettuce as a salad or as a stuffing for vegetables, as it is here, paired with acorn squash.

PICADILLO-STUFFED ACORN SQUASH

2 acorn squash, each 1¼ lb/570 g

Kosher salt and freshly ground black pepper

PICADILLO

2 Tbsp olive oil

1 yellow onion, chopped

1 small green bell pepper, cored, seeded, and chopped

2 garlic cloves, minced

1 lb/455 g ground round beef (85 percent lean)

2 Roma (plum) tomatoes, seeded and chopped

1 tsp ground cumin

1 tsp dried oregano

1 tsp kosher salt

¼ tsp freshly ground black pepper

¼ tsp red pepper flakes

⅛ tsp ground cinnamon

1 bay leaf

1 Tbsp tomato paste

¾ cup/180 ml hot water

⅓ cup/50 g sliced pimiento-stuffed olives

⅓ cup/60 g seedless raisins

2 Tbsp chopped fresh cilantro or flat-leaf parsley, for serving

1 To roast the acorn squash: Position a rack in the center of the oven and preheat the oven to 425°F/220°C. Oil a roasting pan large enough to hold the acorn squash halves.

2 Cut each squash in half lengthwise through its stem and scoop out the seeds. Season to taste with salt and pepper. Place the squash halves, cut side down, in the prepared pan. Add ½ cup/120 ml water and tightly cover the pan with aluminum foil. Roast until the squash is tender when pierced with the tip of a small sharp knife, 30 to 40 minutes.

3 Meanwhile, make the picadillo: Heat 1 Tbsp of the oil in a medium skillet over medium heat. Add the onion, bell pepper, and garlic and cook, stirring occasionally, until softened, about 3 minutes. Transfer to a plate and tent with aluminum foil to keep warm.

4 Heat the remaining 1 Tbsp oil in the skillet. Add the ground beef and cook, stirring occasionally and breaking up the meat with the side of the spoon, until it loses its raw look, about 5 minutes. Drain off the excess fat. Stir in the tomatoes and cook for 1 minute. Stir in the reserved onion mixture. Stir in the cumin, oregano, salt, black pepper, red pepper flakes, cinnamon, and bay leaf. Dissolve the tomato paste in the hot water, add to the skillet, and stir well. Reduce the heat to medium-low. Simmer, stirring occasionally, until the liquid has evaporated and the picadillo is well flavored, about 30 minutes. During the last 5 minutes, stir in the olives and raisins. Discard the bay leaf.

5 Place each acorn squash, cut side up, in a wide soup bowl. Divide the picadillo among the squash, filling each one with a heaping portion. Sprinkle with the cilantro and serve.

MAKES 4 SERVINGS

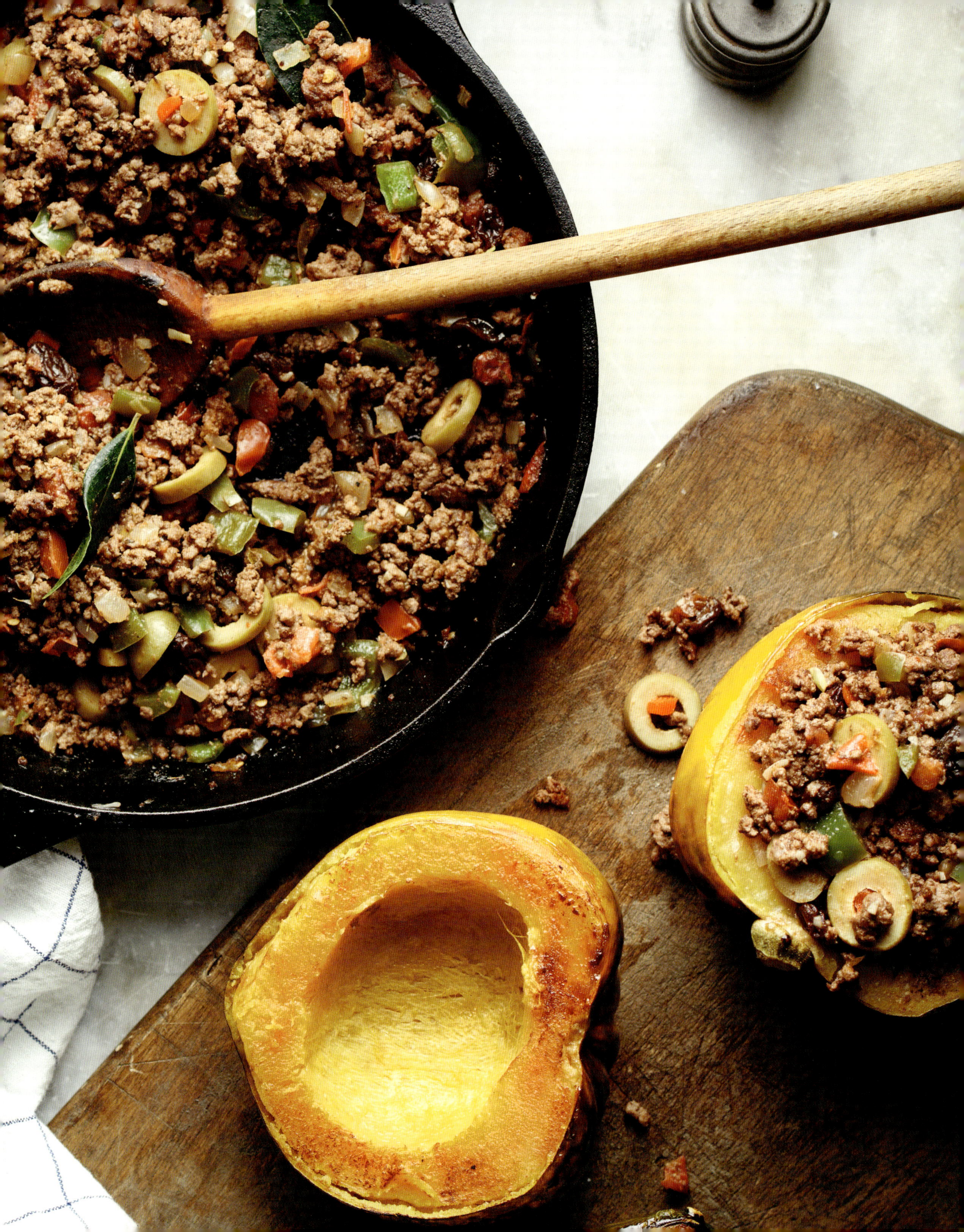

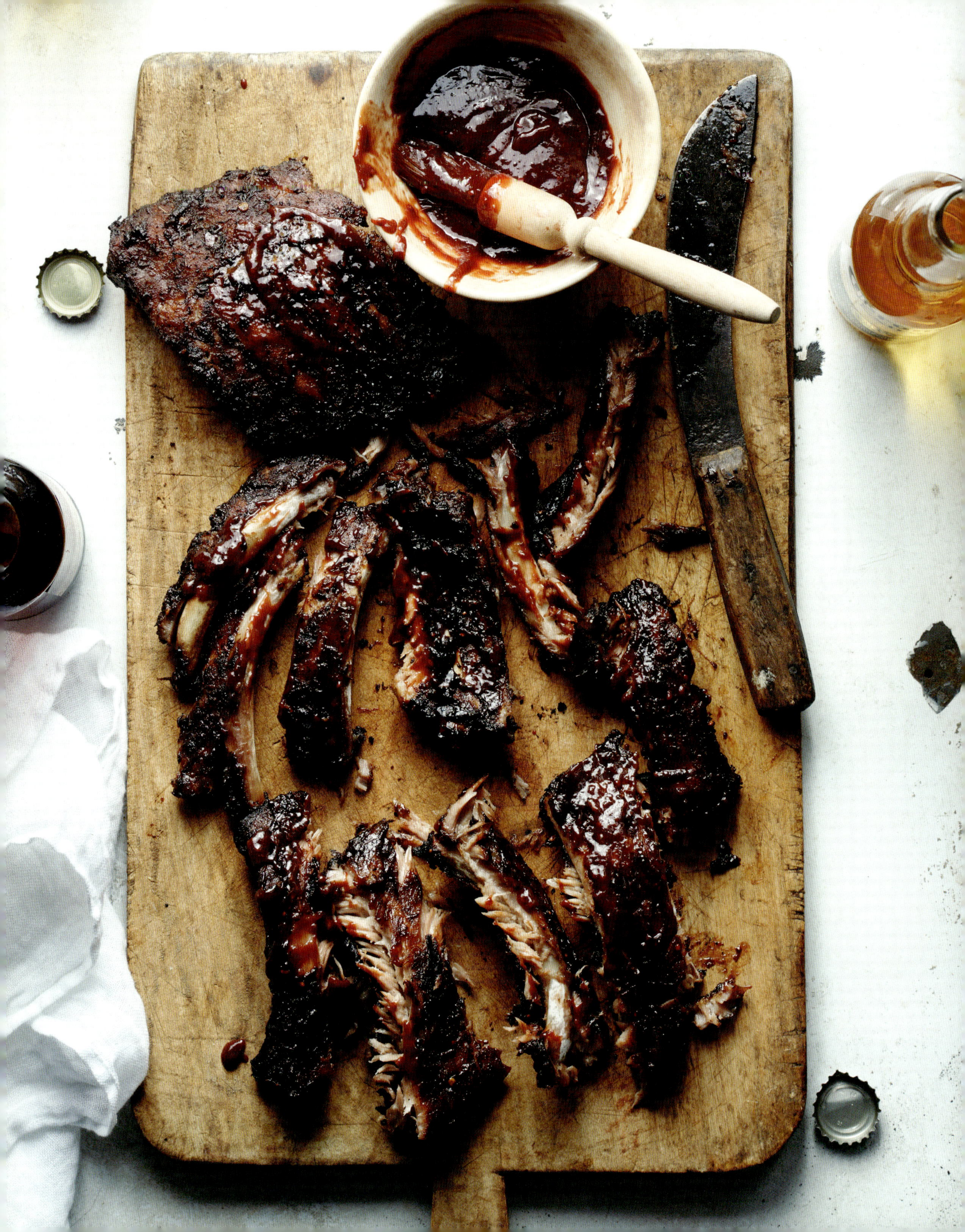

At our restaurants, we are famous for serving the tastiest, stickiest, lick-your-fingers, falling-off-the-bone ribs in town. Here's how we do it: with a spicy rub, a slow braise in the oven, and a final glazing with a sensational blackberry sauce. We prefer baby back ribs because they are naturally less chewy than spareribs. Removing the tough membrane from each rack is optional, but we like to do it for increased tenderness.

BABY BACK RIBS WITH BLACKBERRY BRANDY BBQ SAUCE

RIBS

3 racks baby back ribs, each about 2½ lb/1.2 kg

1 cup/200 g packed light brown sugar

2 Tbsp kosher salt

⅓ cup/35 g plus 1 Tbsp Cajun Seasoning (page 213) or commercial Cajun seasoning

4 teaspoons Dry Jerk Seasoning (page 213) or commercial jerk seasoning

2 cups/480 ml hot water

One 12-oz/360-ml bottle cola (1½ cups)

¼ cup/60 ml hickory-flavored liquid smoke

1 Tbsp Worcestershire sauce

SAUCE

1 Tbsp olive oil

3 Tbsp minced shallots

1 tsp granulated onion

½ cup/120 ml blackberry brandy

1 cup/240 ml ketchup

½ cup/120 ml Worcestershire sauce

½ cup/120 ml blackberry purée (from one 6-oz/170-g container fresh blackberries)

¼ cup/60 ml red wine vinegar

¼ cup/60 ml honey

Island Slaw (page 209), for serving

1 To cook the ribs: Position a rack in the center of the oven and preheat the oven to 350°F/180°C.

2 Cut each rack in half to make 6 slabs, each about 1¼ lb/570 g. If desired, remove the membrane from the bone side of each slab. (To do this, slip a small, sharp knife under the membrane at one corner of a slab to loosen it. Using a paper towel, grab the membrane at the cut and pull to strip off the membrane. It may take a few tries.) Mix the brown sugar, salt, Cajun seasoning, jerk seasoning together in a small bowl. Season the ribs all over with the brown sugar mixture.

3 Stack the ribs, meaty side up, in a very large roasting pan. Mix the hot water with the cola, liquid smoke, and Worcestershire sauce together, and pour over the ribs gently, to avoid washing away the rub. Cover tightly with a double thickness of aluminum foil.

4 Bake until the ribs are very tender and the meat has pulled away from the bone end by about ½ in/12 mm, 2 to 2¼ hours. Remove from the oven, uncover, and let cool completely in the liquid.

5 To make the sauce: Heat the oil in a medium saucepan over medium heat. Add the shallots and cook, stirring occasionally, until lightly browned, about 3 minutes. Add the granulated onion and stir well. Increase the heat to high. Stir in the blackberry brandy, bring to a boil, and cook until reduced by one-fourth, about 1 minute.

6 Stir in the ketchup, Worcestershire sauce, blackberry purée, vinegar, and honey. Bring to a boil and reduce the heat to medium-low. Simmer, stirring occasionally, until thickened and reduced to 2 cups/480 ml, about 30 minutes. Using an immersion blender, purée the sauce in the saucepan. Let cool. (Or let cool completely and purée in a standing blender.)

7 Position the grill rack about 6 in/15 cm from the source of heat. Broil the ribs on the broiler pan, occasionally brushing with some of the sauce, until glazed and hot, about 6 minutes. (Or prepare an outdoor grill for direct cooking over medium heat; see page 19. Grill the ribs, with the lid closed as much as possible, occasionally brushing with the sauce, until heated through, about 8 minutes.)

8 Serve the ribs hot, with the slaw.

MAKES 6 SERVINGS

Pernil, the garlicky Puerto Rican pork roast, produces one of the most intoxicating aromas that can come out of a kitchen. This dish yields succulent shreds of meat, with crunchy cracklings (chicharrónes) as a bonus. The sauce is entirely optional, but the pan drippings are so tasty they should not be wasted. Be sure to allow at least twelve hours for marinating.

PUERTO RICAN PORK ROAST

1 pork picnic shoulder with skin and bone (see below), about 9 lb/4 kg

12 garlic cloves, crushed under the flat side of a knife and peeled

3 tsp kosher salt

2 Tbsp dried oregano

1 Tbsp ground cumin

1½ tsp freshly ground black pepper

2 Tbsp distilled white or cider vinegar

2 Tbsp olive oil

1 cup/240 ml reduced-sodium chicken broth

SPECIAL EQUIPMENT: 1 turkey-sized oven roasting pan or similar very large food-safe plastic bag.

1 The day before cooking, use a thin, sharp knife to cut the skin and fat cap from the top of the roast in one piece, leaving the cap attached at one side of the roast. With the fat cap pulled back, slash the exposed meat on the top of the roast from one side to the other with about 6 diagonal cuts about 1 in/2.5 cm apart and ½ in/12 mm deep. Do not crosshatch the cuts in the opposite direction.

2 Use a large knife to coarsely chop the garlic on a chopping board. Sprinkle it with 2 tsp of the salt and continue chopping and mashing with the flat side of the knife to make a paste. Transfer to a small bowl and stir in the oregano, cumin, and 1 tsp of the pepper. Add the vinegar and oil and stir well. Spread about half of the paste over the top of the roast, working it into the cuts. Replace the fat cap. Using the thin knife, score the skin in a crosshatch pattern with shallow diagonal cuts about 1 in/2.5 cm apart, taking care to not cut completely through the skin. Season the skin with the remaining 1 tsp salt and ½ tsp pepper. Turn the pork over, slash the exposed meat, and spread it with the remaining garlic paste, working it into the cuts.

3 Put the pork in a very large turkey-sized oven roasting bag (or similar food-safe plastic bag) and refrigerate for at least 12 or up to 24 hours.

4 Position a rack in the center of the oven and preheat the oven to 350°F/180°C.

5 Place the roast, skin side up, on a rack in a large, deep roasting pan. Bake, uncovered, basting about every 45 minutes with the drippings, and adding 1 cup/240 ml water to the pan if the drippings threaten to burn, until the skin is very crisp and an instant-read thermometer inserted in the thickest part of the roast but not touching a bone registers 185°F/85°C, about 6½ hours. Do not cover the roast at any time during cooking. Transfer the roast to a carving board and let it stand for 20 to 45 minutes.

Pork Shoulder

Before sale, a whole pork shoulder is divided into two cuts: picnic (the lower half, with top part of the shank attached) and butt (upper half, going up to the shoulder). While both cuts work for this recipe, the picnic (also called pernil at Latino grocers) is traditional and preferred. Shoulder has the distinction of being not only one of the most delicious of all pork cuts, but the cheapest, even if it takes a long time to cook properly.

6 Pour off all of the fat from the pan. Taste the drippings; they should be deeply caramelized but not burned. Place the pan over high heat and heat until the drippings are sizzling. Add the broth and bring to a boil, scraping up the browned bits from the bottom of the pan with a wooden spoon. Pour into a small saucepan and keep the sauce warm over very low heat.

7 Chop the crisp skin cracklings into pieces about 2-in/5-cm square. Carve the falling-apart-tender meat into irregular chunks and shreds, mixing to distribute the garlic paste well. Transfer the pork meat and cracklings to a serving platter. Moisten the meat with some of the sauce. Serve immediately.

MAKES 10 TO 12 SERVINGS

Tenderloin is one of the leanest pork cuts, which is its blessing—and its curse. Care must be taken to avoid overcooking, as it can dry out. This excellent Caribbean-inspired recipe uses a garlicky brine to infuse the meat with extra moisture. The spicy jerk rub, sweet and savory pineapple sauce, and mango salsa will turn this familiar cut into a very special dish.

JERK PORK TENDERLOIN WITH PINEAPPLE-RUM SAUCE

BRINE

2 cups/480 ml hot water

½ cup/100 g sugar

¼ cup /55 g kosher salt

1 Tbsp coarsely ground black pepper

4 bay leaves, crumbled

4 garlic cloves, finely chopped

6 cups/1.4 L ice water

PORK

2 pork tenderloins, trimmed of excess fat and silver skin, each about 1¼ lb/570 g

2 Tbsp olive oil

2 Tbsp Dry Jerk Seasoning (page 213) or commercial jerk seasoning

SAUCE

1 Tbsp olive oil

1 Tbsp finely chopped shallot

1 garlic clove, minced

1 cup/180 g finely chopped fresh pineapple

3 Tbsp spiced rum, such as Captain Morgan, or golden rum

1 cup/240 ml unsweetened pineapple juice

1½ Tbsp rice vinegar

1½ Tbsp Thai sweet chili sauce

2 whole star anise pods

Pinch of ground cloves

Pinch of Chinese five-spice powder

1 Tbsp minced fresh cilantro

MANGO SALSA

1 ripe mango, pitted, peeled, and cut into ½-in/12-mm dice

2 Tbsp diced (¼ in/6 mm) red bell pepper

2 Tbsp thinly sliced green onion, white and green parts, cut on a sharp diagonal

1 Tbsp finely chopped fresh cilantro

1 Tbsp fresh lime juice

1 Tbsp olive oil

2 tsp minced jalapeño chile

Kosher salt and freshly ground black pepper

Sweet Potato Mofongo (page 172), for serving

6 long fried plantain chips (available at Latino markets), for garnish

1 To make the brine: Early in the day, combine 2 cups/480 ml water with the sugar, salt, pepper, and bay leaves in a small saucepan. Stir over medium heat until the mixture comes to a boil and the sugar dissolves. Transfer to a large bowl and add the garlic. Let cool to lukewarm. Stir in the ice water.

2 Place the pork in a 1-gl/3.8-L resealable plastic bag. Pour in the brine, seal the bag, and refrigerate for at least 2 or up to 4 hours.

3 Drain the pork well (do not rinse) and pat it dry. Brush the pork with the oil and sprinkle with the jerk seasoning. Transfer the pork to another 1-gl/3.8-L resealable plastic bag and refrigerate for at least 2 or up to 24 hours.

4 To make the sauce: Heat the oil in a medium saucepan over medium heat. Add the shallot, garlic, and pineapple and cook, stirring occasionally, until the onion softens, about 3 minutes. Increase the heat to high, add the spiced rum, and cook until the rum is almost entirely evaporated, about 2 minutes. Add the pineapple juice, rice vinegar, chili sauce, star anise, cloves, and five-spice powder and bring to a boil. Reduce the heat to low and simmer until the pineapple is very tender and the liquid is reduced by about three-fourths, about 30 minutes. Discard the star anise. Purée in a blender with the lid ajar until the sauce is smooth. Transfer to a small bowl and stir in the cilantro. (The sauce can

(continued)

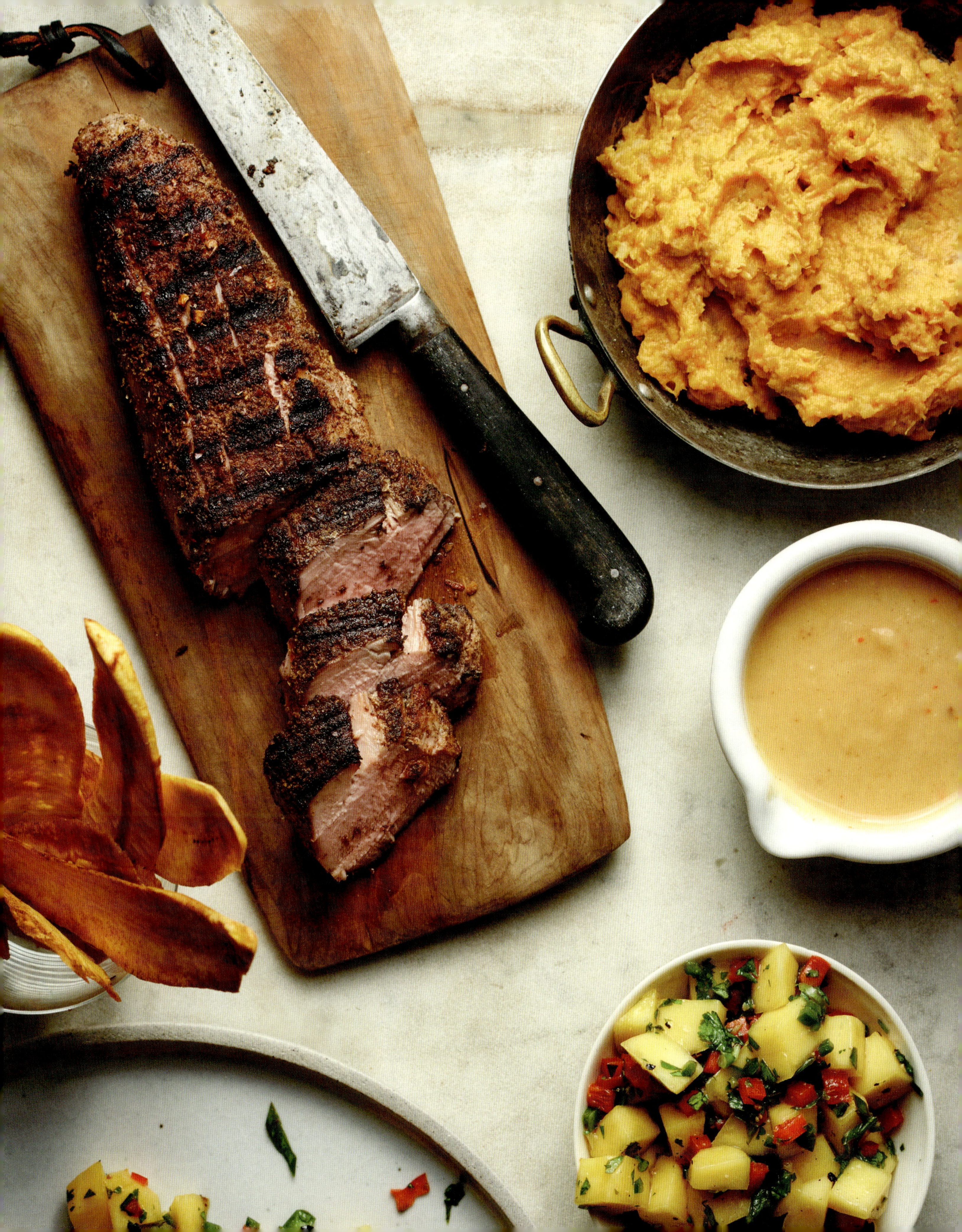

JERK PORK TENDERLOIN WITH PINEAPPLE-RUM SAUCE, continued

be cooled, covered, and refrigerated for up to 4 days. Reheat before serving.)

5 To make the salsa: Mix all of the ingredients together in a small bowl, seasoning to taste with the salt and pepper. Cover and refrigerate until chilled, at least 1 hour or up to 1 day.

6 Prepare an outdoor grill for direct cooking over medium-high heat (see page 19). Place the pork on the grill and cook with the lid closed as much as possible, turning the pork occasionally, until it is browned and an instant-read thermometer inserted in the center reads 145°F/63°C, about 15 minutes. Transfer to a cutting board and let stand for 5 minutes.

7 Cut the pork across the grain into slices about ½ in/12 mm thick. Divide the mofongo among 6 dinner plates, spooning it on the upper third of each plate. Spread equal amounts of the sauce on the bottom third of the plates, followed by pork slices. Add a portion of mango salsa to each plate and garnish by sticking a plantain chip on a diagonal into the mofongo. Serve immediately.

MAKES 6 SERVINGS

Brining has long been favored by savvy grilling fans because it adds moisture and flavor to lean meats and poultry. This brine has a good dose of bourbon, which adds a subtle kick and intensifies the flavors of the other ingredients. Rubbed with spices, and glazed with a quick peach preserves sauce, the chops are served on a colorful vegetable hash that can be made ahead and reheated.

BOURBON-BRINED PORK CHOPS WITH PEACH GLAZE AND CORN-BACON HASH

PORK AND BRINE

2 cups/480 ml hot tap water

½ cup/120 ml packed light brown sugar

¼ cup/60 g fine sea or table salt

2 Tbsp stone-ground mustard

5½ cups/1.3 L ice water

¾ cup/180 ml bourbon

4 double-cut, bone-in pork chops, each about 14 oz/400 g and 1½ in/4 cm thick

RUB

1½ tsp smoked paprika (pimentón)

½ tsp granulated garlic

½ tsp granulated onion

½ tsp dry mustard

½ tsp freshly ground black pepper

1/16 tsp cayenne pepper

Vegetable oil, for brushing

GLAZE

½ cup/140 g peach preserves

1 Tbsp bourbon

1 Tbsp stone-ground mustard

CORN-BACON HASH

2 slices bacon, coarsely chopped

½ bell pepper, cored, seeded, and cut into ½-in/12-mm dice

1 green onion, white and green parts, finely chopped

1 Tbsp seeded and minced jalapeño chile

1 garlic clove, minced

1½ cups/255 g fresh corn kernels, cut from 2 ears corn

1 cup/135 g fresh cooked or thawed frozen peas

Kosher salt and freshly ground black pepper

1 **To make the brine:** Whisk the hot water, sugar, salt, and stone-ground mustard together in a large bowl to dissolve the sugar. Stir in the ice water and bourbon.

2 Place the pork chops in a jumbo 2-gl/7.5-L self-sealing plastic bag. Pour in the brine and close the bag. Refrigerate, turning occasionally, for at least 4 but not more than 6 hours.

3 Prepare an outdoor grill for two-zone cooking with medium-high heat (see page 19).

4 **To make the rub:** Mix all of the ingredients together in a small bowl. Remove the pork from the brine and pat it dry with paper towels. Lightly brush the pork with oil. Season all over with the rub. Let stand at room temperature for 15 to 30 minutes.

5 **To make the glaze:** Bring the preserves to a simmer in a small saucepan over medium heat. Remove from the heat and whisk in the bourbon and stone-ground mustard. Transfer to a small bowl and set aside.

6 **Meanwhile, make the hash:** Cook the bacon in a large skillet over medium heat, stirring occasionally, until crisp and browned, about 5 minutes. Using a slotted spoon, transfer the bacon to paper towels to drain.

(continued)

BOURBON-BRINED PORK CHOPS WITH PEACH GLAZE AND CORN-BACON HASH, continued

Add the bell pepper, green onion, jalapeño, and garlic to the fat in the pan and cook, stirring occasionally, until the bell pepper is tender, about 4 minutes. Add the corn and peas and cook, stirring occasionally, until heated through, 3 to 5 minutes. Season to taste with salt and pepper. Remove from the heat and set aside while cooking the pork.

7 Brush the grill grate clean. Grill the pork chops over the side with direct medium-high heat, with the lid closed, turning once or twice, until well browned, about 10 minutes. Move to the side with indirect heat and grill, occasionally turning the chops and brushing with the glaze, until they are slightly pink when cut at the bone or an instant-read thermometer inserted horizontally into the center of a chop registers 145°F/63°C, about 5 minutes longer. Remove from the grill and let rest for 3 to 5 minutes.

8 Stir the reserved bacon into the hash and reheat the hash over medium-high heat, stirring occasionally, until hot, about 2 minutes. Divide the hash among 4 dinner plates. Top each with a pork chop and serve.

MAKES 4 SERVINGS

Curry goat is probably the national dish of Jamaica: a spicy stew with chunks of meat falling off the bone. Because goat is not always easy to come by, our version uses lamb. Part of the delight of this dish is eating the meat from the bones, so don't bother with boneless cuts. Look for Jamaican curry powder, which has more warm spices than the typical blend, at Latino markets.

JAMAICAN CURRY LAMB

2 Tbsp vegetable oil

3½ lb/1.6 kg bone-in lamb neck or shoulder, sawed by the butcher into 2-in/5-cm chunks

Kosher salt and freshly ground black pepper

1 yellow onion, chopped

1 green bell pepper, cored, seeded, and chopped

1 Tbsp peeled and minced fresh ginger

4 garlic cloves, chopped

1 tsp seeded and minced Scotch bonnet or habanero chile, plus more as needed

4 green onions, white and green parts, thinly sliced

2 Tbsp curry powder, preferably Jamaican (see Note, page 94)

1 tsp dried thyme

½ tsp ground allspice

One 14-oz/400 g can coconut milk (not cream of coconut)

5 red-skinned potatoes, about 1½ lb/680 g total, each cut into sixths

4 carrots, peeled and cut into ½-in/12-mm rounds

2 Tbsp coarsely chopped fresh cilantro, for garnish

Lime wedges, for serving

1 Position a rack in the center of the oven and preheat the oven to 350°F/180°C.

2 Heat the oil in a large Dutch oven or flameproof casserole over medium-high heat. Season the lamb with 1½ tsp salt and 1 tsp pepper. In batches, add the lamb and cook, turning occasionally, until browned, about 5 minutes. Using tongs, transfer the lamb to a plate.

3 Add the onion, bell pepper, ginger, garlic, and chile to the pot and cook, stirring occasionally, until the vegetables soften, about 5 minutes. Add the green onions, curry powder, thyme, and allspice and cook, stirring often, until the green onions are wilted, about 1 minute. Add the coconut milk and bring to a boil, scraping up the browned bits in the bottom of the pot with a wooden spoon. Return the lamb to the pot, add enough water to barely cover the ingredients, and bring to a boil over high heat.

4 Cover tightly and bake for 1 hour. Add the potatoes and carrots and continue baking until the lamb and vegetables are tender, about 1 hour more. Season to taste with salt and pepper. Sprinkle with the cilantro. Serve hot, with the lime wedges.

MAKES 6 SERVINGS

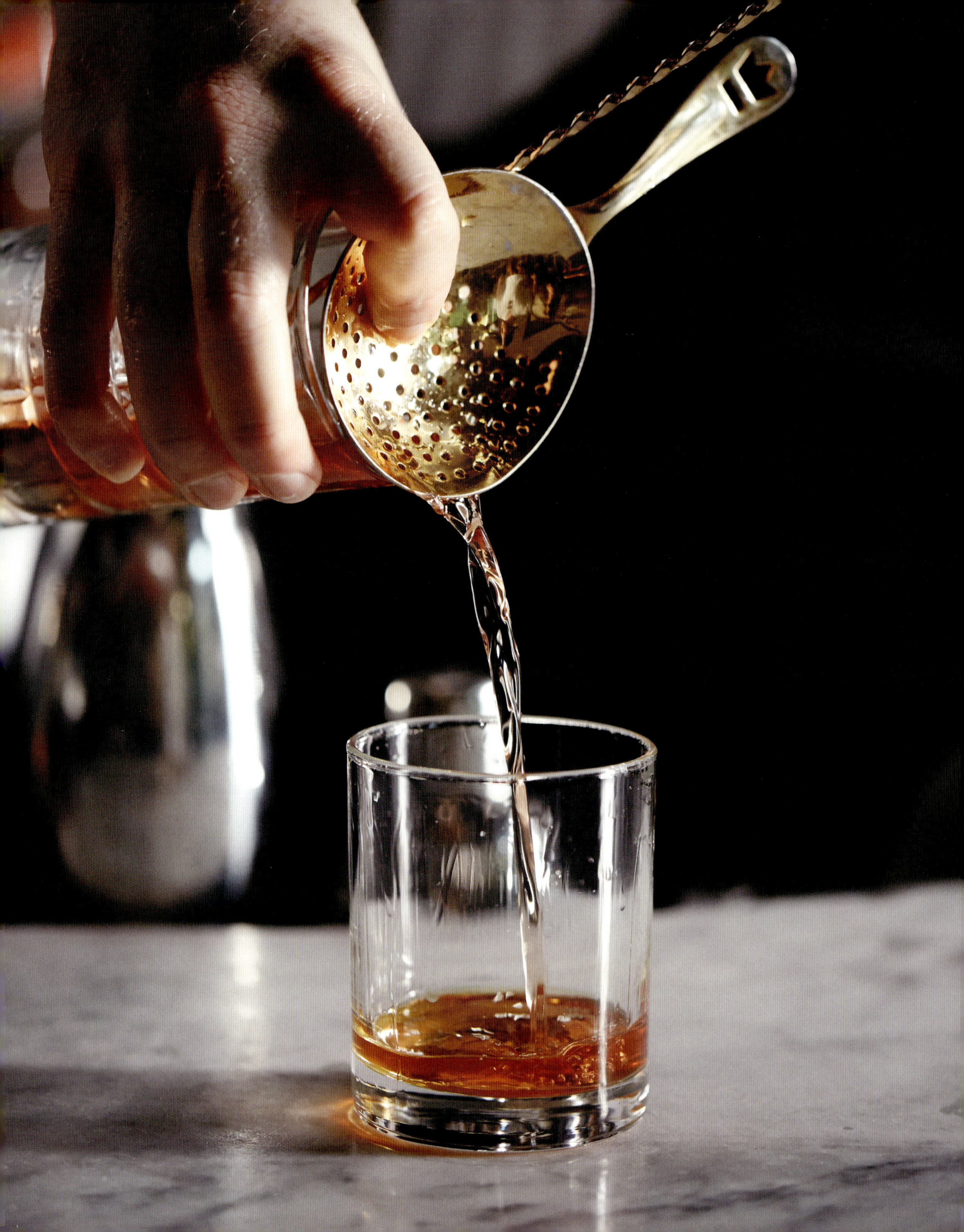

Why is the Sazerac considered "history in a glass"? Created in New Orleans around 1850, its name comes from the brand of Cognac used in the original recipe. Rye became the liquor of choice when French grapevines were destroyed by blight during the late 1800s and Cognac became unavailable. Here's our version of this venerable drink, which is as tasty as it is historical.

SAZERAC

RICH DEMERARA SYRUP

½ cup/100 g Demerara sugar

2½ fl oz/75 ml rye, bourbon, or Cognac

1 tsp Rich Demerara Syrup, above

4 dashes Peychaud's bitters

2 dashes Angostura bitters

½ tsp absinthe or Herbsaint

GARNISH: 1 strip lemon zest

1 **To make the Demerara syrup:** Bring the Demerara sugar and ¼ cup/60 ml water to a boil in a small saucepan over high heat, stirring constantly to dissolve the sugar. Let cool. (Makes about ⅔ cup/165 ml. The syrup can be refrigerated in a covered container for up to 1 month.)

2 Fill an Old-Fashioned glass with ice and set aside to chill. (This is the traditional glass for this drink, although you can use a Martini glass.) Add the rye, syrup, and both bitters to an ice-filled shaker. Stir well.

3 Empty the ice from the glass. Add the absinthe to the glass, swirl to coat, and pour out the excess absinthe. Strain the cocktail into the glass. Twist the lemon zest over the cocktail, rub the zest around the edge of the glass, and drop it in.

MAKES 1 DRINK

When rum was not as carefully made as it is today, it could be pretty fiery, so it's easy to see how the Mojito came to be, with lots of spearmint and sugar to sweeten up the brew. That world-class drinker, Ernest Hemingway, named it as one of his favorites, especially the version at La Bodeguita del Medio in Havana. In African dialect, mojo means a "magic spell"; therefore mojito means a "little spell maker." This one will definitely give reality a magical glow.

MOJITO

5 large fresh mint leaves, preferably spearmint

1 fl oz/30 ml fresh lime juice

2½ fl oz/75 ml citrus-flavored rum, such as Cruzan

¾ fl oz/22.5 ml cane sugar syrup (see Note)

2 fl oz/60 ml club soda

GARNISH: Lime wedge

1 Muddle the mint and lime juice together in a cocktail shaker. Add the rum and syrup and half fill with ice. Shake well.

2 Pour (do not strain) into a tall Collins glass. Fill with more ice and top with the club soda. Garnish with the lime wedge and serve.

MAKES 1 DRINK

NOTE: Cane sugar syrup, available in both domestic and imported versions, is a beige sweetener sold at supermarkets, in the ethnic department of some supermarkets, and online.

Tarpon Springs, near Tampa, boasts the largest Greek-American population in the nation. Souvlaki, grilled lamb skewers, is one of the great dishes of this cuisine. It's best to cook the meat and vegetables separately, as the moisture in the vegetables keeps the lamb from browning. Tzatziki, the classic Greek cucumber-yogurt sauce, finishes off the dish perfectly

GREEK LAMB SOUVLAKI WITH VEGETABLE KEBABS AND TZATZIKI

TZATZIKI

1 large cucumber, peeled

Kosher salt

½ cup/120 ml plain Greek yogurt

2 Tbsp fresh lemon juice

2 Tbsp finely chopped fresh dill

1 garlic clove, minced

Freshly ground black pepper

MARINADE

⅓ cup/75 ml fresh lemon juice

⅓ cup/75 ml extra-virgin olive oil

2 garlic cloves, minced

1½ tsp dried oregano

1½ tsp dried cumin

1 tsp Aleppo pepper flakes (see Note), or ½ tsp pure ground ancho chile

1 tsp kosher salt

½ tsp freshly ground black pepper

1 boneless leg of lamb, about 4 lb/1.8 kg

2 large bell peppers (preferably 1 red and 1 yellow), cored, seeded, and cut into 1½-in/4-cm squares

1 large red onion, cut into eighths and separated into sections of 2 or 3 layers

Extra-virgin olive oil, for brushing and drizzling

Kosher salt and freshly ground black pepper

2 teaspoons chopped fresh oregano or basil

SPECIAL EQUIPMENT: 9 long bamboo skewers, soaked in water for at least 30 minutes and drained

1 To make the tzatziki: Shred the cucumber lengthwise on the large holes of a box grater over a medium bowl, discarding the seeded core. Toss the cucumber with 1 tsp salt. Transfer to a sieve and let drain for 1 hour.

2 A handful at a time, squeeze the excess liquid from the cucumber. Mix the cucumber, yogurt, lemon juice, dill, and garlic together in a medium bowl. Season with salt and pepper to taste. Cover and refrigerate until chilled, at least 1 hour or up to 2 days.

3 To make the marinade: Whisk the ingredients together in a small bowl.

4 Trim the lamb well of all fat and gristle. (Contrary to common belief, marinating will not tenderize tough meat.) Cut the lamb into 30 equal chunks, each about 1½ in/4 cm square. Place the lamb in a 1-gl/3.8-L self-sealing plastic bag. Pour in the marinade and close the bag. Refrigerate, occasionally turning the bag, for at least 2 hours or up to 18 hours.

5 Remove the lamb from the marinade. Thread 5 cubes onto each of 6 skewers, leaving a little space between the meat. Thread the bell peppers and the red onion sections onto the remaining 3 skewers, dividing the vegetables as evenly as possible and again not packing the ingredients on the skewers. Lightly brush the vegetable skewers with oil and season to taste with salt and pepper. Let the skewers stand at room temperature for 15 to 30 minutes.

6 Prepare an outdoor grill for two-zone cooking with high heat (see page 19).

7 Brush the grill grate clean. Place the lamb and vegetable kekabs on the grill, sliding strips of aluminum foil under the "handles" and tips to protect them from the heat. Grill the kebabs, with the lid closed, turning occasionally, until the vegetable kebabs are lightly charred and crisp-tender, about 6 minutes. Transfer the vegetable kebabs to a platter and tent with aluminum foil to keep warm. Continue grilling the lamb until it is pink when pierced with the tip of a small, sharp knife, about 4 minutes more. Transfer the lamb skewers to the platter.

8 Slide the vegetables off their skewers into a serving bowl. Toss the vegetables with the fresh oregano, a drizzle of olive oil, and a sprinkling of salt and pepper. Place each lamb skewer on a dinner plate and add a spoonful of the tzatziki. Serve immediately, with the vegetables.

MAKES 4 SERVINGS

NOTE: Aleppo pepper, a moderately hot seasoning made of crushed dried Aleppo chiles from Syria and Turkey, is sold at Middle Eastern and Mediterranean grocers and online. It is excellent sprinkled on salads, pizzas, and more.

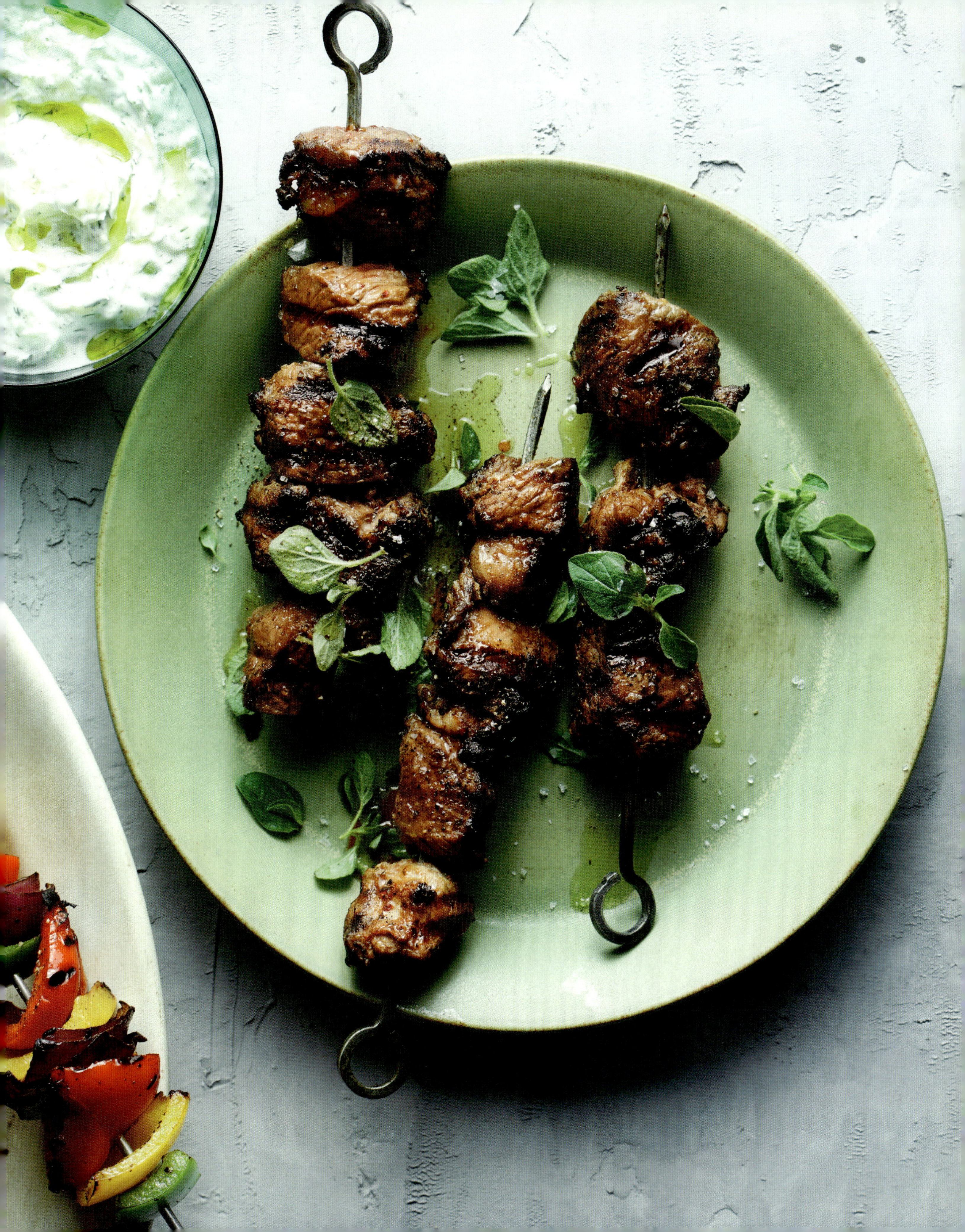

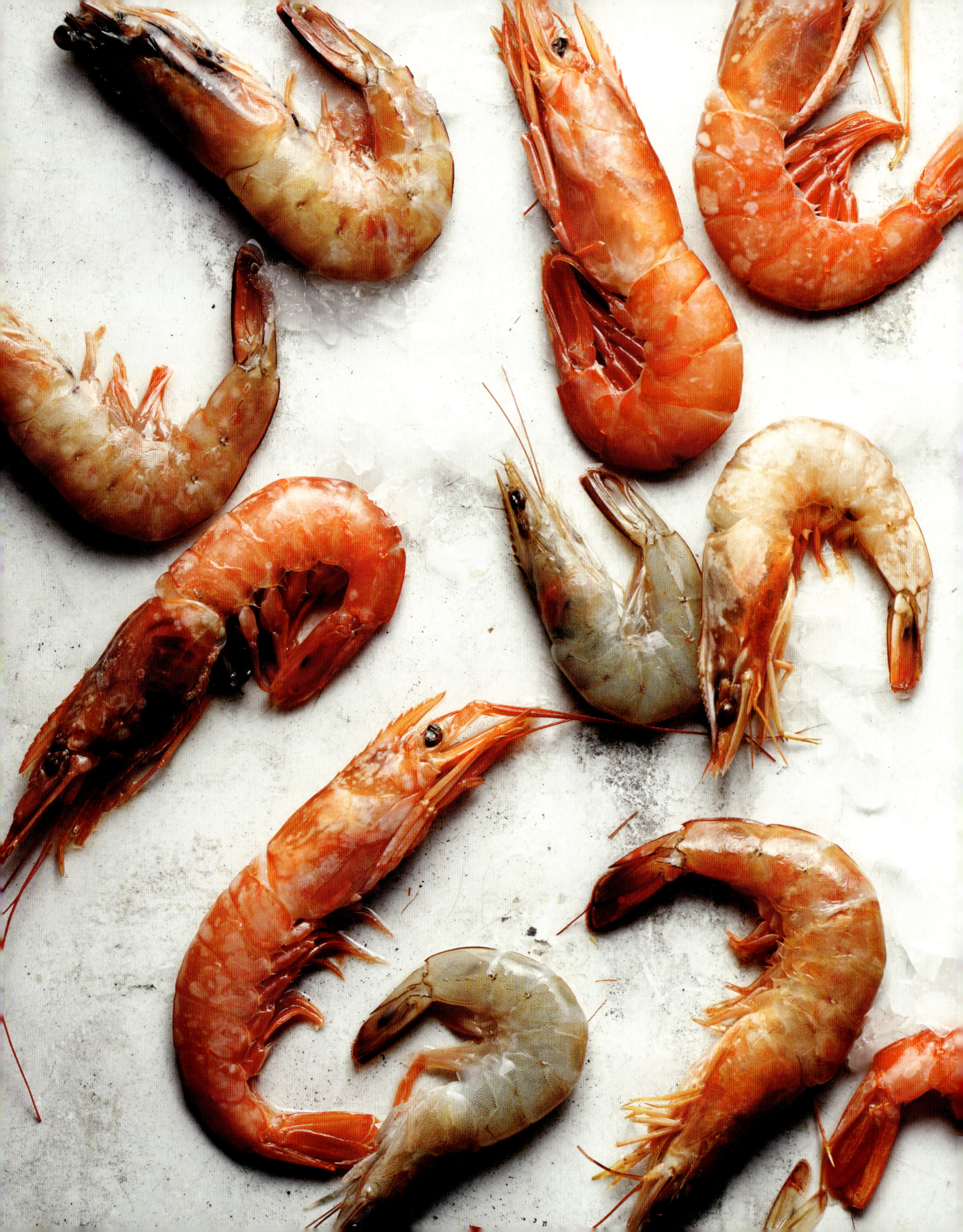

Shrimp is the most popular seafood in the United States: the nation consumes over a billion pounds annually. Only 10 percent of this amount is domestic shrimp, as the remaining 90 percent is imported frozen product, which is mostly farm-raised. The naturally grown wild shrimp of the Gulf Coast states make up about 70 percent of the domestic crop, and sweeter, more succulent shrimp is impossible to find.

Fried, boiled, broiled, sautéed, gumbo-ed, and étouffée-ed—there are countless ways to cook the tasty little crustaceans. Of the more than nineteen hundred species, only the brown, white, and pink shrimp are commercially viable. While they are available all year, the peak season runs from May to September. Shrimp are nocturnal, so trawling occurs at night. Wild shrimp are a sustainable food, as a new crop is available every year, and females lay from 100,000 to a million eggs at a time. The warm Gulf waters encourage rapid growth, and a shrimp can grow an inch every week or so until it reaches maturity. Government regulations allow for escape traps in the nets for larger turtles and fish.

The shrimp industry is in large part the story of people who came from other countries to ply the waters. Biloxi (once known as the Seafood Capital of the World not only for shrimp, but for the vast amounts of oysters dredged from its shores) thrived because of the arrivals of Bohemians (from present-day Czech Republic), Croatians, and recently, Vietnamese working the boats. At the wharf-side restaurants today, you are as likely to see báhn mì on the menus as po' boys—which, of course, they resemble!

GULF SHRIMP

SEAFOOD

The Gulf region is blessed with thousands of miles of coastline, and its cooks are famous for their acumen with fish and shellfish. Here are some of the most delectable seafood recipes from Texas to Florida.

115
BAKED GROUPER WITH DILL-YOGURT SAUCE

117
CARIBBEAN MAHI MAHI WITH QUINOA SUCCOTASH

119
CRAYFISH ÉTOUFFÉE

120
JAMAICAN FISH RUNDOWN

121
MARINATED SWORDFISH WITH SKORDALIA AND HORTA

122
TUNA IN VERACRUZ SAUCE

125
CRAB ENCHILADAS IN GREEN SAUCE

126
CRAB-STUFFED SHRIMP WITH TWO SAUCES

129
BBQ SHRIMP WITH SPICY BEER SAUCE

132
SHRIMP AND ANDOUILLE WITH CHEESE GRITS

You will find yourself turning to this simple fish main course with Greek flavors again and again for a light and healthy meal. A bold sauce complements the mild flesh of groupers or flounders, and this one, made with fresh dill, garlic, and yogurt, is anything but shy. For side dishes, consider roasting asparagus spears separately from the fish, and steamed baby potatoes, both perfect partners for the sauce.

BAKED GROUPER WITH DILL-YOGURT SAUCE

SAUCE

½ cup/120 ml whole milk or low-fat Greek yogurt

½ cup/15 g dill sprigs

1 green onion, white and green parts, coarsely chopped

1 garlic clove, crushed under a knife and peeled

2 Tbsp extra-virgin olive oil

1 Tbsp fresh lime juice

Milk, if needed

Kosher salt and freshly ground black pepper

4 skinless grouper or flounder fillets, each about 5 oz/140 g

2 Tbsp extra-virgin olive oil

½ tsp kosher salt

¼ tsp freshly ground black pepper

Lime wedges, for serving

1 Position a rack in the upper third of the oven and preheat the oven to 400°F/200°C. Oil a large baking dish.

2 To make the sauce: Purée the yogurt, dill, green onion, garlic, oil, and lime juice in a blender. (If the sauce is too thick, thin it with a little milk.) Season to taste with salt and pepper. Transfer to a serving bowl, cover, and let stand at room temperature to blend the flavors while baking the fish.

3 Fold each fillet in half so the pointed ends meet. Arrange the fillets in the baking dish, drizzle with oil, and season with the salt and pepper. Bake until the fish is barely opaque when flaked in the thickest part with the tip of a small, sharp knife, about 10 minutes.

4 Transfer each fillet to a dinner plate. Top each with a spoonful of the sauce. Serve with the lime wedges and the remaining sauce on the side.

MAKES 4 SERVINGS

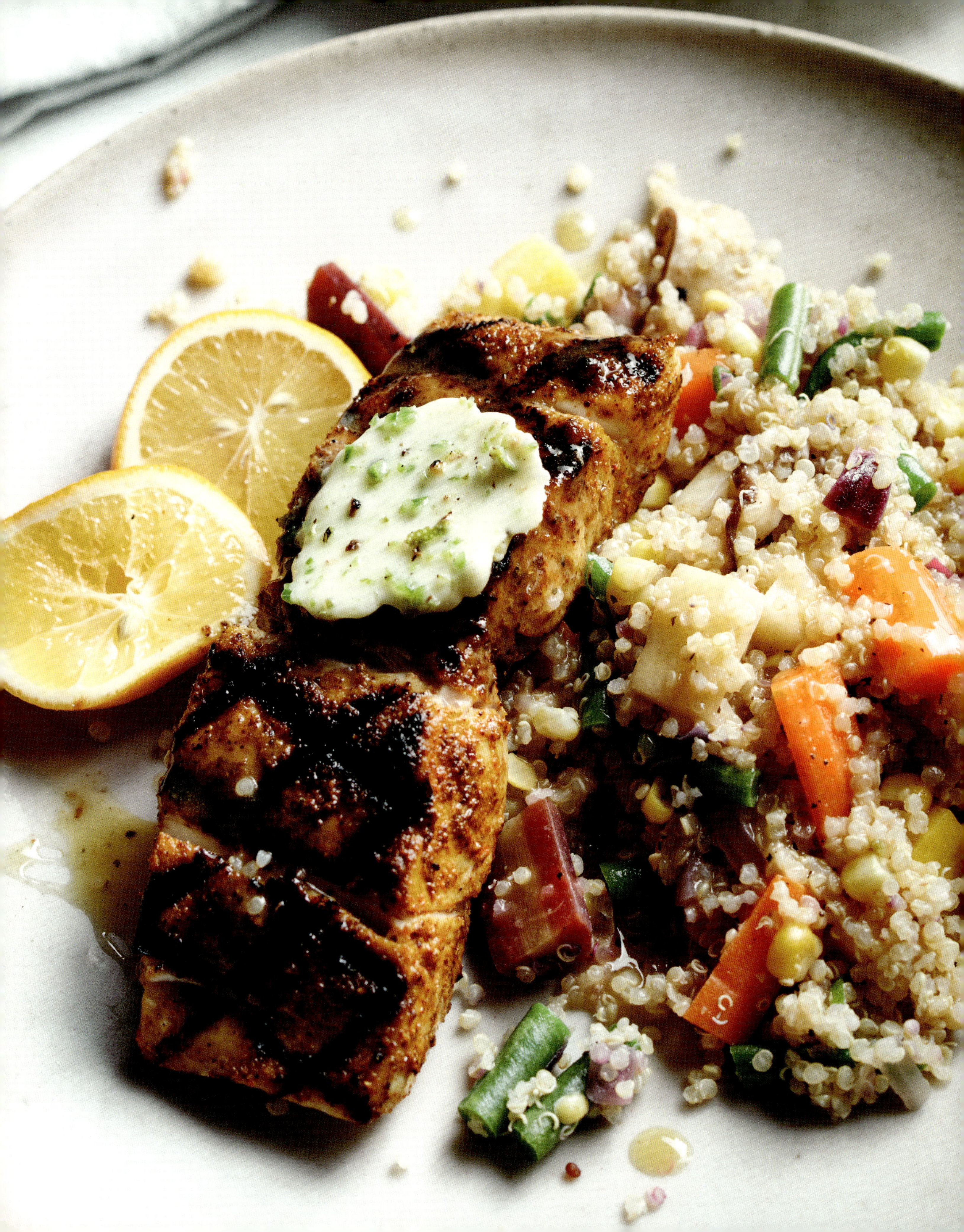

Here's an elegant recipe from our restaurants that blends the flavors of many coastal cuisines for a harmonious result. Although it has a Hawaiian name, mahi mahi is also fished in Gulf waters. The fish fillet is seasoned with a spicy rub inspired by Jamaican flavors, with an update of Southern succotash, and a topping of jalapeño butter from the Mexican cooking canon.

CARIBBEAN MAHI MAHI WITH QUINOA SUCCOTASH

CARIBBEAN RUB

2 tsp kosher salt

1 tsp curry powder, preferably Jamaican (see Note, page 94)

1 tsp ground cumin

1 tsp chili powder

1 tsp ground cinnamon

1 tsp freshly ground black pepper

½ tsp cayenne pepper

½ tsp ground allspice

6 mahi mahi fillets, each about 6 oz/170 g

Vegetable oil, for brushing

Quinoa Succotash (page 170), for serving

6 Tbsp/85 g Jalapeño-Lime Butter (page 211), for topping

6 Tbsp/90 ml Meyer Lemon Vinaigrette (page 211), for drizzling

1 To make the rub: Mix all of the ingredients together in a small bowl.

2 Prepare an outdoor grill for direct cooking over high heat (see page 19).

3 Lightly brush the mahi mahi with the oil. Season the fillets all over with about 2 tsp of the rub. (The remaining rub can be stored in an airtight container in a cool, dark place for up to 3 months.)

4 Brush the grill grate clean. Grill the mahi mahi, with the lid closed, turning once, until opaque throughout, about 6 minutes. Remove from the grill.

5 Divide the succotash among 6 dinner plates. Top each serving with a mahi mahi fillet. Add 1 Tbsp of the jalapeño butter to each fillet. Drizzle 1 Tbsp of vinaigrette around the succotash and serve.

MAKES 6 SERVINGS

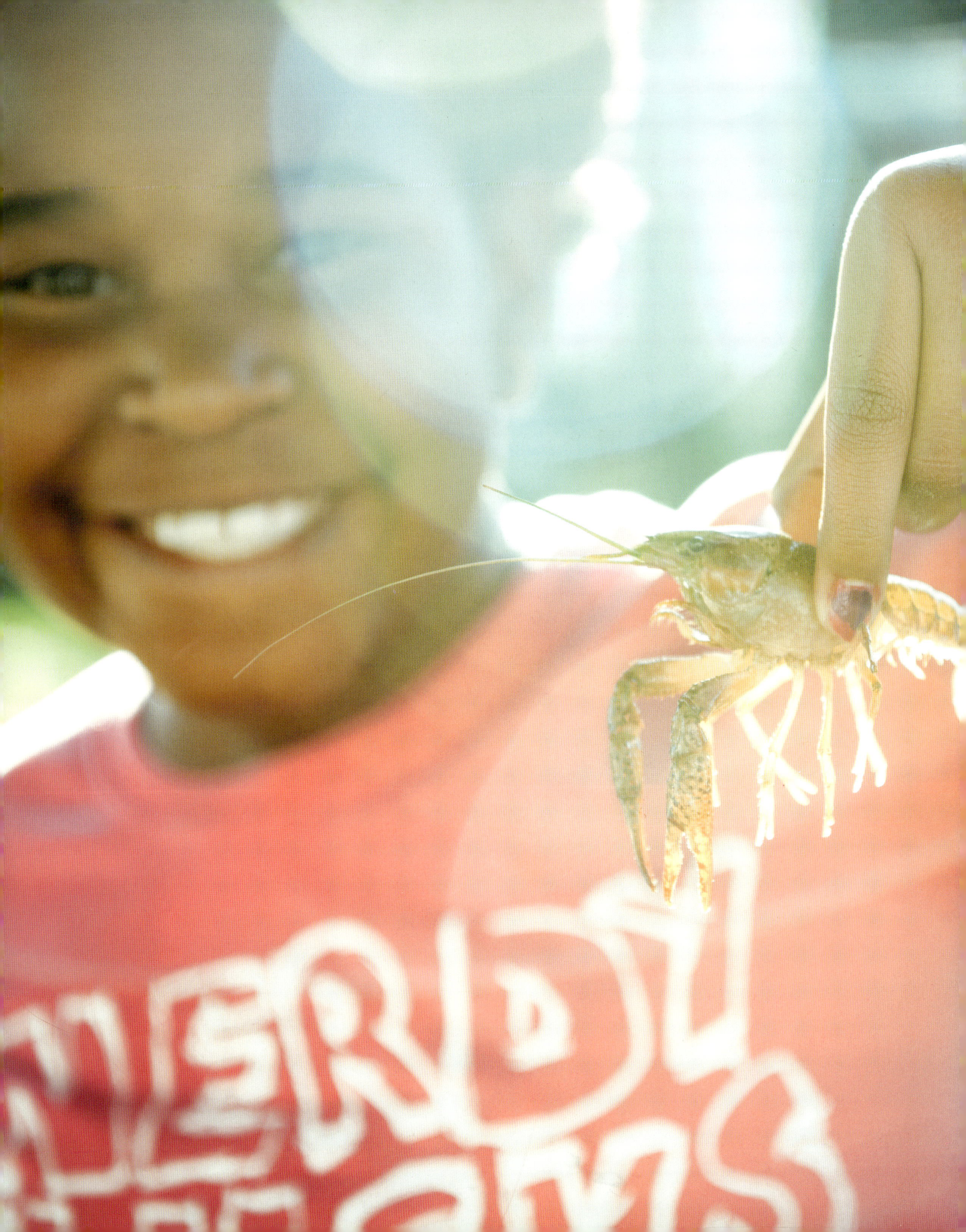

When visitors to New Orleans savor that city's many culinary delights, one elusive flavor is often hard to pinpoint. Chances are it's the long-cooked roux that thickens and flavors many Creole and Cajun dishes. Étouffée (from the French word for "smother") is one of those recipes. This version uses crayfish, a favorite locally sourced ingredient, but we've also included a shrimp variation.

CRAYFISH ÉTOUFFÉE

- ½ cup/120 ml vegetable oil
- ½ cup/70 g unbleached all-purpose flour
- 5 green onions, white and green parts
- 4 celery stalks, cut into ½-in/12-mm dice
- 1 yellow onion, chopped
- 1 small green bell pepper, cored, seeded, and cut into ½-in/12-mm dice
- 4 garlic cloves, minced
- 4 cups/960 ml Shrimp Stock (page 210) or bottled clam juice
- One 28-oz/785-g can plum tomatoes in juice, drained and chopped
- 1½ tsp Worcestershire sauce
- 1 tsp red pepper sauce, such as Tabasco
- 2 tsp Cajun Seasoning (page 213) or commercial Cajun seasoning
- 1½ lb/680 g cooked and cleaned crayfish tails (see Note)
- Basic Rice (page 209), for serving

1 Heat the oil in a large, heavy skillet over medium heat. Whisk in the flour. Reduce the heat to medium-low and cook, whisking very often, until the roux is medium beige and smells toasty, about 10 minutes.

2 Finely chop the green onions, reserving 1 for garnish. Carefully add the celery, the remaining green onions, the yellow onion, bell pepper, and garlic (they will splatter when they hit the roux). Return the heat to medium and cook, stirring often, until the onion is translucent, about 10 minutes.

3 Gradually stir in the stock and ½ cup/120 ml water. Add the tomatoes, Worcestershire, and hot sauce and mix well. Simmer, stirring often, until the sauce is lightly thickened, about 30 minutes. Sprinkle in the Cajun seasoning and stir well.

4 Stir in the crayfish tails and cook, stirring often, just until they are heated through, about 3 minutes. For each serving, spoon about 1 cup/155 g cooked rice into a shallow soup bowl. Spoon in the étouffée, sprinkle with the reserved green onion, and serve hot.

MAKES 4 SERVINGS

NOTE: Unless you are on the Gulf Coast, crayfish are usually sold cooked and whole, and some fish stores sell cooked crayfish tail meat. Usually, the cook will have to obtain the meat for this recipe from cooked crayfish. For 1½ lb/680 g tail meat, purchase about 3 lb/1.4 kg cooked whole crayfish. For each, break off the tail where it meets the head, reserving the head (the yellow fat in that area is very flavorful). Peel off the first two rings of the tail shell to reveal the meat. Pinch and grab the top of the tail meat and pull it out of the shell. Use the shells to make Crayfish Stock (page 210). If you don't have the crayfish shells, just use bottled clam juice for the étouffée sauce.

SHRIMP ÉTOUFFÉE: Substitute 2 lb/910 g jumbo (21 to 25 count) shrimp, peeled and deveined, for the crayfish. If desired, reserve the shells to make the Shrimp Stock on page 210.

The most famous fish dish of Veracruz, on the western edge of the Mexican Gulf Coast, has traveled up to the States, where it is found on just about every Mexican-restaurant menu. Instead of cooking the tuna in the tomato, chile, and olive sauce, we cook it separately to keep it rare. The slight smokiness of the fish is a great complement to the sauce. You might want to serve warm tortillas to sop up the sauce.

TUNA IN VERACRUZ SAUCE

SAUCE

1 Tbsp extra-virgin olive oil, plus more for brushing

1 white onion, chopped

1 Tbsp seeded and minced jalapeño chile

2 garlic cloves, minced

½ tsp dried oregano

½ tsp dried cumin

One 28-oz/785-g can plum tomatoes in juice, drained and chopped, juices reserved

½ cup/120 ml dry white wine, such as Pinot Grigio

½ cup/75 g sliced pimiento-stuffed green olives

3 Tbsp drained nonpareil capers

Kosher salt and freshly ground black pepper

4 skinless tuna steaks, each about 6 oz/170 g and 1½ in/4 cm thick

Extra-virgin olive oil, for brushing

½ tsp kosher salt

½ tsp freshly ground black pepper

2 Tbsp chopped fresh cilantro, for garnish

Lime wedges, for serving

1 To make the sauce: Heat the oil in a medium skillet over medium heat. Add the onion and cook, stirring occasionally, until translucent, about 4 minutes. Stir in the chile, garlic, oregano, and cumin and cook until the garlic is fragrant, about 1 minute. Stir in the tomatoes with their juices and the wine and bring to a simmer. Reduce the heat to medium-low and simmer until the sauce is slightly reduced, about 20 minutes. During the last 5 minutes, stir in the olives and capers. Season to taste with salt and pepper.

2 Lightly brush the tuna with the oil and season with the salt and pepper. Let stand at room temperature for 15 to 30 minutes.

3 Meanwhile, prepare an outdoor grill for direct cooking over high heat (see page 19).

4 Brush the grill grate clean. Grill the tuna, turning once, until seared well on both sides, about 6 minutes for rare tuna. Transfer to a carving board and let stand for about 2 minutes. Using a sharp, thin knife, cut the tuna across the grain into ½-in/12-mm slices.

5 Divide the sauce among 4 shallow soup bowls and top with equal amounts of the sliced tuna, fanning the slices in the sauce. Sprinkle with cilantro and serve hot, with lime wedges.

MAKES 4 SERVINGS

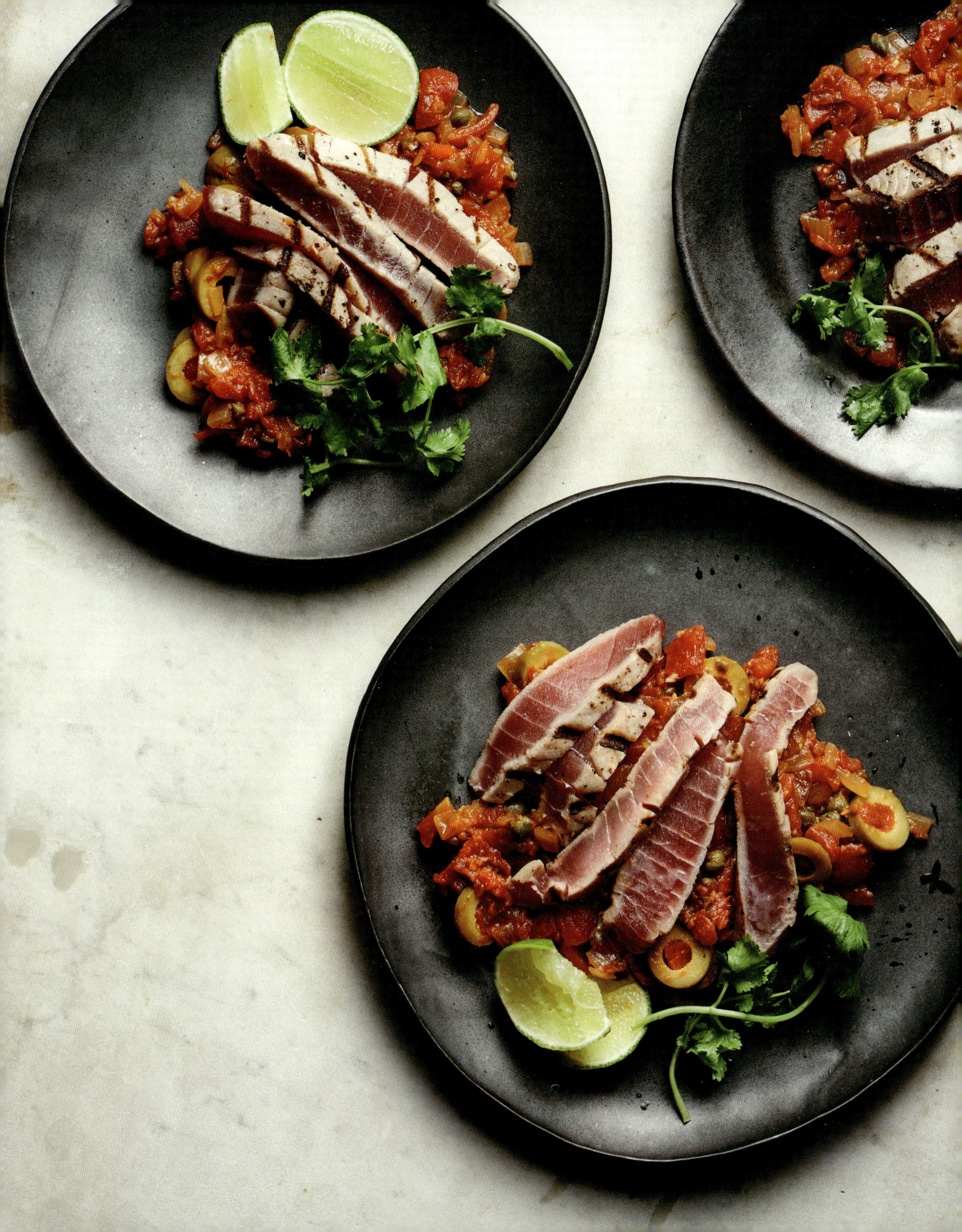

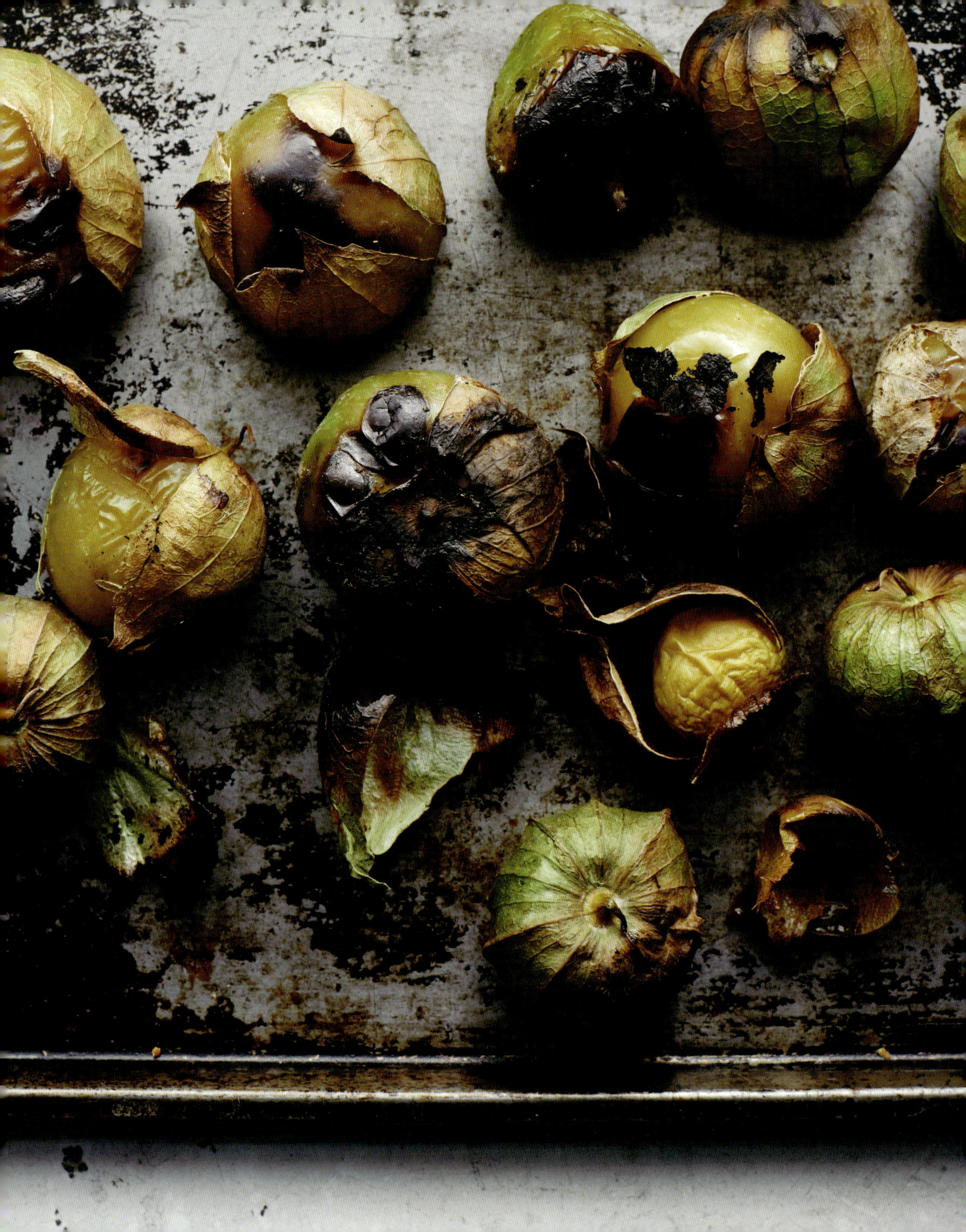

Mexican cooks use local seafood to make specialties like these enchiladas in a creamy green tomatillo and chile sauce. This dish is often called *enchiladas suizas* ("Swiss enchiladas" in Spanish), because it uses generous amounts of cream and cheese, dairy products associated with Switzerland. Crabmeat stays relatively moist when baked, making it the best choice for the filling.

CRAB ENCHILADAS IN GREEN SAUCE

SALSA VERDE

2½ lb/1.2 kg fresh tomatillos, husked, rinsed, and patted dry

2 poblano chiles, or 1 large green bell pepper and 1 jalapeño

¾ cup/180 ml Mexican crema (see below), crème fraîche, or sour cream

⅔ cup/100 g chopped white or yellow onion

½ cup/15 g packed fresh cilantro leaves with tender stems

4 garlic cloves

Pinch of sugar

Kosher salt

1 lb/455 g crabmeat, picked over for cartilage

1½ cups/165 g shredded Monterey jack cheese

¼ cup/60 ml vegetable oil, for frying

12 corn tortillas

Chopped fresh cilantro, for garnish

1 To make the salsa: Position the broiler rack about 6 in/15 cm from the heat source and preheat the broiler on high.

2 Add the tomatillos and poblanos to the broiler pan and broil, turning occasionally, until the skins are blackened and blistered, about 10 minutes (the tomatillos may be done earlier, depending on their size). Taking care not to squeeze and burst the soft tomatillos, transfer them and the poblanos to separate bowls. Cover the poblanos and let stand for 10 minutes. Peel, devein, and seed the poblanos and coarsely chop them. In batches, purée the poblanos, tomatillos, crema, onion, the cilantro with its stems, and the garlic and sugar in a blender. Season to taste with salt. Transfer the salsa to a bowl.

3 Position a rack in the center of the oven and preheat the oven to 350°F/180°C.

4 Mix the crabmeat and 1 cup/115 g of the cheese in a medium bowl. Lightly oil a 10-by-15-in/25-by-38-cm baking dish. Spread ½ cup/120 ml of the salsa in the dish.

5 Heat the oil in a medium skillet over medium heat. One at a time, add a tortilla to the skillet and cook, turning once, just until pliable, about 15 seconds. Do not brown the tortilla. Transfer the tortilla to a plate, add about 3 Tbsp of the filling, and roll it up. Arrange the tortillas in the prepared baking dish, smooth sides up. Spread the remaining salsa over the enchiladas and sprinkle with the remaining ½ cup/55 g cheese.

6 Bake until the salsa is bubbling and the cheese is melted, about 30 minutes. Let stand for 5 minutes. Serve hot, sprinkling each serving with cilantro.

MAKES 4 TO 6 SERVINGS

Crema and Tomatillos

Crema is a Latino cultured cream with a thick texture and a mild tang. It is similar to crème fraîche, which is a good substitute. Sour cream can also be used, although it is more tart than the other two. When buying, look carefully at the label, because many Latin American countries make versions of crema with subtle differences from the Mexican version called for in this recipe. Usually, the type of crema is identified by a picture of the country or its flag on the label.

Tomatillos are related to the cape gooseberry, which explains their distinctive papery husk. Before using, discard the husks and rinse the tomatillos under cold running water to wash off the natural sticky coating.

Both crema and tomatillos are sold at Latino markets and, increasingly, at many standard supermarkets, especially in areas with Mexican communities.

For a special dinner party, you can count on these plump stuffed shrimp to be a showstopper. They are beautifully seasoned with flavors from around the world: a Thai sweet-hot sauce, Caribbean spices, and cilantro. For the most dramatic presentation, look for super-sized shrimp, usually sold frozen at supermarkets or thawed at wholesale clubs.

CRAB-STUFFED SHRIMP WITH TWO SAUCES

ASIAN CHILI SAUCE

½ cup/140 ml Thai sweet chili sauce, such as Mae Ploy

1 tsp sambal olek (see Notes, page 128)

1½ tsp drained and minced pickled ginger for sushi

1 tsp minced fresh cilantro

¾ tsp bottled yuzu juice (see Notes, page 128) or fresh lime juice

STUFFING

2 Tbsp unsalted butter

¼ cup/40 g minced yellow onion

2 Tbsp minced celery

2 Tbsp minced green bell pepper

2 Tbsp minced fresh flat-leaf parsley

2 garlic cloves, minced

2 Tbsp mayonnaise

1 large egg yolk

1½ tsp fresh lemon juice

1½ tsp Worcestershire sauce

1 tsp red pepper sauce, preferably Frank's RedHot Original Cayenne Pepper Sauce

½ tsp Caribbean Rub (page 117)

⅛ tsp kosher salt

⅛ tsp freshly ground black pepper

8 oz/225 g lump crabmeat, picked over for cartilage

½ cup/25 g finely crushed buttery snack crackers, such as Ritz

16 colossal (13 to 15 count) shrimp

1 tsp Caribbean Rub (page 117)

3 Tbsp unsalted butter, melted

3 Tbsp finely crushed buttery snack crackers, such as Ritz

SPINACH

1 Tbsp olive oil

2 garlic cloves, minced

5 oz/140 g baby spinach (about 5 cups)

Kosher salt and freshly ground black pepper

Coconut-Almond Rice (page 174)

2 Tbsp Cilantro Oil (page 211), or as needed

1 To make the Asian chili sauce: Whisk all of the ingredients together in a small bowl. (The sauce may be covered and refrigerated for up to 3 days. Bring to room temperature before using.)

2 To make the stuffing: Melt the butter in a small skillet over medium heat. Add the onion, celery, and green pepper and cook, stirring often, until the onion is tender but not browned, about 4 minutes. Stir in the parsley and garlic and cook until the garlic is fragrant, about 1 minute. Transfer to a medium bowl and let cool.

3 Add the mayonnaise, egg yolk, lemon juice, Worcestershire sauce, hot sauce, Caribbean rub, salt, and pepper to the cooled stuffing and mix well. Add the crabmeat and crackers and mix well to combine. (The stuffing can be covered and refrigerated for up to 1 day.)

4 Peel and devein the shrimp, leaving the bottom two segments at the tail intact. Butterfly the shrimp at the deveining incision, making sure not to cut all the way through the shrimp. Toss the shrimp with the Caribbean rub, making sure to distribute the spices evenly. Brush a 10-by-15-in/25-by-38-cm baking dish with some of the butter. Arrange the shrimp, cut side down, with the tail segment curling up, in the dish. Divide the stuffing into 16 balls and place a ball in the curve of each shrimp. (The shrimp can be

(continued)

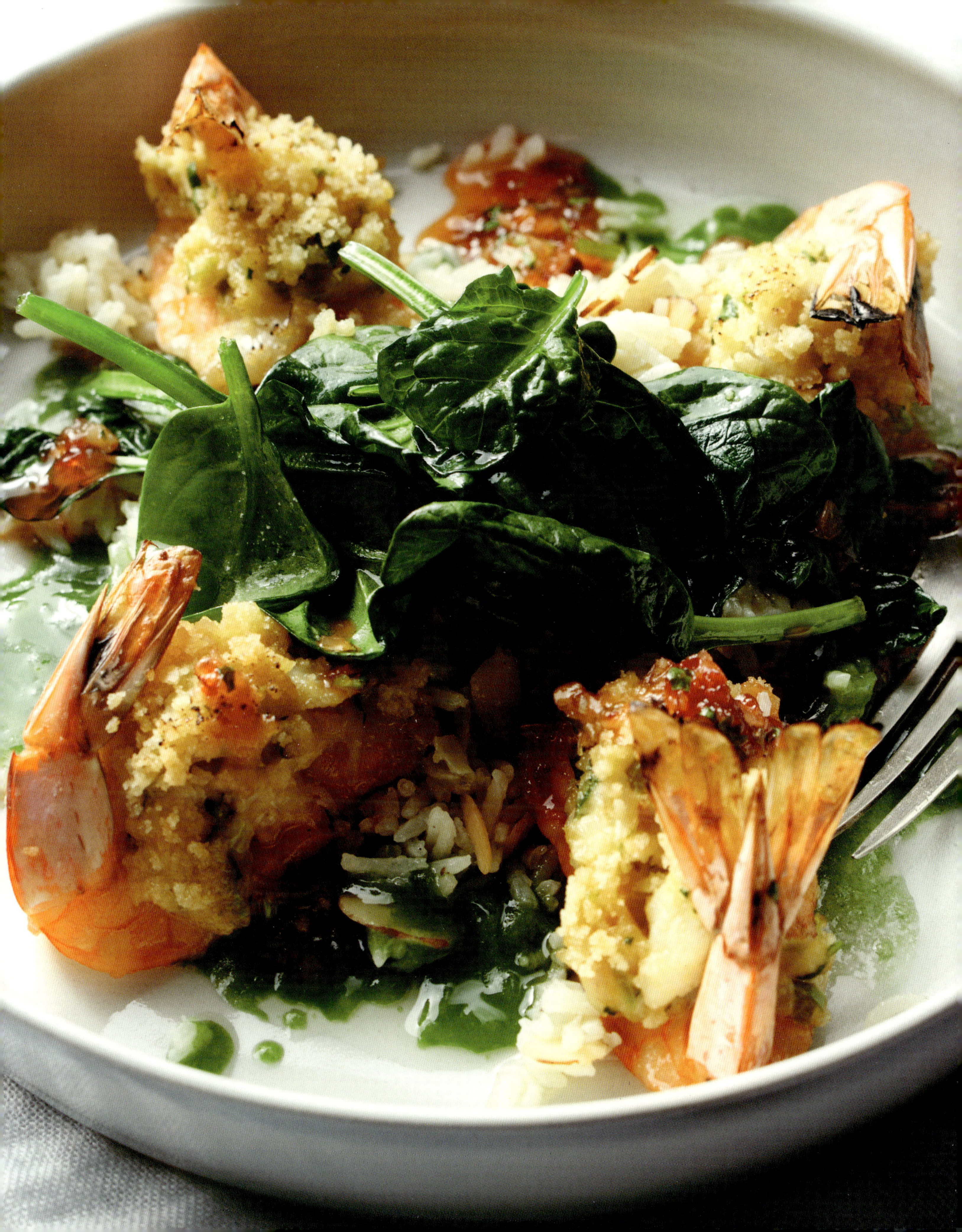

CRAB-STUFFED SHRIMP WITH TWO SAUCES, continued

covered with plastic wrap and refrigerated for up to 6 hours.)

5 Position a rack in the top third of the oven and preheat the oven to 400°F/200°C. Brush the stuffing with melted butter (you will have to move the tails), sprinkle with the crumbs, and drizzle with the remaining butter. Bake until the topping is golden brown and the shrimp are opaque, 12 to 15 minutes.

6 Just before the shrimp is done, make the spinach: Heat the oil and garlic together in a large skillet (preferably nonstick) over high heat, just until the garlic is fragrant but not browned, about 2 minutes. Add the spinach and cook, tossing constantly with kitchen tongs, just until it is just heated but not wilted (you want the spinach to provide some height to the dish), about 30 seconds. Season to taste with salt and pepper. Remove from the heat.

7 Spoon equal amounts of the rice into the center of each of 4 dinner plates. Spoon about 2 Tbsp of the Asian chili sauce around the rice, then drizzle with about 2 tsp of the cilantro oil. Place the shrimp, tails up, equally spaced around the rice. Using the tongs, divide the spinach evenly over the rice. Serve immediately.

MAKES 4 SERVINGS

NOTES: Sambal olek (sometimes called sambal or sambal oelek) is an Indonesian seasoning made of ground chiles, vinegar, and salt. It's easy to find at Asian markets, but more and more supermarkets are carrying it, too.

Yuzu is a Japanese citrus fruit with a slightly bitter juice. It is rarely available fresh, but bottled juice is available at Japanese grocers and online. Fresh lime juice is a good substitute.

In New Orleans, "barbecued shrimp" has nothing to do with firing up the grill. Instead, shrimp (preferably the head-on variety, sold at Asian markets) are cooked in an aromatic butter sauce redolent with the familiar BBQ spices. This dish is made for sopping up with crusty bread, so be sure to have some on the table and offer plenty of napkins, as finger licking cannot be avoided.

BBQ SHRIMP WITH SPICY BEER SAUCE

2 Tbsp olive oil

1½ lb/680 g jumbo (21 to 25 count) shrimp, preferably with heads and tails, deveined but not peeled

1½ tsp smoked paprika (pimentón)

1 tsp dried oregano

1 tsp dried thyme

Kosher salt

¼ tsp freshly ground black pepper

Pinch of cayenne pepper

1 cup/225 g cold unsalted butter, cut into ½-in/12-mm cubes

2 green onions, white and pale green parts finely chopped, dark green tops thinly sliced for serving

2 garlic cloves, minced

1 cup/240 ml lager beer

2 Tbsp fresh lemon juice

2 Tbsp Worcestershire sauce

Red pepper sauce, such as Tabasco

Lemon wedges, for serving

1 Heat the oil in a very large skillet over medium-high heat until shimmering but not smoking. Add the shrimp and cook, stirring occasionally, just until they turn opaque, 2 to 3 minutes. Transfer to a platter.

2 Whisk the paprika, oregano, thyme, ½ tsp salt, the black pepper, and cayenne pepper together in a small bowl. Melt 1 Tbsp of the butter in the skillet over medium heat. Add the white part of the green onions with the garlic and cook, stirring occasionally, until softened, about 1 minute. Stir in the spice mixture. Add the beer, lemon juice, Worcestershire sauce, and ½ tsp red pepper sauce and bring to a boil over high heat, scraping up any browned bits in the bottom of the skillet with a wooden spoon. Boil until the liquid is reduced by half, about 5 minutes. Remove the skillet from the heat to stop the sauce from boiling.

3 Return the skillet to very low heat. A few cubes at a time, whisk the remaining butter into the sauce, letting each piece soften (it should not melt into a liquid) before adding the next piece, until the butter has emulsified with the liquid to make a smooth sauce. If the sauce starts to boil, remove the skillet from the heat. Season to taste with salt and red pepper sauce. Stir in the reserved shrimp and cook just to warm it through, about 1 minute.

4 Divide among 4 shallow bowls, sprinkle with the green onion leaves, and serve hot, with lemon wedges.

MAKES 4 SERVINGS

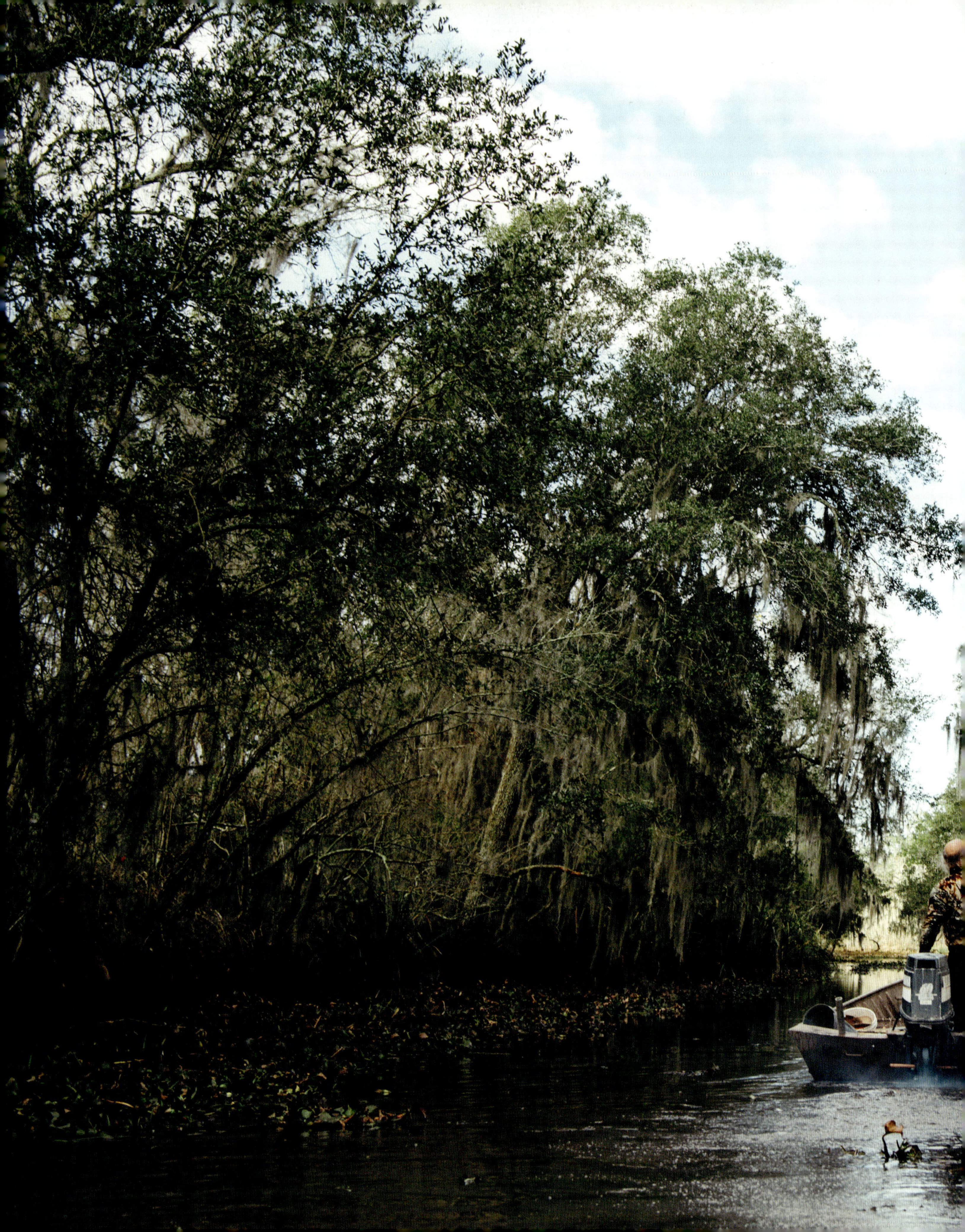

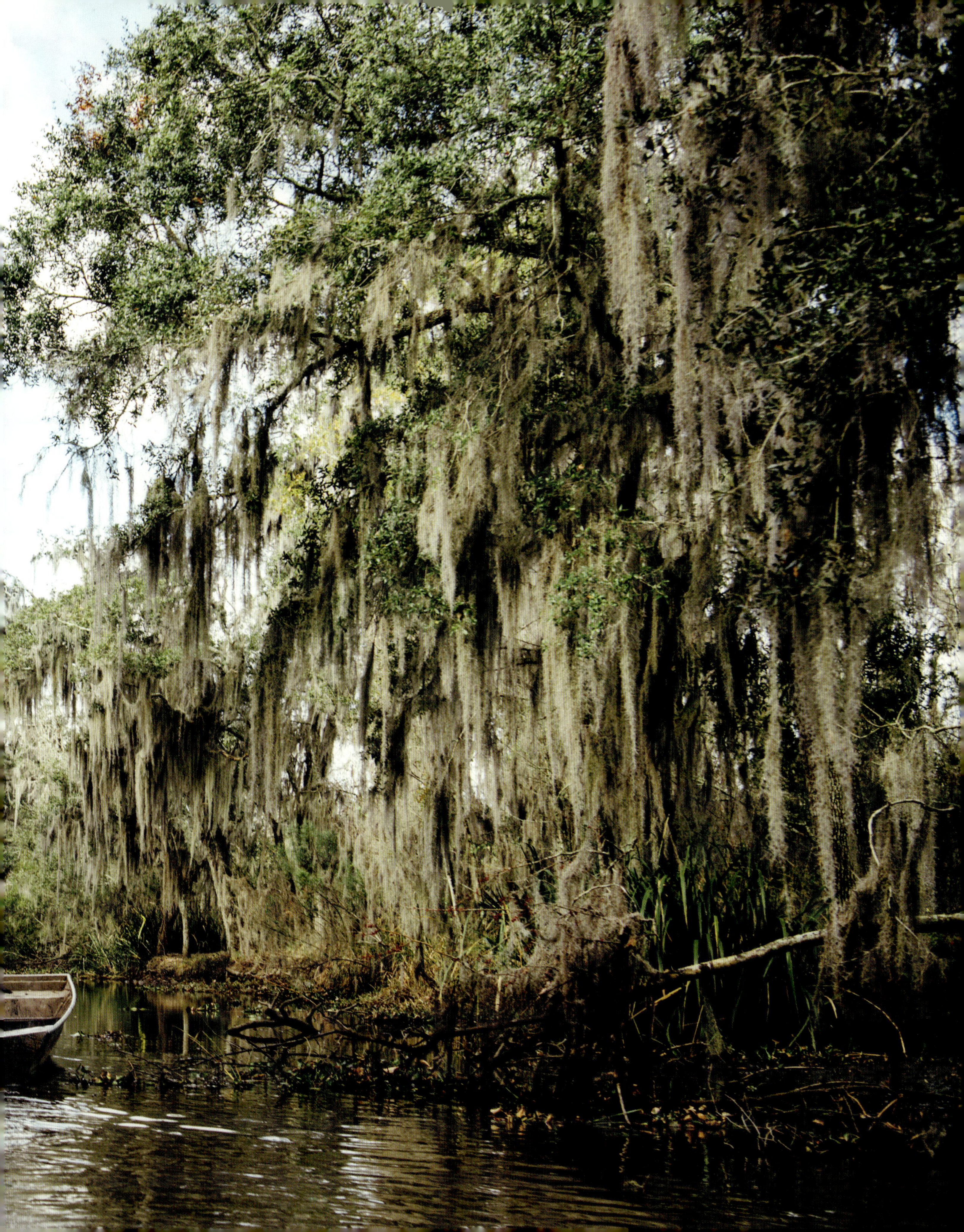

Shrimp and grits is served everywhere along the Gulf Coast, from the most humble seafood shack to white-tablecloth "fine dining" establishments. Therefore, it can be dressed up or dressed down. This version falls in the middle, with cheese added to the grits, and andouille sausage and extra vegetables flavoring the sauce. Flip a coin to choose whether to drink cold beer or chilled white wine with this dish.

SHRIMP AND ANDOUILLE WITH CHEESE GRITS

GRITS

2 cups/480 ml canned reduced-sodium chicken broth

1 cup/240 ml whole milk

½ teaspoon kosher salt

1 cup/200 g supermarket old-fashioned grits (not instant)

SHRIMP AND ANDOUILLE

1 Tbsp olive oil

6 oz/170 g andouille or other spicy smoked sausage, cut into ½-in/12-mm dice

1 lb/455 g jumbo (21 to 25 count) shrimp, peeled and deveined

1 tsp Cajun Seasoning (page 213)

2 Tbsp unsalted butter

½ yellow onion, chopped

4 green onions, thinly sliced

1 large celery stalk, diced

½ large red bell pepper, cored and diced

2 garlic cloves, minced

2 Tbsp unbleached all-purpose flour

2 cups/480 ml Shrimp Stock (page 210) or canned reduced-sodium chicken broth

1 Tbsp Worcestershire sauce

½ tsp red pepper sauce

Kosher salt and black pepper

1 cup/110 g shredded sharp Cheddar cheese, for serving

Chopped fresh flat-leaf parsley, for garnish

1 To start the grits: Bring the broth, milk, 1 cup/240 ml water, and salt to a simmer in a medium, heavy saucepan over medium heat, taking care that the mixture does not boil over. Whisk the grits into the saucepan and return the mixture to a simmer. Reduce the heat to medium-low. Simmer, whisking often, until the mixture is thick and smooth, about 20 minutes.

2 Meanwhile, make the shrimp and andouille: Heat the oil in a large skillet over medium-high heat. Add the andouille and cook, stirring occasionally, until the andouille browns and renders some of its fat, about 5 minutes. Using a slotted spoon, transfer the andouille to paper towels. Pour out all but 1 Tbsp fat from the skillet.

3 Toss the shrimp with the Cajun seasoning. Add the shrimp to the skillet and cook, stirring occasionally, just until it turns opaque, about 4 minutes. Transfer the shrimp to the andouille.

4 Melt the 2 Tbsp butter in the skillet. Add the yellow onion, green onions, celery, bell pepper, and garlic and cook, stirring occasionally, until the vegetables soften, about 3 minutes. Sprinkle in the flour and mix well. Whisk in the broth, Worcestershire sauce, and pepper sauce and bring to a boil. Reduce the heat to low and simmer until no raw flour taste remains, about 5 minutes. Return the shrimp and andouille to the skillet and mix well. Season to taste with salt and pepper. Remove from the heat.

5 Add the cheese to the grits and stir until the cheese melts. Divide the grits among 4 wide soup bowls. Top with equal amounts of the shrimp mixture, sprinkle with the parsley, and serve immediately.

MAKES 4 SERVINGS

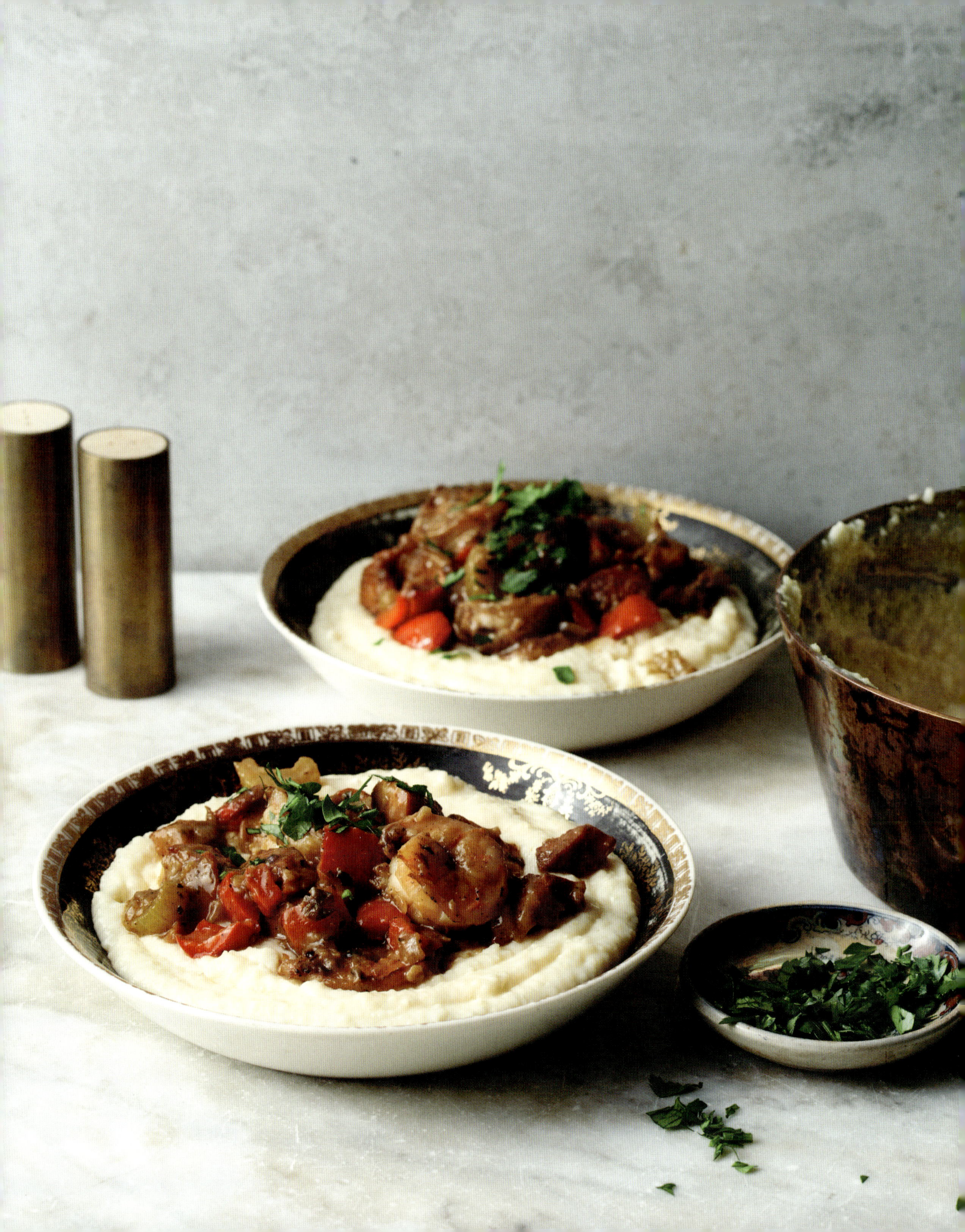

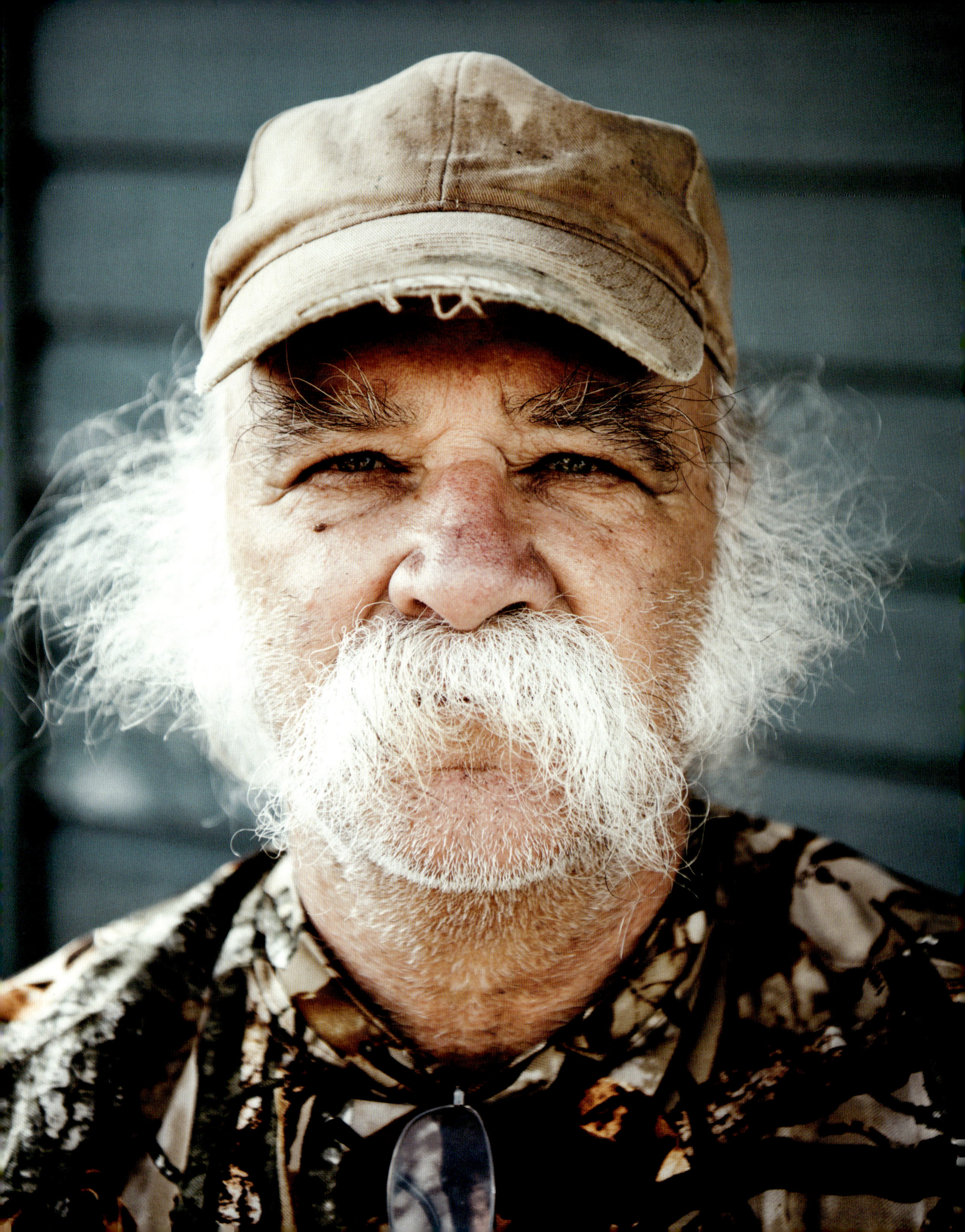

JOEY FONSECA, CATFISH FISHERMAN

Des Allemands is a small town (2,500 inhabitants) with a big title: the Catfish Capital of the Universe. We're talking wild catfish here, harvested directly from their natural habitat in the bayous, and not the farmed variety raised in tanks. The village is also home to Raymond Joseph "Joey" Fonseca and his family, third-generation fishermen, and owners of Des Allemands Outlaw Katfish Company, who sell their products (including crab, crawfish, and alligator sausage) to some of the best restaurants in Louisiana.

But what does "Outlaw" mean in Joey's company's name? "The status quo in Baton Rouge only recognized hook-and-line fishing for catching catfish—or you could catch them with your hands. My father and other fishermen around here knew a better way. They'd punch up a paint can or big metal drum can and let it slime up in the water so it looked like a log. The fish would go into the can, and it was just a question of getting them out of the can water and into your partner's net on the boat." Because the state was promoting catfish farming at the time, "can fishing" was discouraged and bayou fishermen were considered outlaws. The effort to support big business over local entrepreneurs fell apart when it was proven that the old methods were not harmful to the environment.

And then there is the matter of whether wild catfish taste better than farmed. "It's a simple fact that they taste better, and they are better for you," says Joey, who points to a study by Louisiana State University that specifies the differences between the two fish. One finding was especially surprising: the wild fish have more omega-3 fatty acids (which help raise "good" HDL cholesterol) and are lower in fat. "The farms hoped the study would show that their fish were just as good, but it was a flop for them," says Joey. Once again, the inhabitants of the Gulf Coast have proven the value of a sustainable lifestyle.

There's nothing more to this cocktail than lemonade spiked with bourbon and fresh mint—but sometimes the simplest combinations are the most resonant. The key word here is *fresh*, as this would not be the same if you made the lemonade from a mix. This drink is similar to that cocktail classic the Whiskey Sour; the mint makes all the difference.

BOURBON-MINT LEMONADE

LEMONADE

1 cup/240 ml fresh lemon juice

¾ cup/150 g sugar, preferably superfine

5 large fresh mint leaves

3½ fl oz/105 ml lemonade, above

1½ fl oz/45 ml high-quality bourbon, such as Bulleit

1 slice lemon

GARNISH: 1 lemon wheel

1 To make the lemonade: Shake the lemon juice and sugar together in a jar to dissolve the sugar. Pour into a pitcher. Add 4 cups/960 ml water and mix well. (Makes about 5 cups/1.2 L.)

2 Muddle the mint in a mixer glass. Add about 4 fl oz/120 ml of the lemonade, the bourbon, and the lemon slice and half-fill with ice. Shake well. Strain into an ice-filled tall Collins glass. Garnish with the lemon wheel and serve.

MAKES 1 DRINK

Many Americans know dried hibiscus flowers as the main ingredient in a favorite hot herbal tea. (Hibiscus is also called sorrel in the Caribbean; don't confuse it with the tart green herb.) Steeped with fresh ginger and spices, the brew is perfect for enjoying iced as a nonalcoholic refresher or spiking with a bit of rum for a very refreshing cocktail.

HIBISCUS-GINGER PUNCH

1 cup/200 g sugar

2 Tbsp shredded fresh ginger (use the large holes on a box grater)

2 tsp whole allspice

1 cup/45 g dried hibiscus flowers (also called *flor de jamaica* or sorrel, sold at Latino markets and online)

3 Tbsp fresh lime juice

GARNISH: 8 lime or lemon wheels and 8 fresh mint sprigs

1 Bring 8 cups/2 L water and the sugar, ginger, and allspice to a boil in a medium saucepan over high heat, stirring often to dissolve the sugar. Remove from the heat. Add the hibiscus flowers and stir well. Let steep for 5 to 10 minutes.

2 Strain the mixture through a sieve into a bowl, pressing hard on the contents in the sieve with the back of a spoon. Stir in the lime juice. Let cool.

3 Pour into ice-filled tall Collins glasses. Garnish each with a lime or lemon wheel and a mint sprig.

MAKES 8 SERVINGS

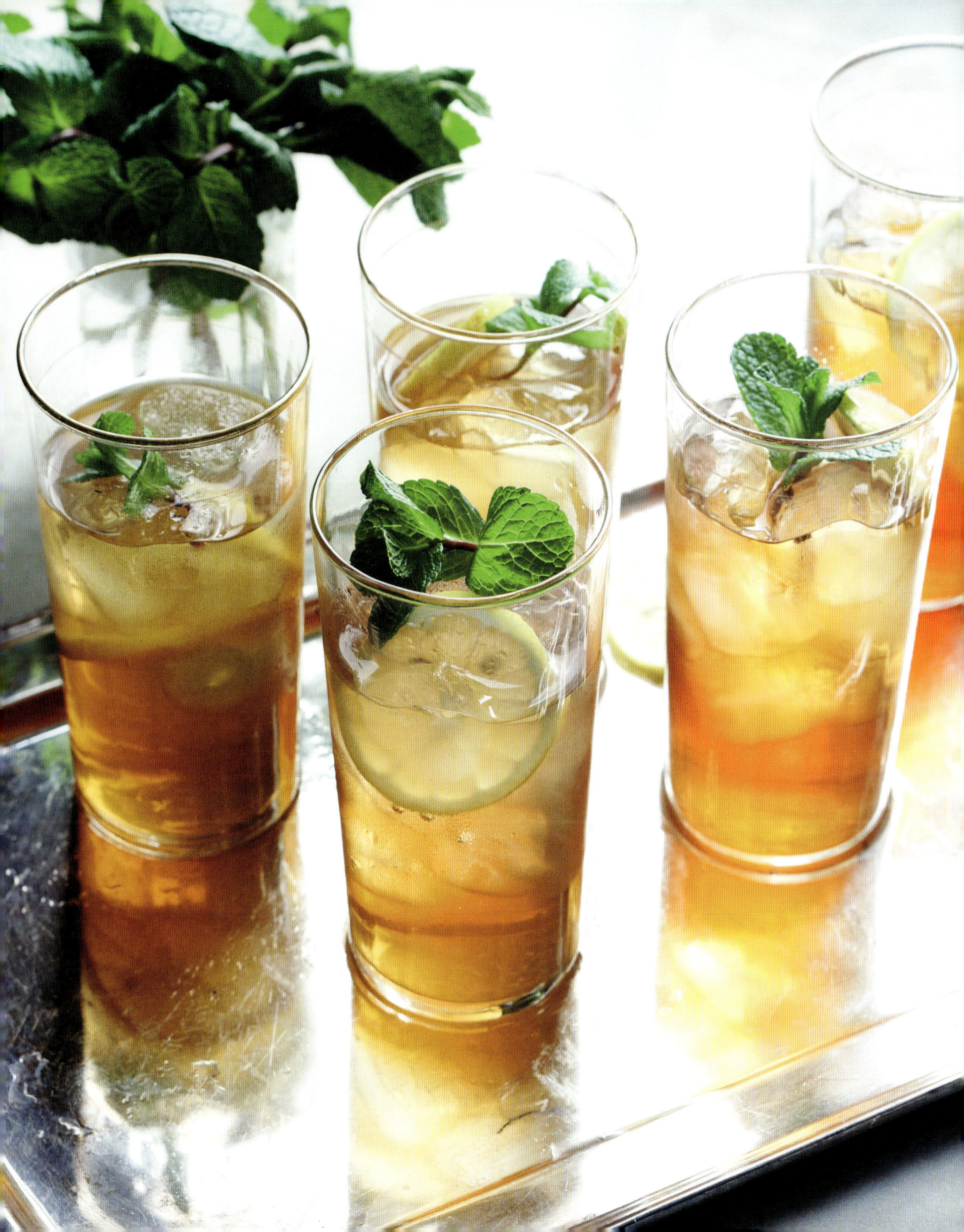

You'll find these frita-style burgers at Cuban restaurants all around Florida. What makes a burger a frita? The addition of smoked chorizo to the beef patties, a topping of crisp shoestring potatoes, and a spiced (if not spicy) "secret sauce." Be sure to use Spanish-style smoked chorizo links, and not uncooked Mexican chorizo.

CUBAN "HAMBURGERS" WITH CHORIZO AND SHOESTRING POTATOES

SAUCE

½ cup/120 ml ketchup

2 Tbsp distilled white vinegar

1 Tbsp Worcestershire sauce

½ tsp sugar

½ tsp Spanish sweet smoked paprika (pimentón)

½ tsp ground cumin

1 garlic clove, crushed through a press

PATTIES

2 garlic cloves

1 cup/140 g chopped yellow onion

½ cup/75 g chopped green bell pepper

10 oz/280 g Spanish-style smoked chorizos, casings removed, thinly sliced

1¼ lb/570 g ground beef (85 percent lean)

½ cup/55 g plain dried bread crumbs

1 large egg, beaten

2 Tbsp ketchup

1 Tbsp Worcestershire sauce

1 tsp kosher salt

6 hamburger buns, split

One 5-oz/140-g can shoestring potatoes (also called potato sticks)

1 To make the sauce: Whisk the ketchup, vinegar, Worcestershire sauce, sugar, paprika, cumin, garlic, and ¼ cup/60 ml water together in a small saucepan. Bring to a simmer over medium heat. Reduce the heat to medium-low and simmer, whisking occasionally, until the mixture thickens slightly and is reduced to ¾ cup/180 ml, about 10 minutes. Transfer to a small bowl and let cool.

2 To make the patties: With the machine running, drop the garlic cloves through the feed tube of a food processor to finely chop them. Add the onion and bell pepper to the food processor and pulse a few times until they are finely chopped. Add the chorizo and pulse until the entire mixture is minced but not a paste. Transfer to a large bowl.

3 Add the ground beef, bread crumbs, egg, ketchup, Worcestershire sauce, and salt and mix gently but thoroughly with your hands; do not overhandle the meat mixture. Divide into 6 equal patties, each about 4 in/10 cm wide. Poke an indentation about 1 in/2.5 cm wide in the center of each patty (this reduces shrinkage during cooking). Transfer the patties to a waxed paper–lined baking sheet, cover, and refrigerate for at least 30 minutes or up to 4 hours.

4 Heat a large griddle or two large skillets over medium-high heat. Reduce the heat to medium and lightly oil the griddle. Place the patties on the griddle and cook until the underside is browned, about 4 minutes. Carefully flip the patties over and cook until the other side is browned and the patties feel somewhat firm when pressed on the top in the center, about 4 minutes more for medium. (These burgers should be cooked until at least medium—they will not dry out.)

5 For each frita, place a bun on a plate. Spread the bottom with about 1 Tbsp sauce. Add a patty, a generous handful of the potatoes (they will spill over), and another Tbsp of the sauce. Finish with the roll top and serve immediately.

MAKES 6 SERVINGS

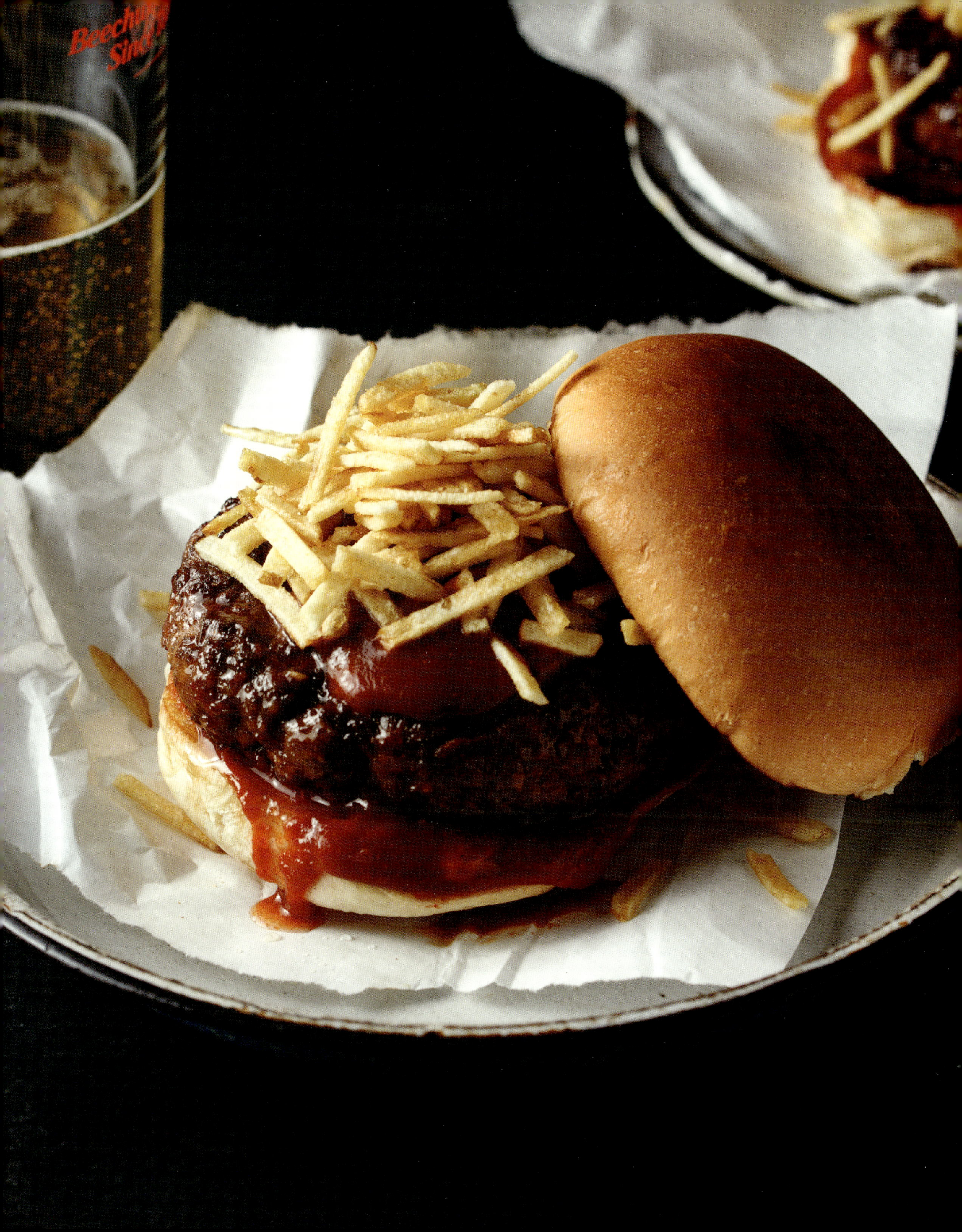

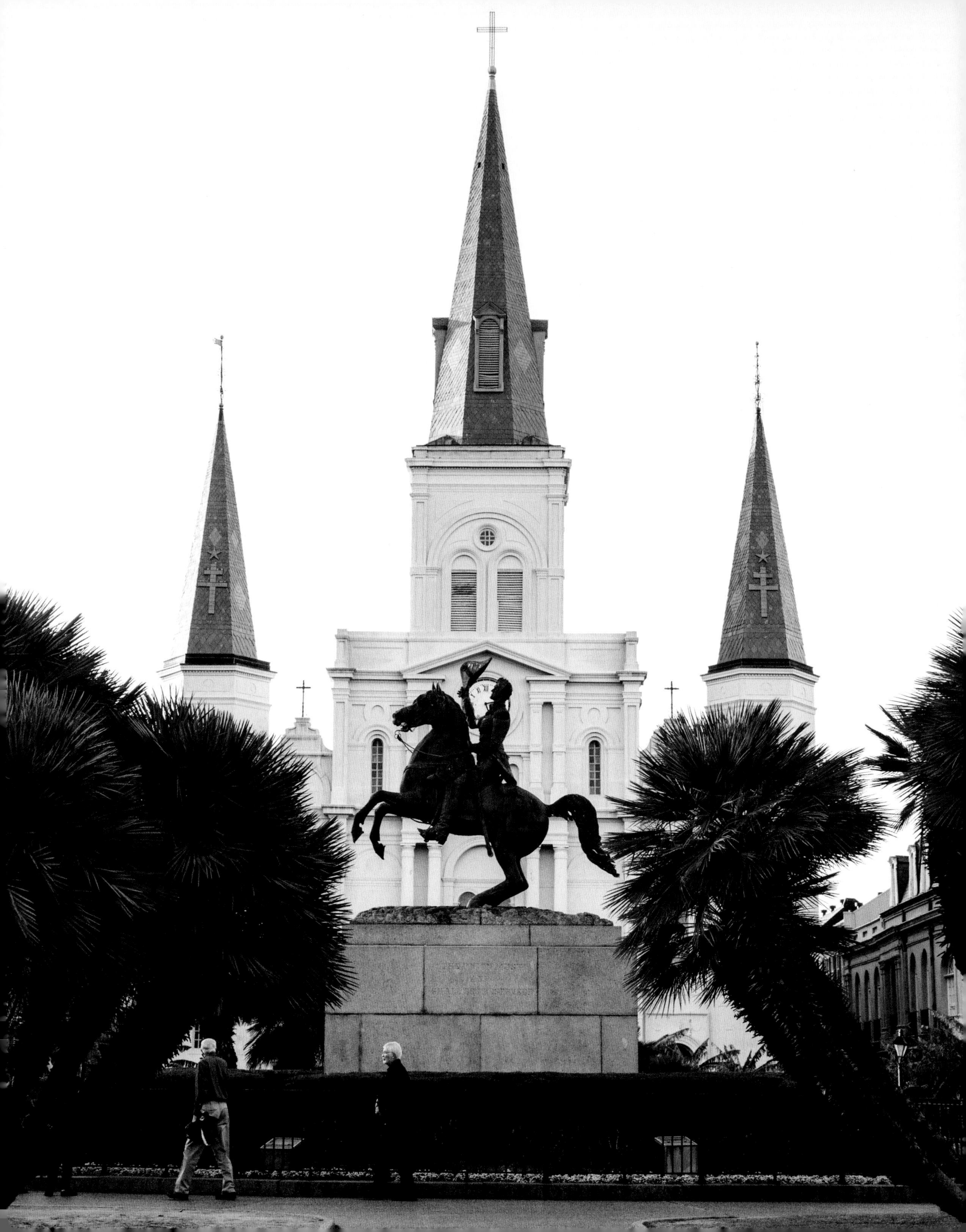

Yes, Beef Debris Po' Boy is an unattractive name for such an appealing sandwich: falling-apart shards of beef piled into a roll and doused with a rich gravy. You might consider the mayonnaise, lettuce, and tomato as extraneous additions, but they are the very things that separate this po' boy from a standard hot beef sandwich. Well, that and the number of napkins you'll use eating it . . .

BEEF DEBRIS PO' BOYS WITH GRAVY

BEEF

1 chuck roast, 3 lb/1.4 kg and about 2 in/5 cm thick

½ tsp kosher salt

½ tsp freshly ground black pepper

2 Tbsp vegetable oil

1 yellow onion, coarsely chopped

1 carrot, peeled and coarsely chopped

1 celery stalk, coarsely chopped

6 garlic cloves, coarsely chopped

1¾ cups/420 ml reduced-sodium beef broth

2 Tbsp tomato paste

2 Tbsp Worcestershire sauce

½ tsp dried thyme

1 bay leaf

GRAVY

3 Tbsp unsalted butter

3 Tbsp all-purpose flour

2½ cups/600 ml reduced beef cooking liquid, above

Kosher salt and freshly ground black pepper

6 oblong French rolls, split

½ cup/120 ml mayonnaise

½ head iceberg lettuce, cored and shredded

2 beefsteak tomatoes, sliced

1 Position a rack in the center of the oven and preheat the oven to 325°F/165°C.

2 Season the beef all over with the salt and pepper. Heat 1 Tbsp of the oil in a large Dutch oven or flameproof casserole over medium-high heat. Add the beef and cook, turning once, until well browned on both sides, about 8 minutes. Transfer the beef to a plate.

3 Add the remaining 1 Tbsp oil to the pot. Add the onion, carrot, celery, and garlic and reduce the heat to medium. Cook, stirring occasionally, until the vegetables soften, about 3 minutes. Add the beef broth, tomato paste, Worcestershire sauce, thyme, and bay leaf and bring to a simmer, scraping up the browned bits in the bottom of the pot with a wooden spoon and dissolving the tomato paste. Return the beef to the pot, add enough water to barely cover the beef, and bring to a boil over high heat. Cover the pot and bake until the beef is very tender, about 2 hours. Remove from the oven. Let the beef cool in its cooking liquid for about 1 hour. Discard the bay leaf.

4 Transfer the beef to a carving board and tent it with aluminum foil to keep the beef from drying out. Strain the cooking liquid through a sieve into a medium bowl. Let stand for 5 minutes, then skim off the fat on the surface. Return the cooking liquid to the pot and boil over high heat until reduced to 2½ cups/600 ml, about 20 minutes.

5 To make the gravy: Melt the butter in a medium saucepan over medium-low heat. Sprinkle in the flour and whisk until smooth. Let the roux bubble without browning for 1 minute. Whisk in the reduced cooking liquid and bring to a simmer. Reduce the heat to medium-low and simmer, whisking occasionally, until the gravy thickens and no raw flour taste remains, about 5 minutes. Season to taste with salt and pepper.

6 Slice the beef across the grain into thick slices and pull the meat into shreds, discarding any fat. Add the beef to the simmering gravy and cook to reheat the beef, about 2 minutes.

7 Spread each roll with mayonnaise and place on a dinner plate. Using a large spoon, divide the sliced beef and gravy among the bottom halves of the rolls and add the lettuce, tomatoes, and roll tops. Cut each sandwich in half and serve hot, with plenty of napkins.

MAKES 6 SERVINGS

When the Spaniards stumbled on the West Indies, they discovered the native method of pit-cooking, a technique they dubbed *barbacoa*, the original version of BBQ. We've developed an indoor, slow-cooked version of Southern pulled pork that borrows from this ancient method by wrapping the meat in banana leaves to hold in the steam. The end result is a melt-in-your-mouth sandwich.

PULLED PORK SANDWICHES WITH BLACKBERRY BRANDY BBQ SAUCE

PORK

1 bone-in pork butt, about 5.5 lb/2.5 kg

1½ tsp coarse salt, preferably red Hawaiian

2 large thawed banana leaves, each measuring about 24 by 12 in/ 60 by 30.5 cm

1 cup/240 ml hot tap water

1 Tbsp hickory liquid smoke

Blackberry Brandy BBQ Sauce (page 99)

10 hamburger buns, toasted

2 cups/300 g Island Slaw (page 209)

Crispy Onions (page 209)

1 Position a rack in the center of the oven and preheat the oven to 350°F/180°C.

2 Cut off the skin and fat in one piece from the top of the pork; set aside. Butterfly the pork on both sides of the bone (butterflying the pork will distribute the salt throughout the meat, and not just on the top and bottom): Make a deep vertical cut into the meatiest side of the pork, next to the bone, stopping the cut about 1 in/2.5 cm from the bottom of the roast. Starting about halfway into the cut, turn the knife to make a horizontal cut, stopping about 1 in/2.5 cm from the side of the pork. Open the meat into a flap. Repeat on the other side of the pork bone (although this area does not have as much meat).

3 Season the pork all over with the salt. Fold the pork back into its original shape and put the skin and fat piece back in place. Cross the banana leaves in a roasting pan, with one leaf running west-east, and the other running north-south. Place the pork, skin side up, on the intersection of the leaves and completely wrap in the leaves. Mix the hot water with the liquid smoke and pour into the pan. Cover the pan tightly with a double thickness of aluminum foil. Bake until the pork is fork-tender and an instant-read thermometer inserted in the thickest part but not touching bone reads 195°F/90°C, about 2¼ hours. Let cool in the pan for 30 minutes. Transfer the pork to a carving board, discarding the banana leaves. Pour the cooking liquid into a small bowl and set aside.

4 Using your fingers or two dinner forks, pull the pork into shreds. Transfer to a large bowl. Skim off and discard the fat on the cooking liquid and mix the liquid into the pork. (The pork can be covered and refrigerated for up to 2 days.)

5 Cook the pork with its juices and in a very large skillet over medium-high heat, stirring occasionally, until the pork is hot and steaming, about 5 minutes. Add ½ cup/120 ml of the blackberry sauce and mix well. Reduce the heat to very low and cover with the lid ajar to keep warm.

6 Fill the buns with pork mixture and slaw. Top with the crispy onions. Serve immediately, with the remaining sauce passed on the side.

MAKES 10 SANDWICHES

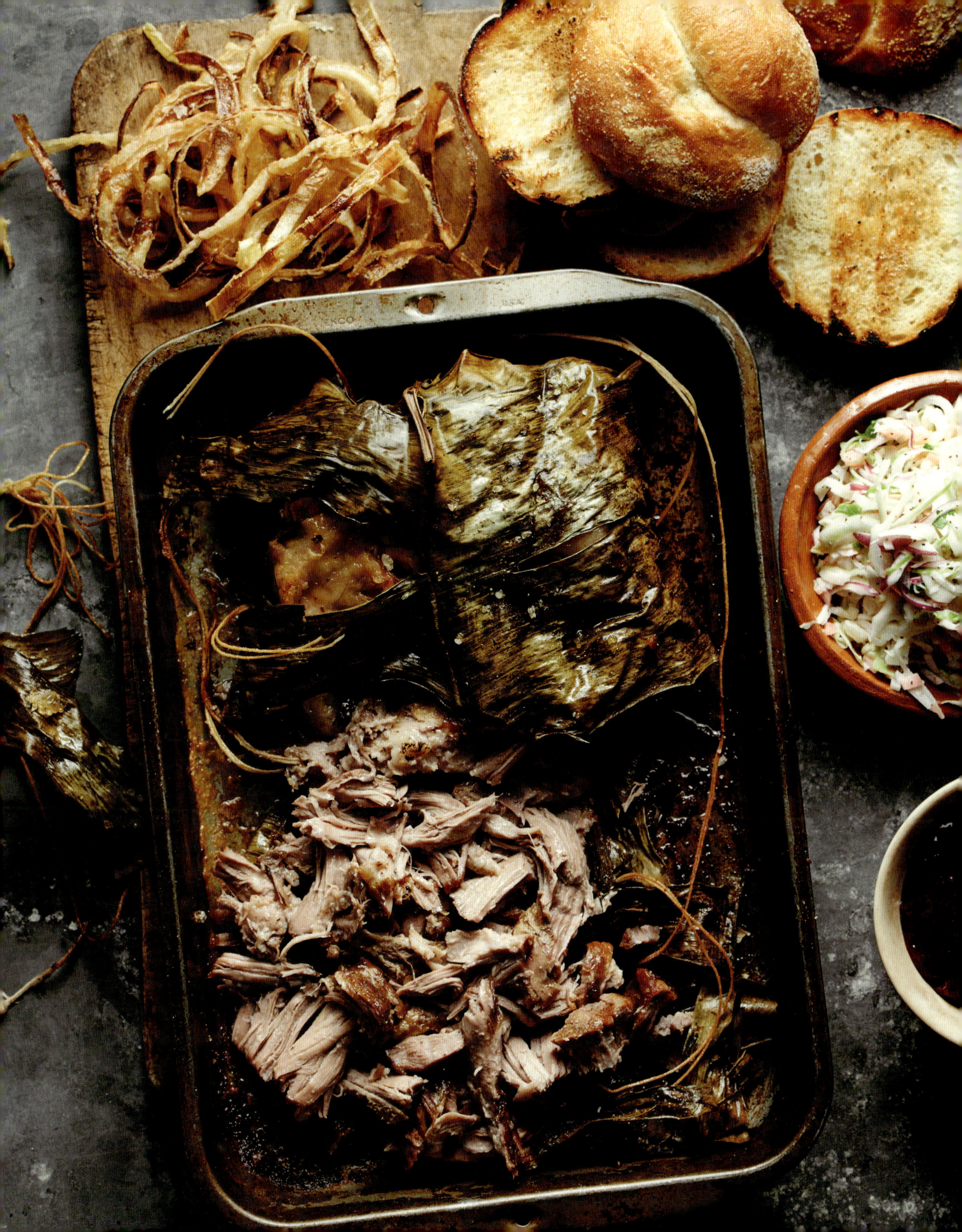

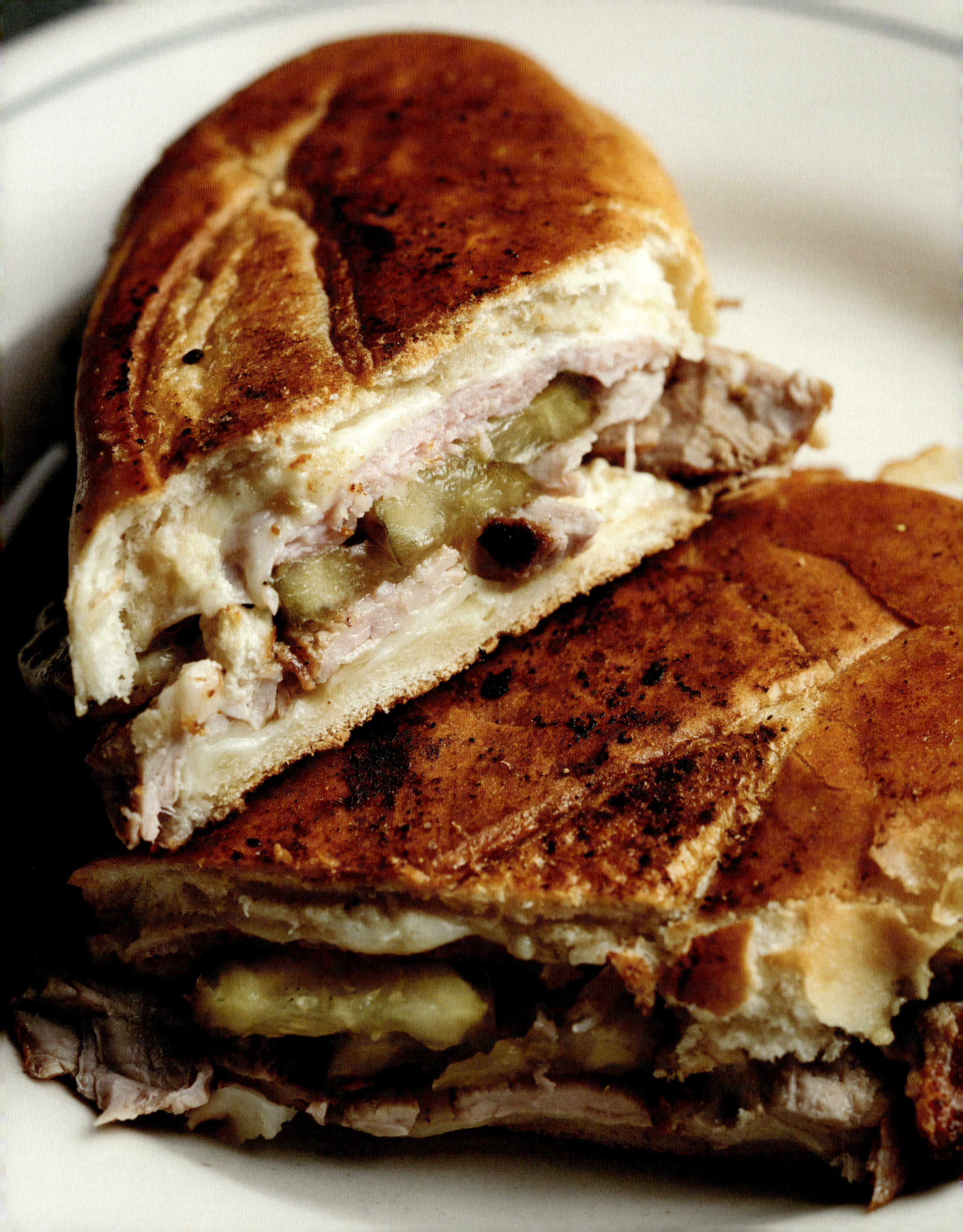

For many years, Cuban sandwiches—ham, Swiss cheese, roast pork, and dill pickles pressed together in a crunchy roll—were only served in Florida at casual Latino restaurants. Too good to remain a secret, they are now served around the country. This recipe makes a quartet of sandwiches at the same time, so you can share your Cubanos with friends.

OLD-SCHOOL CUBAN SANDWICHES WITH GARLIC MAYONNAISE

GARLIC MAYONNAISE

⅓ cup/75 ml mayonnaise

2 Tbsp Dijon mustard

1 garlic clove, crushed through a garlic press

PORK

1 pork tenderloin, about 1 lb/455 g

¾ tsp kosher salt

¼ tsp granulated onion

¼ tsp granulated garlic

¼ tsp freshly ground black pepper

1 Tbsp olive oil

8 slices boiled ham, about 8 oz/225 g, cut to fit rolls

4 oblong soft rolls, about 6 in/15 cm long, split lengthwise

8 slices Swiss cheese, about 8 oz/225 g total, cut to fit rolls

8 long dill pickle slices

3 Tbsp unsalted butter, at room temperature

SPECIAL EQUIPMENT: A large griddle

1 To make the mayonnaise: Whisk all of the ingredients together in a small bowl to combine. Cover and set aside.

2 To make the pork tenderloin: Position a rack in the center of the oven and preheat the oven to 350°F/180°C.

3 Using a thin, sharp knife, trim the silver skin and excess fat from the pork. Mix the salt, granulated onion and garlic, and pepper in a small bowl. Season the pork all over with the salt mixture. Let stand at room temperature for 15 minutes.

4 Heat the oil in a large ovenproof skillet over medium-high heat. Add the pork and cook, turning occasionally, until browned, about 5 minutes. Transfer the skillet with the pork to the oven. Bake until the tenderloin reaches 145°F/63°C on an instant-read thermometer, 10 to 15 minutes. Transfer the pork to a carving board and let stand for 5 minutes. Cut the pork crosswise into slices about ¼ in/6 mm thick.

5 Heat a large griddle or 2 large skillets over medium heat. Cook the ham on the griddle, turning once, just until it is heated but not browned, about 30 seconds, and transfer the ham to a plate. Quickly wipe the griddle clean with a moistened paper towel.

6 Spread the rolls with the mayonnaise. Divide the cheese, ham, roast pork, and dill pickle slices evenly among the rolls. Close the rolls and press them firmly with your hands to compress them. Spread the sandwich exteriors with the butter. Place the sandwiches on the griddle. Cover them loosely with a large sheet of aluminum foil, then top with a large baking sheet. Weight the sheet evenly with heavy saucepans, skillets, cans of food, or foil-wrapped bricks. Cook, adjusting the heat as needed so the sandwiches cook evenly without burning, turning once, until they are crisp and golden brown, about 6 minutes.

7 Transfer the sandwiches to the carving board and let them stand for a few minutes. Using a serrated knife, cut each sandwich crosswise in half on a diagonal and serve immediately.

MAKES 4 SERVINGS

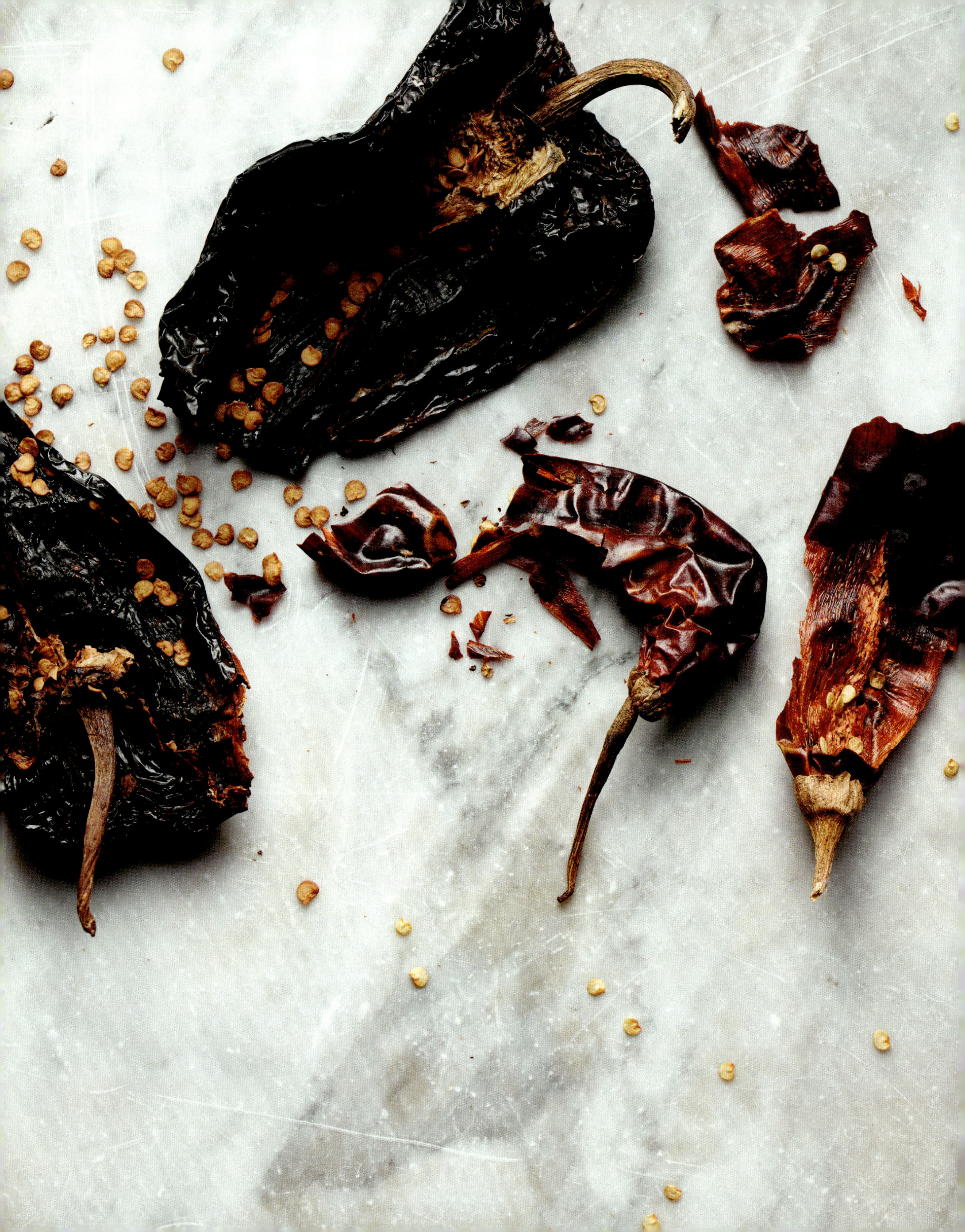

This is a simplified indoor recipe for *barbacoa*-style lamb—originally smothered in a chili sauce, wrapped in banana leaves, and slowly cooked in a pit or grill. The lamb shanks braise to a succulent tenderness, and the meat is removed from the bones to create a filling for soft tacos. The pickled onions cut through the richness and only take a few minutes to make, so don't skip them.

LAMB SHANKS ADOBO SOFT TACOS

PICKLED ONIONS

¾ cup/180 ml distilled white vinegar

1½ tsp sugar

¾ tsp kosher salt

8 black peppercorns

1 red onion, thinly sliced and separated into rings

ADOBO

5 ancho chiles, stemmed, seeded, and deveined

6 guajillo chiles, stemmed, seeded, and deveined

3 garlic cloves, crushed under a knife and peeled

2 Tbsp distilled white vinegar

1½ tsp ground cumin

1½ tsp dried oregano, preferably Mexican, crumbled

1 tsp kosher salt

½ tsp freshly ground black pepper

¼ tsp ground cloves

2 Tbsp vegetable oil

4 lamb shanks, each about 1 lb/455 g

12 corn tortillas, warmed according to package directions

½ cup/55 g crumbled goat cheese

1 cup/90 g shredded green cabbage

2 limes, cut into wedges, for serving

Chopped fresh cilantro, for serving

1 To make the onions: Bring the vinegar, ½ cup/120 ml water, the sugar, salt, and peppercorns to a boil over high heat in a small saucepan. Put the onion rings in a small heatproof bowl. Pour in the vinegar mixture. Let cool completely. (The onion rings can be covered and refrigerated for up to 5 days.) Drain before serving.

2 To make the adobo: Heat a large skillet over medium-high heat. In batches, add the chiles and toast, pressing the chiles against the skillet with a spatula, until they turn brick red, about 30 seconds. Transfer the chiles to a medium bowl. Add enough cold water to cover the chiles. Let stand until softened, 15 to 30 minutes. Strain the chiles, reserving the soaking liquid.

3 Transfer the chiles, garlic, vinegar, cumin, oregano, salt, pepper, and cloves to a blender. With the machine running, add enough of the soaking liquid to make a thick sauce. You should have about 1½ cups/360 ml.

4 To cook the lamb: Position a rack in the center of the oven and preheat the oven to 325°F/165°C. Heat the oil in a large Dutch oven over high heat. In batches, without crowding, add the lamb shanks and cook, turning occasionally, until browned, about 5 minutes. Transfer the shanks to a plate.

5 Return all of the lamb to the pot and add the adobo. Stir in enough water to barely cover the lamb. Bring to a simmer over medium heat. Cover tightly and bake until the lamb is very tender, occasionally turning the lamb, about 2 hours. Transfer the lamb to a carving board and let stand for 10 minutes. Using two forks, shred the warm lamb meat, discarding the bones.

6 Let the cooking liquid in the pot stand for 3 minutes. Skim off and discard any fat that rises to the surface. Bring to a boil over high heat and cook, stirring often, until the adobo is reduced to about 1½ cups/360 ml, about 10 minutes. (The lamb and sauce can be cooled, covered separately, and refrigerated for up to 1 day. Reheat the lamb and sauce separately.)

7 Transfer the lamb to a serving bowl and stir in about ⅓ cup/75 ml sauce to moisten the meat. Pour the remaining sauce into another serving bowl. Drain the red onions and place in a small serving bowl. Serve the lamb with the tortillas, red onions, cheese, cabbage, lime wedges, and cilantro, allowing the guests to make their own tacos with the ingredients.

MAKES 4 TO 6 SERVINGS

Many Tommy Bahama regulars believe that our fish fillet sandwich is every bit as satisfying as a beef burger. Use any white fish that suits your fancy; we prefer grouper. Commercial seafood seasoning gives the fish an exceptionally light coating. And be sure to make your own slightly spicy tartar sauce—it's delicious, and leftovers will keep well in the fridge.

CRISPY FISH FILLET SANDWICHES WITH ISLAND TARTAR SAUCE

TARTAR SAUCE

1 cup/240 ml mayonnaise

2 Tbsp sweet relish

1 Tbsp fresh lemon juice

1 Tbsp minced celery

1 Tbsp minced yellow onion

2 tsp coarsely chopped capers

2 tsp minced fresh flat-leaf parsley

Pinch of cayenne pepper

Pinch of granulated onion

HONEY ONIONS

1 Tbsp olive oil

1 lb/455 g yellow onions, cut into ¼-in/6-mm rounds

1 Tbsp honey

2 tsp molasses

Kosher salt and freshly ground black pepper

Pinch of red pepper flakes

FILLETS

¾ cup/90 g plus ½ cup/60 g fish-fry seasoning mix, such as Zatarain's

⅔ cup/165 ml lager beer

¾ tsp dried thyme

½ tsp freshly ground black pepper

½ tsp kosher salt

Vegetable oil, for frying

4 skinless fish fillets, such as grouper, catfish, or tilapia, each about 6 oz/170 g

4 hamburger buns, toasted

4 slices beefsteak tomato

4 Bibb lettuce leaves

1 To make the sauce: Mix all of the ingredients together in a medium bowl. Cover and refrigerate for at least 1 hour or up to 1 week to blend the flavors.

2 To make the onions: Heat the oil in a large skillet over medium heat. Add the onions and cook, stirring occasionally, until softened, about 5 minutes. Stir in the honey and molasses and season with ¼ tsp salt, ¼ tsp black pepper, and the red pepper flakes. Reduce the heat to medium-low and cook, uncovered, stirring occasionally, until the onions are very tender and glazed, 20 to 30 minutes. If the glaze threatens to burn, stir in 1 to 2 Tbsp of water. Remove from the heat. (The onions can be cooled, covered, and refrigerated for up to 3 days. Reheat gently in a skillet or microwave oven before serving.)

3 To cook the fish: Whisk ¾ cup/90 g of the fish-fry seasoning with the beer, thyme, pepper, and salt just until the batter is smooth. Spread the remaining ½ cup/60 g fish-fry seasoning on a plate. Place the batter and seasoning next to the stove.

4 Position a rack in the center of the oven and preheat the oven to 200°F/95°C. Pour 2 in/5 cm oil into a deep, heavy saucepan and heat over high heat to 350°F/180°C on a deep-frying thermometer. Line a large, rimmed baking sheet with brown paper or paper towels.

5 One at a time, coat a fish fillet with the seasoning mix. Dip in the batter, letting the excess drip back into the bowl, and carefully transfer to the oil, making sure that the batter does not stick to the sides of the saucepan. Repeat with another fish fillet. Deep-fry, turning halfway through cooking, until golden brown, 2½ to 3 minutes. Using a wire spider or slotted spoon, transfer to the baking sheet and keep warm in the oven while frying the remaining fillets.

6 To serve, place a bun on each of 4 dinner plates and spread each bun with 2 Tbsp of the tartar sauce. Top each bun with a tomato slice and a lettuce leaf. Add a fish fillet and top with one-fourth of the onions. Serve immediately, with the remaining tartar sauce passed on the side.

MAKES 4 SERVINGS

One of our most popular restaurant dishes, blackened fish tacos are a mouthwatering mash-up of Cajun and Mexican cuisines. A combination of easy-to-make sauces gives the tacos their special flavor. You can assemble the tacos and serve them on a platter, or simply present all of the components at the table and let your guests make their own.

BLACKENED FISH TACOS

PICO DE GALLO

2 (Roma) plum tomatoes, seeded and cut into ¼-in/6-mm dice

1 Tbsp minced white or yellow onion

1 tsp minced fresh cilantro

1 tsp fresh lime juice

1 tsp olive oil (not extra-virgin)

Kosher salt and freshly ground black pepper

LIME SOUR CREAM

½ cup/120 ml sour cream

1 Tbsp fresh lime juice

Chipotle Aïoli (page 210)

FISH

4 cod or basa fillets, about 6 oz/170 g each

4 tsp Cajun Seasoning (page 213) or commercial Cajun seasoning

4 Tbsp/60 ml Clarified Butter (see below) or canola oil

12 corn tortillas, heated

2 cups/455 g Island Slaw (page 209), drained well

Lime wedges, for serving

SPECIAL EQUIPMENT: 2 food-service plastic squeeze bottles

1 **To make the pico de gallo:** Mix all of the ingredients in a small bowl, seasoning to taste with salt and pepper.

2 **To make the lime sour cream:** Whisk the sour cream and lime juice together in a small bowl until combined.

3 Purée the aïoli in a mini-food processor, being sure the purée is very smooth and can pass through the opening of a squeeze bottle.

4 Transfer the lime sour cream and aïoli to separate food-service plastic squeeze bottles. (Or put them in small self-sealing plastic bags and snip off one corner of each bag to make an opening ¼ in/6 mm wide.)

5 **To cook the fish:** Position a rack in the center of the oven and preheat the oven to 200°F/95°C. Season the cod all over with the Cajun seasoning. Heat a large skillet, preferably cast iron, over high heat until it is very hot. Add 2 Tbsp of the clarified butter. Add half of the cod and cook, turning once, until well browned on both sides, about 4 minutes. Transfer to a baking sheet and keep warm in the oven. Repeat with the remaining butter and cod.

6 Working with 4 warm tortillas at a time, place them on a work surface and top with equal amounts of the cod, slaw, and pico de gallo. Squirt zigzags of the lime sour cream and aïoli over the tacos. Fold the tortillas and place the tacos on a dinner plate. Add the lime wedges and serve immediately.

MAKES 4 SERVINGS

Clarified Butter

Regular butter burns easily when used for sautéing or frying because its dairy solids scorch when exposed to high temperatures. Clarified butter has had the dairy solids removed, making it a perfect flavorful medium for these high-heat cooking methods.

To clarify butter, melt at least 1 cup/225 g (2 sticks) unsalted butter in a small saucepan over medium heat and heat until the butter comes to a full boil. Pour the melted butter into a 1-cup/240-ml glass measuring cup or small heatproof bowl and let it stand for 5 minutes. Using a soup spoon, skim off and discard the scum from the surface. Carefully pour the clear yellow clarified butter into a covered container, leaving the white solids behind in the glass. The clarified butter can be cooled, covered, and refrigerated for up to 4 weeks.

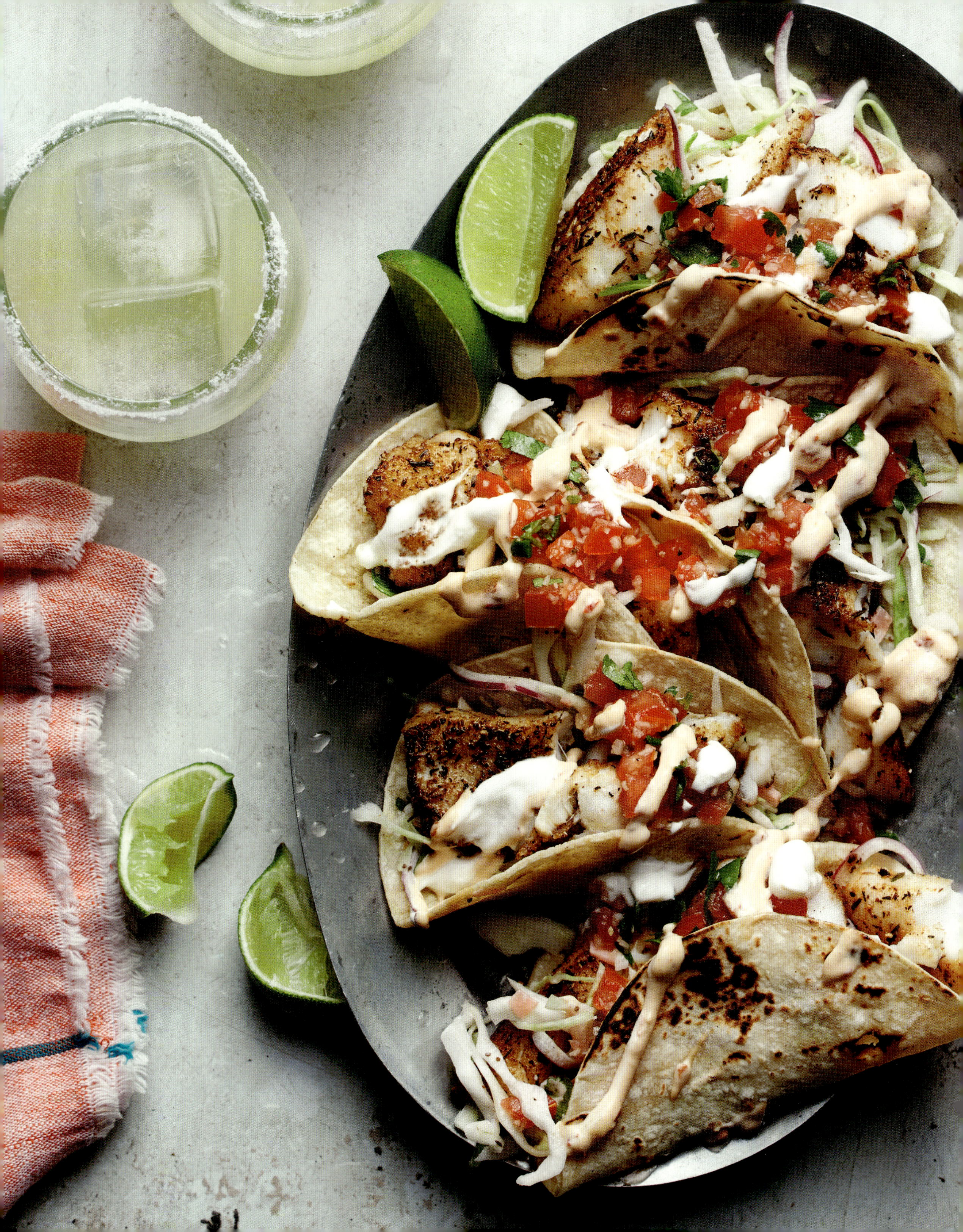

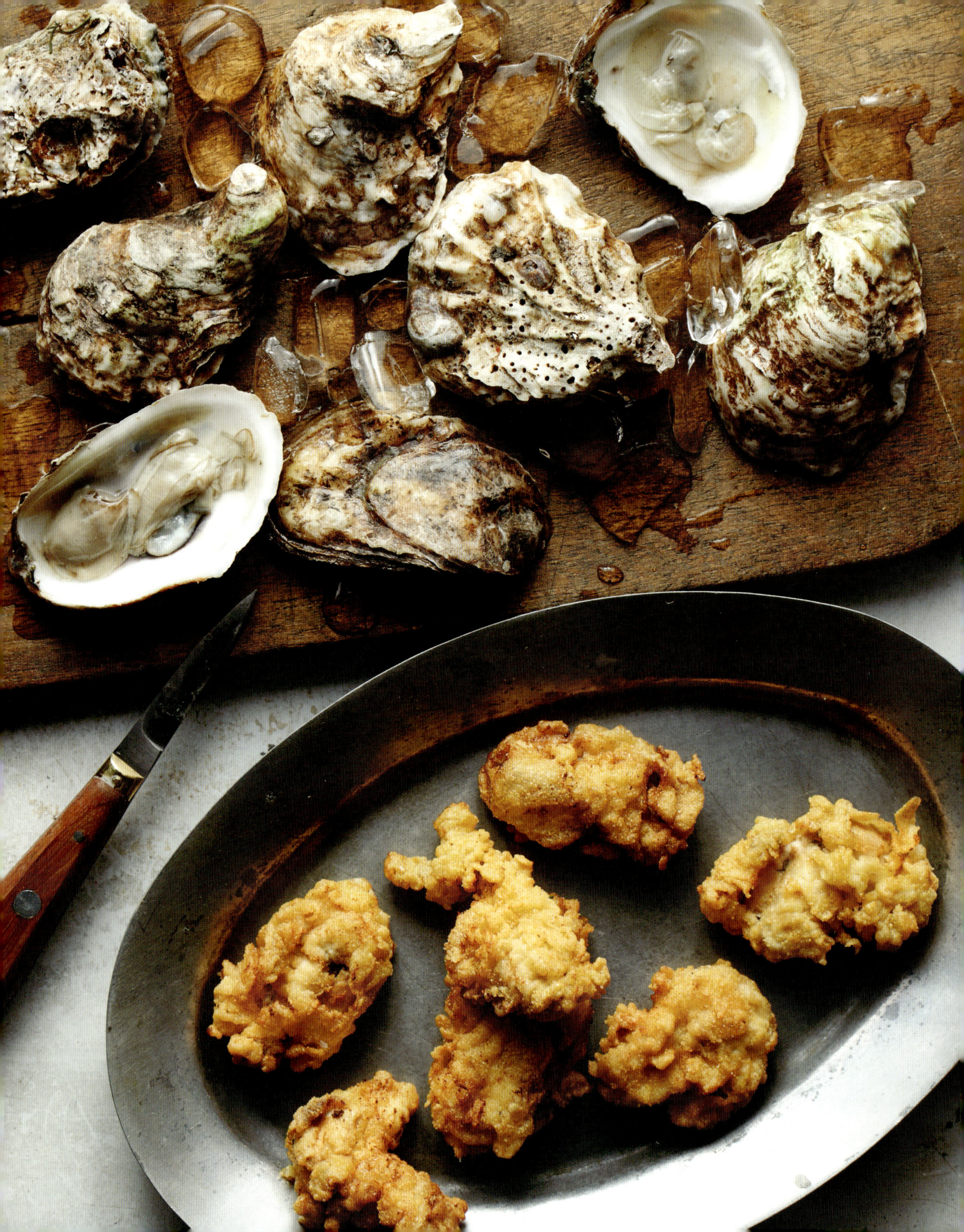

Here's another outstanding po' boy, with cornmeal-dusted and deep-fried oysters tucked into the bread rolls. This sandwich is usually dressed with mayonnaise but is even better with "comeback sauce," which hails from restaurants in Jackson, Mississippi, and is similar to Russian dressing. Reportedly, this sauce is so good that it will make the diner come back to the restaurant for more.

OYSTER PO' BOYS WITH MISSISSIPPI COMEBACK SAUCE

COMEBACK SAUCE

¾ cup/180 ml mayonnaise

¼ cup/60 ml ketchup-style chili sauce, such as Heinz

¼ cup/60 ml canola or vegetable oil

2 Tbsp fresh lemon juice

½ yellow onion, shredded on the large holes of a box grater

1 garlic clove, crushed through a garlic press

1 tsp spicy brown mustard

1 tsp Worcestershire sauce

½ tsp red pepper sauce, such as Tabasco

½ tsp celery salt

¼ tsp freshly ground black pepper

OYSTERS

1 large egg

1 cup/240 ml whole milk

½ tsp sweet paprika

½ tsp Italian seasoning or dried oregano

½ tsp granulated garlic

½ tsp freshly ground black pepper

¼ tsp granulated onion

¼ tsp kosher salt

⅛ tsp cayenne pepper

16 shucked oysters, from about three 8-oz/225-g containers, drained

½ cup/70 g yellow cornmeal, preferably stone-ground

½ cup/70 g unbleached all-purpose flour

Vegetable oil, for deep-frying

4 thin-crusted oblong rolls

2 cups/160 g shredded iceberg lettuce

2 large ripe tomatoes, cut into 12 rounds

16 dill pickle rounds (optional)

1 To make the comeback sauce: Whisk all of the ingredients together. Cover and refrigerate for at least 1 hour or up to 1 week.

2 To make the oysters: Whisk the egg in a medium bowl. Add the milk, paprika, Italian seasoning, granulated garlic, black pepper, granulated onion, salt, and cayenne and mix well to combine. Add the oysters, cover, and refrigerate for 15 minutes.

3 Whisk the cornmeal and flour together in a large bowl. A few at a time, lift the oysters from the milk mixture and toss in the flour mixture to coat. Transfer to a baking sheet or platter and let stand for 15 minutes.

4 Preheat the oven to 200°F/95°C. Pour 2 in/5 cm oil into a large, heavy saucepan and heat over high heat to 350°F/180°C. Place a wire rack on a rimmed baking sheet. In batches, add the oysters to the hot oil and deep-fry until golden brown, about 2½ minutes. Using a slotted spoon, transfer the oysters to the wire rack and keep warm in the oven while deep-frying the remaining oysters.

5 Split the rolls lengthwise almost all of the way through to "hinge" them. Spread both sides of each roll with about 3 Tbsp of the sauce. Fill the rolls with equal amounts of the oysters, lettuce, tomatoes, and dill pickles, if using. Serve immediately, with the remaining sauce passed on the side.

MAKES 4 SERVINGS

Tomatoes thrive in the hot summers of the Gulf Coast, but in the fall, there always seems to be a surplus of hard, unripened green tomatoes that refuse to turn color on the vine. That's when it's time to pull out the skillet and make this delicious hybrid of a BLT and grilled cheese. Be sure to use sandwich bread with a firm crust and not a cottony variety—a crusty sourdough, without too many holes, would work well.

FRIED GREEN TOMATO AND PIMENTO CHEESE BLTS

GREEN TOMATOES

½ cup/70 g all-purpose flour

½ tsp kosher salt

¼ tsp freshly ground black pepper

2 large eggs

¼ tsp red pepper sauce, such as Tabasco

½ cup/75 g yellow cornmeal, preferably stone-ground

2 large green tomatoes, cut crosswise into ¼-in/6-mm rounds

½ cup/120 ml vegetable oil

8 slices firm white sandwich bread, such as Pepperidge Farm

12 Tbsp/180 ml Zesty Pimento Cheese (page 37)

8 slices bacon, cooked until crisp (see below) and cut in half crosswise

4 large red-leaf lettuce leaves

1 To prepare the green tomatoes: In a wide, shallow bowl, mix the flour, salt, and pepper together. In a second bowl, beat the eggs and hot sauce together until well combined. In a third bowl, spread the cornmeal. One at a time, dip the green tomato slices in the flour mixture to coat, followed by the egg mixture and finally the cornmeal, being sure to coat them completely. Transfer the green tomato slices to a platter.

2 Heat the oil in a large skillet over medium-high heat until shimmering but not smoking. Place a wire rack on a rimmed baking sheet and set the pan near the stove. In batches, add the green tomato slices to the oil and cook, turning once, until golden brown, about 3 minutes. Transfer to the rack.

3 Meanwhile, position the broiler rack about 6 in/15 cm from the heat source and preheat the broiler.

4 Place the bread on the broiler rack and broil, turning once, until lightly toasted, about 1½ minutes. Spread about 3 Tbsp of the pimento cheese on 4 of the toasted bread slices. Return to the broiler and cook just until beginning to melt (take care not to burn the exposed bread), about 30 seconds. The cheese will melt further from the warmth of the other sandwich ingredients. Remove from the broiler.

5 Divide the green tomato slices, bacon slices, and lettuce leaves among the cheese-topped slices and finish with the remaining bread. Cut each sandwich in half crosswise and serve immediately.

MAKES 4 SANDWICHES

Cooking Bacon

The traditional way to cook bacon is in a skillet on top of the stove. But there are other ways that work better, especially when you need more than a few slices. For smaller amounts of bacon (say, up to six slices), you can microwave it according to the package directions. This usually involves layering the bacon in paper towels, but if you have a dedicated microwave bacon cooker, use it. Some brands state a maximum suggested number of slices, so cook the bacon in batches, if necessary.

For larger amounts of bacon (up to a pound), baking is a great method because you don't have to stand over a skillet while the slices cook. Place the slices side by side (they will shrink, so go ahead and crowd them) on a large rimmed baking sheet. Bake in a preheated 350°F/180°C oven, without turning the slices, until browned, about 20 minutes. Immediately transfer the bacon to paper towels to drain. If you wish, for extra flavor, substitute ¼ cup/60 ml of the rendered bacon fat for the vegetable oil when frying the green tomatoes, above.

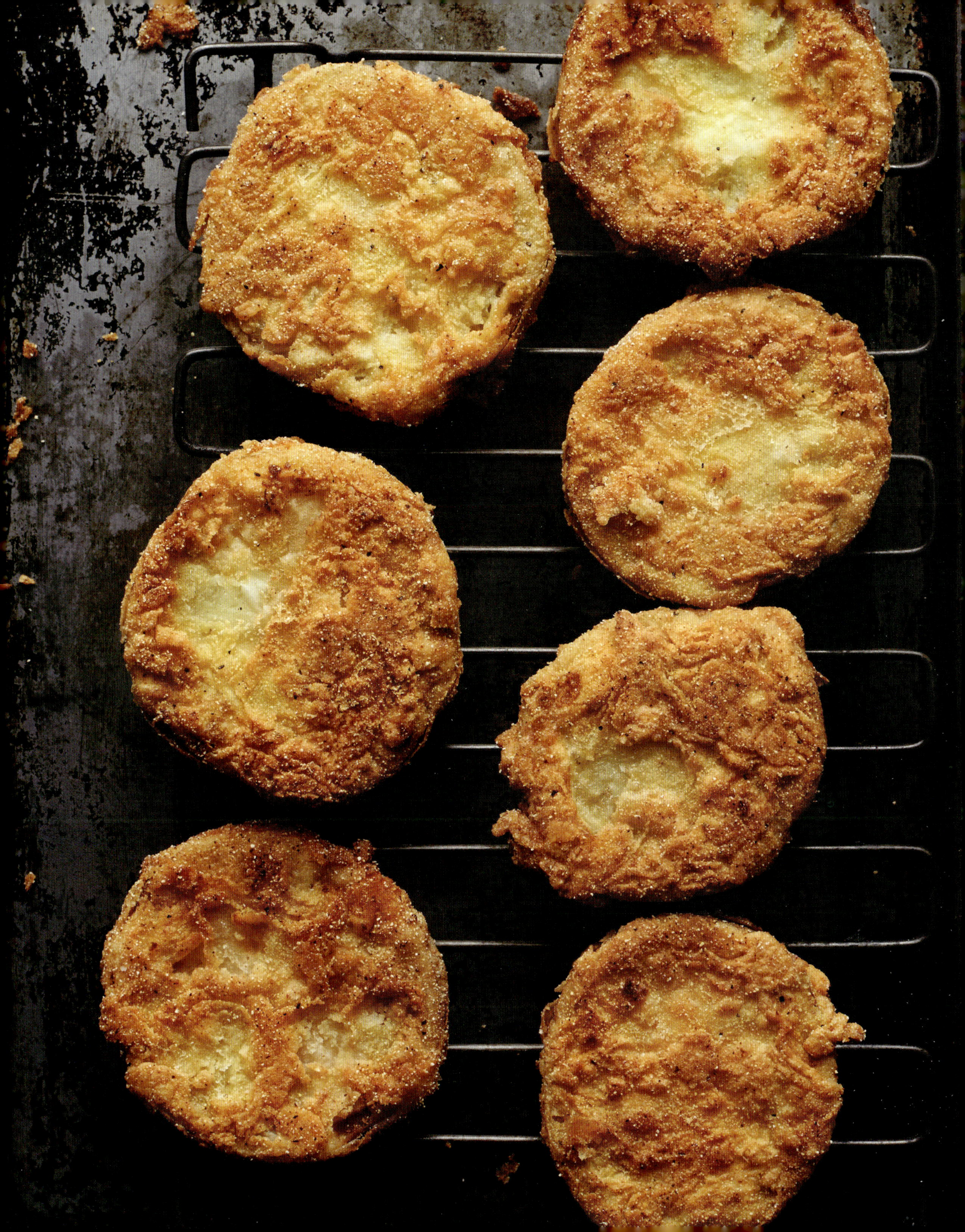

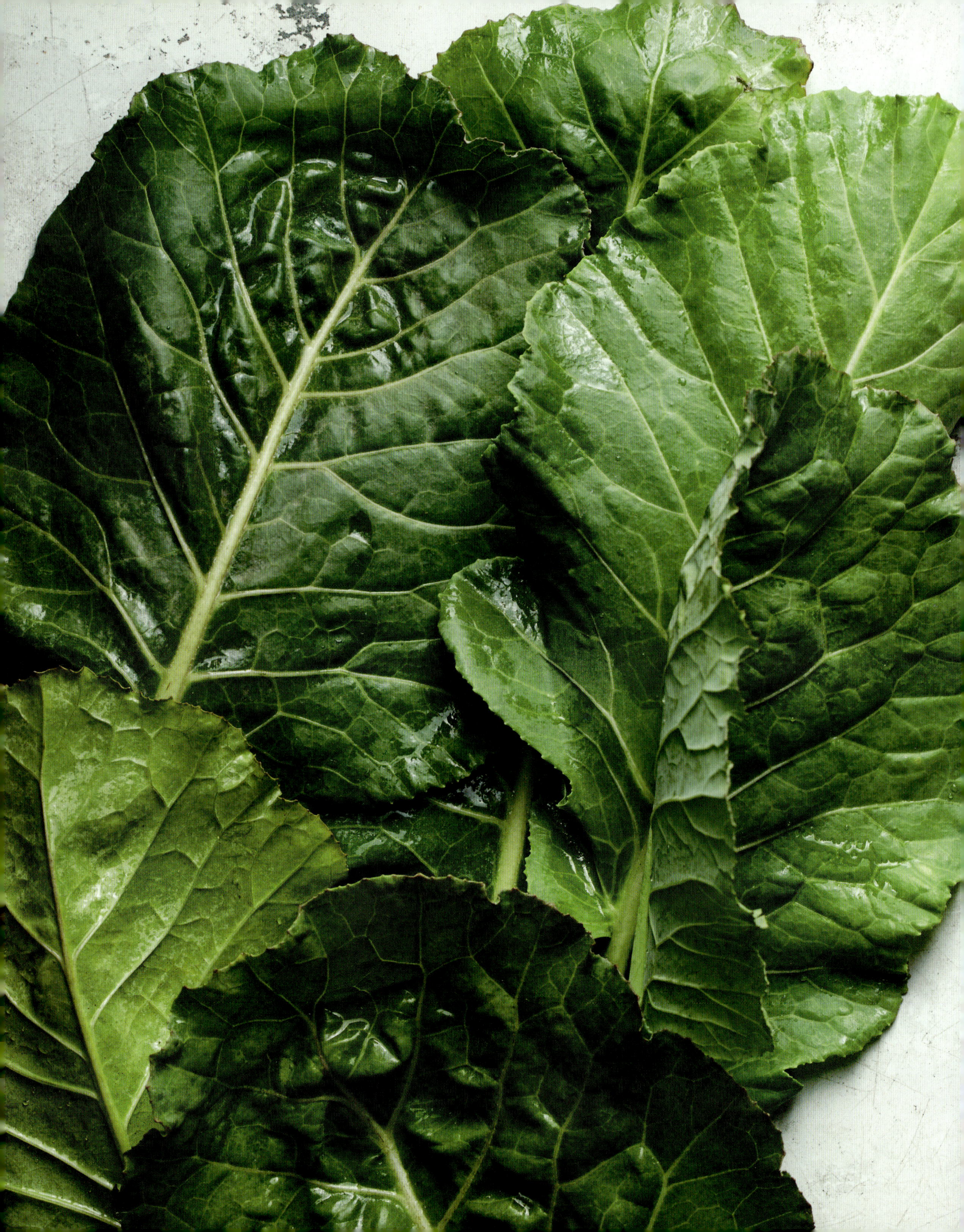

A pot of collard greens simmering with a chunk of smoked pork symbolizes down-home Southern cooking, specifically the rich heritage of soul food. Some historians believe that collard greens arrived in this country with the first African slaves in the early seventeenth century, but that is unlikely as collards had been known in Europe since the Greek era.

Along with other foods that traveled from Africa—black-eyed peas, rice, okra, watermelons, sesame, and *names*, from which we get the word yams—nutritious collard greens helped to sustain generations of Southerners. Like kale, broccoli, cauliflower, and other cousins in the Brassica family of cruciferous vegetables, collards are a well-known "superfood," high in Vitamins K, C, and A, and manganese.

Collards—the word is a corruption of *colewort*, the Old English name for wild cabbage—became a staple food of the displaced Africans, who prepared it according to their preferred method of long cooking in liquid. This technique renders "pot likker," a nutritious broth loaded with vitamins and minerals—which is especially wonderful when used as a dunk for corn bread. To this day, collard greens are an important tradition on New Year's Day, as their green leaves, which resemble dollar bills, represent good fortune. (Black-eyed peas, symbolizing coins, are always served alongside the collards.) Holiday or not, collard greens are now enjoyed at tables all along the Southern Coast.

COLLARD GREENS

The South is dotted with cafeterias, sometimes called "meat and threes" for their standard menu of a main meat course with three vegetable side dishes. You can be assured that one of the sides will be long-cooked greens simmered with pork. To enjoy the pot likker (the savory cooking liquid in a pot of greens) in the classic manner, serve it on the side with a chunk of Moist Corn Bread with Fresh Corn (page 178) for dunking.

COLLARD GREENS WITH BACON AND GARLIC

2 lb/910 g collard greens

1 Tbsp vegetable oil

4 slices bacon, cut into 1-in/ 2.5-cm lengths

1 yellow onion, chopped

4 garlic cloves, finely chopped

1¾ cups/420 ml canned reduced-sodium chicken broth

1 Tbsp sugar

Kosher salt

½ tsp red pepper flakes

Cider vinegar and red pepper sauce, such as Tabasco, for serving

1 Wash the greens well in a sink of cold water, letting any grit fall to the bottom of the sink, changing the water if needed. Lift the greens from the water, shaking off excess water, and place on your drain board. Do not dry the leaves. Tear the thick stems from the leaves and reserve the stems. In batches, stack the leaves and cut them into strips about ½ in/12 mm wide. Transfer them to a large bowl. Chop the stems crosswise into ½-in/12-mm pieces and add to the bowl.

2 Heat the oil in a soup pot over medium heat. Add the bacon and cook, stirring occasionally, until crisp and brown, about 8 minutes. Using a slotted spoon, transfer the bacon to paper towels to drain.

3 Add the onion to the fat in the pot and cook, stirring occasionally, until translucent, about 4 minutes. Add the garlic and cook until fragrant, about 1 minute. Stir in the broth and bring to a simmer.

4 In batches, stir the greens and stems into the pot, covering to let the first batch wilt before adding more. Stir in the sugar, 1 tsp salt, and the red pepper flakes. Reduce the heat to medium-low and cook, stirring occasionally, until the greens and stems are very tender, about 1 hour. Season to taste with salt. (The greens can be cooled, covered, and refrigerated for up to 1 day. Reheat in the pot over medium heat.)

5 Using a slotted spoon, transfer the greens to a serving bowl, adding enough of the cooking liquid to moisten the greens. Sprinkle the bacon on top. Serve hot, with the vinegar and hot sauce alongside, and the cooking liquid (pot likker) passed on the side also, if desired.

MAKES 6 TO 8 SERVINGS

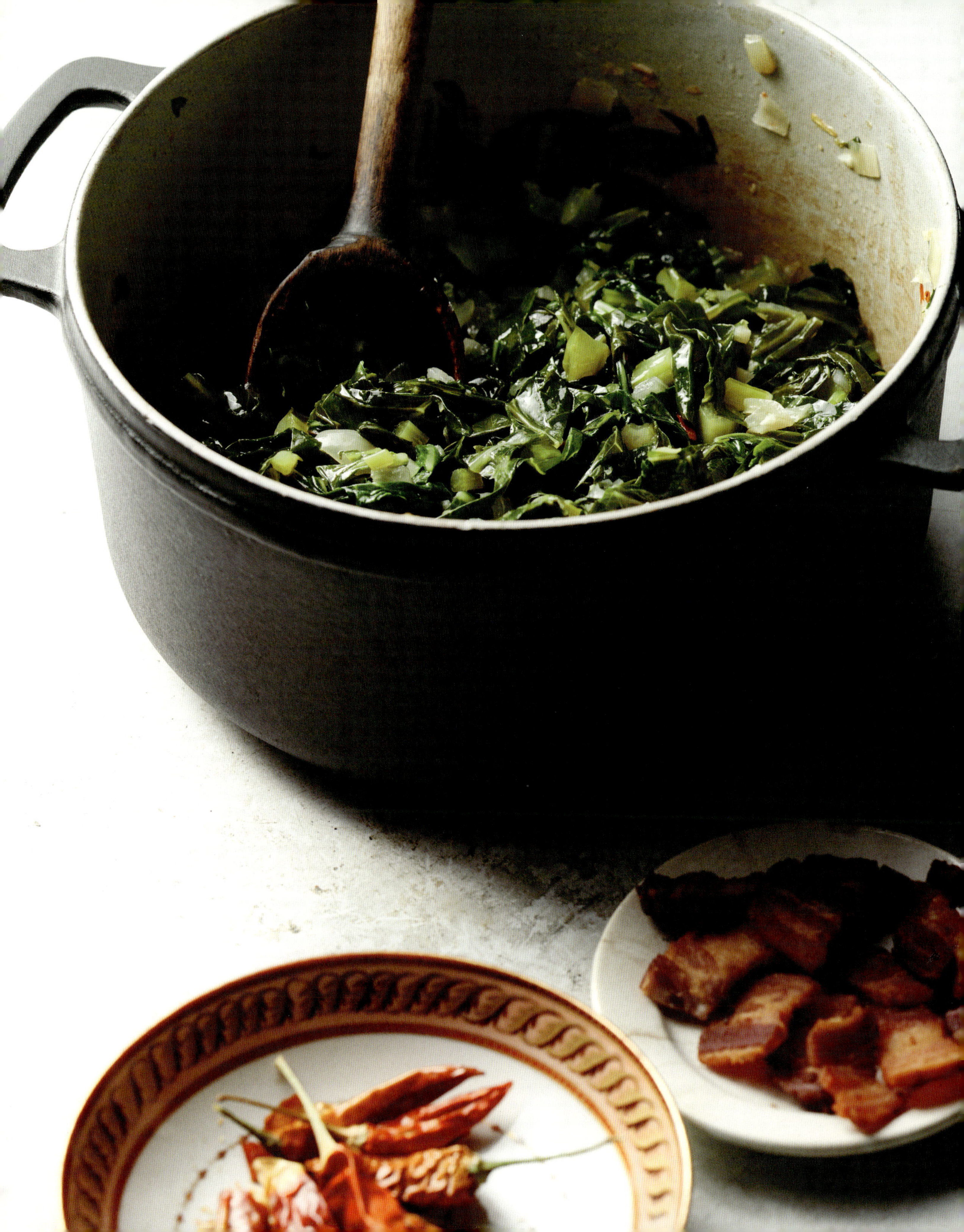

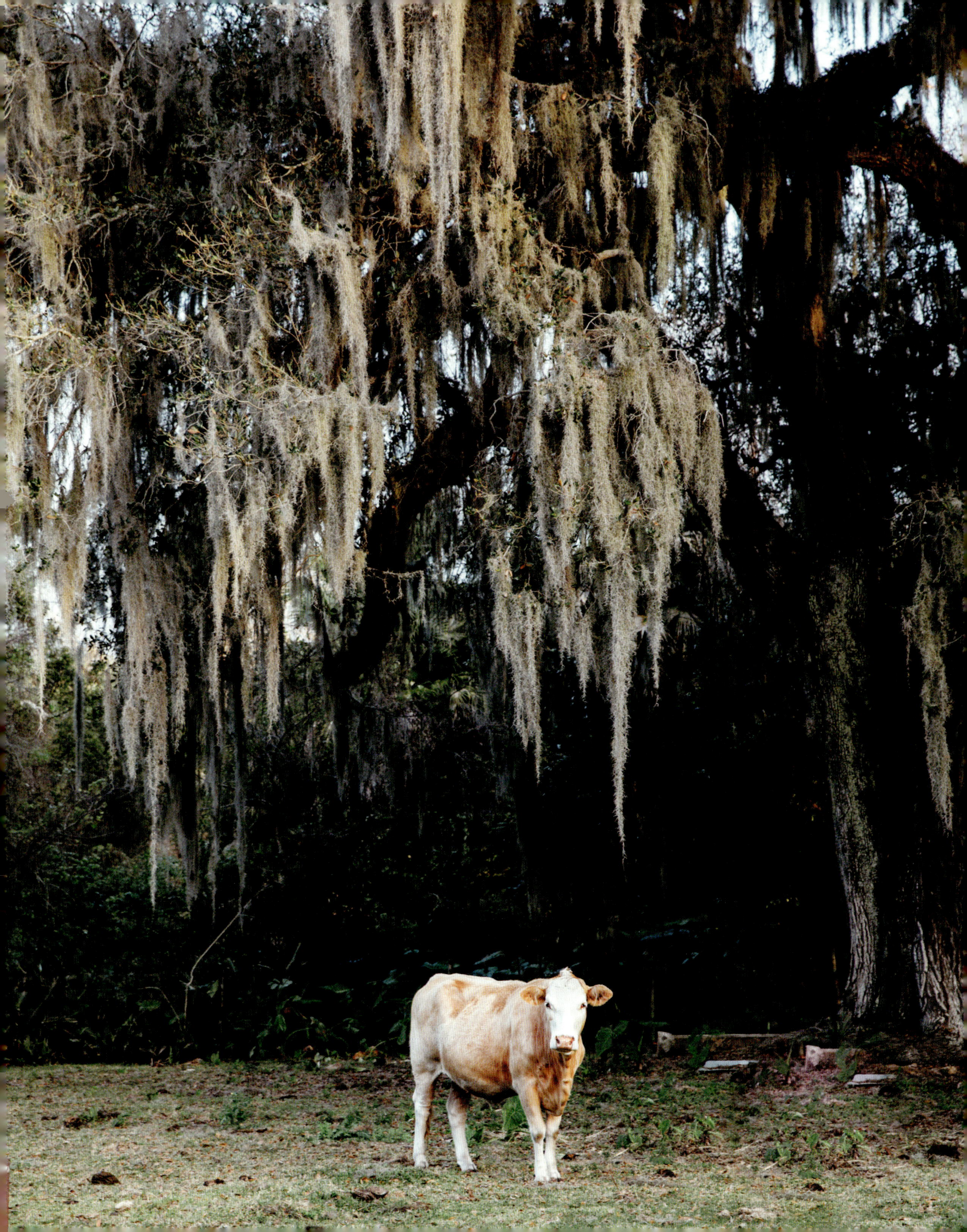

Squash casserole is another Southern "covered dish" that gets huge play at backyard cookouts and community gatherings. It is often made with yellow summer squash, but this variation adds zucchini, red bell peppers, and corn. Allow some time to pre-cook the vegetables—two skillets will come in handy. Don't be tempted to skip this step, or you will end up with very soggy gratin.

SOUTHERN VEGETABLE GRATIN

5 Tbsp/75 ml vegetable oil

1 large yellow onion, chopped

1 red bell pepper, cored, seeded, and cut into ½-in/12-mm dice

2 garlic cloves, minced

1 tsp dried oregano or basil (optional)

1¾ lb/800 g zucchini, cut into ½-in/12-mm rounds

1¾ lb/800 g yellow summer squash, cut into ½-in/12-mm rounds

2 cups/340 g fresh or thawed frozen corn kernels (if fresh, from 3 ears of corn)

2 large eggs

1 cup/240 ml sour cream

½ tsp kosher salt

½ teaspoon red pepper sauce, such as Tabasco

2 cups/120 g bread crumbs, made in a food processor from day-old bread

2 cups/220 g shredded sharp Cheddar cheese

2 Tbsp unsalted butter, melted

1 Position a rack in the center of the oven and preheat the oven to 350°F/180°C. Butter a 9-by-13-inch/23-by-33-cm baking dish.

2 Heat 1 Tbsp of the oil in a large skillet over medium-high heat. Add the onion, bell pepper, and garlic and cook, stirring occasionally, until tender, about 10 minutes. Stir in the oregano, if using. Transfer to a large colander set over a bowl.

3 Heat 2 Tbsp of the oil in the skillet over medium-high heat. Add the zucchini and cook, stirring occasionally, until browned and tender, about 10 minutes. Transfer to the colander. Wash the skillet. Repeat with the remaining 2 Tbsp oil and the yellow squash, cooking for about 10 minutes. Transfer to the colander. Using a rubber spatula, press gently on the squash mixture to remove excess moisture, but keep the squash intact as possible. Stir the corn into the squash.

4 Whisk the eggs in a large bowl. Add the sour cream, salt, and pepper sauce and whisk until combined. Add the squash and onion mixtures with 1 cup/60 g of the bread crumbs and 1 cup/110 g of the Cheddar cheese. Mix well and spread in the prepared dish. Sprinkle with the remaining bread crumbs and cheese and drizzle with the melted butter.

5 Bake until the casserole feels set when pressed gently in the center, about 30 minutes. Let stand for 5 minutes, then serve hot.

MAKES 8 SERVINGS

Succotash is traditionally a mixture of lima beans and corn. This version is succotash for the twenty-first century, mixed with quinoa to make it a bit more substantial so you won't have to cook a separate starch.

QUINOA SUCCOTASH

QUINOA

½ cup/90 g white or red quinoa

1 cup/240 ml reduced-sodium chicken broth

¼ tsp kosher salt

1 Tbsp Jalapeño-Lime Butter (page 211)

3 carrots, preferably tricolor (rainbow) carrots, peeled and cut into 1-by-½-in/2.5-cm-by-12 mm sticks

1 cup/185 g fresh corn kernels (from 1 to 2 ears of corn)

12 green beans or haricot verts, trimmed and cut on the diagonal into 1-in/2.5-cm lengths

3 shiitake mushrooms, stemmed and thinly sliced

1 green onion, white and green parts, thinly sliced on the diagonal

1 Tbsp minced red onion

½ cup/120 ml reduced-sodium chicken broth

Kosher salt and freshly ground black pepper

1 To cook the quinoa: Rinse the quinoa well in a fine-mesh sieve under cold running water. (This is an important step, as it rinses off the bitter, naturally occurring saponins from the grains.) Drain well.

2 Combine the drained quinoa, broth, and salt in a medium saucepan. Bring to a boil over high heat. Reduce the heat to low and cover tightly. Simmer until the quinoa is tender and has absorbed the liquid, about 20 minutes. Remove from the heat and let stand for 5 minutes. Fluff the quinoa with a fork. (The quinoa can be cooled, covered, and refrigerated for up to 1 day.)

3 Meanwhile, melt the jalapeño butter in a large skillet over medium heat. Add the carrots and cook, stirring often, for 1 minute. Stir in the corn, green beans, shiitakes, green onion, and red onion and cook, stirring often, until the vegetables are coated with butter and the carrots are beginning to soften, about 3 minutes. Add the broth, bring to a boil, cook until the liquid is reduced to 1 Tbsp, about 1 minute.

4 Stir in the hot quinoa. (If using cold quinoa, cook, stirring often, until it is heated through, about 2 minutes.) Season to taste with salt and pepper. Serve hot.

MAKES 4 TO 6 SERVINGS

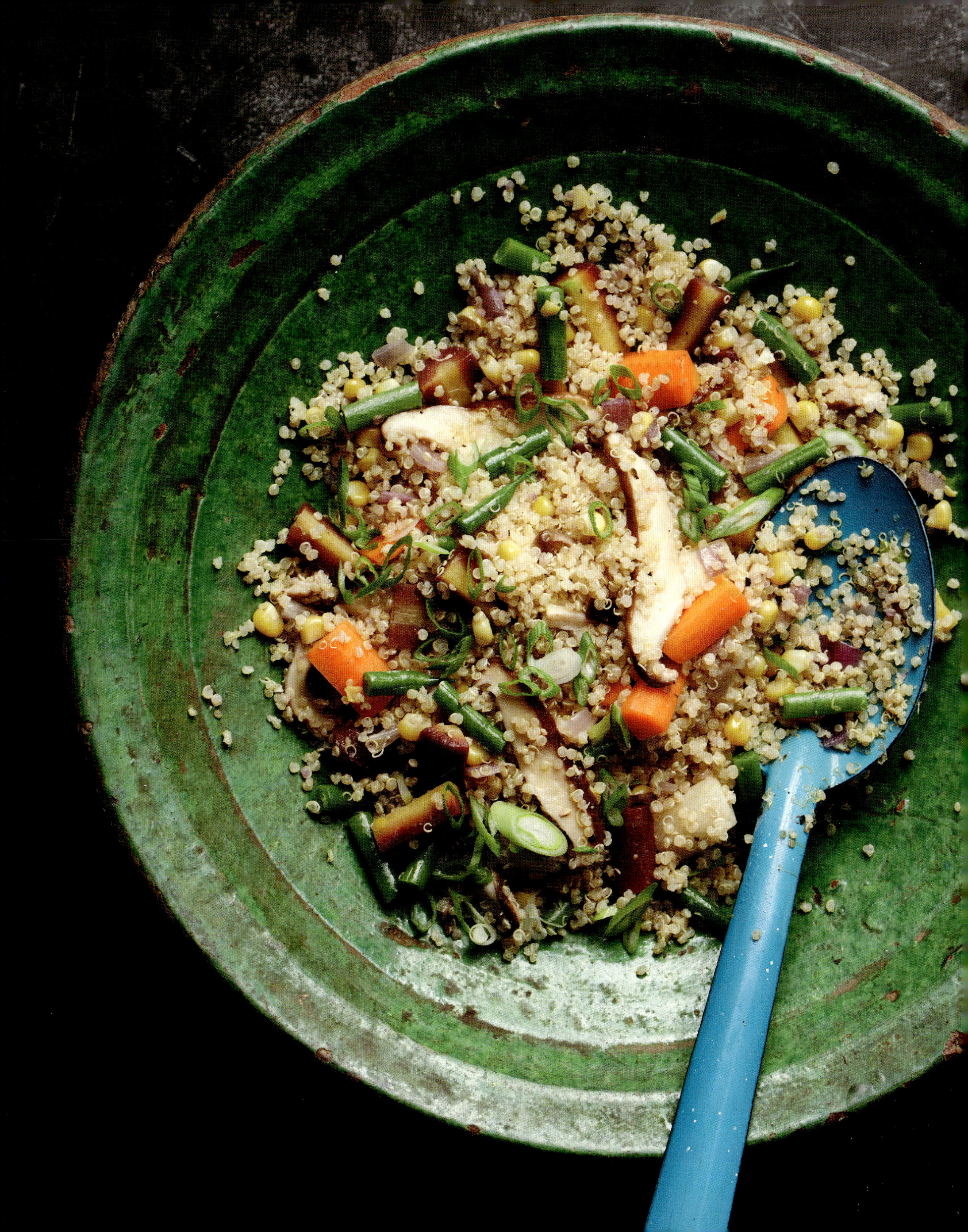

Plain rice has its place (see Basic Rice, page 209), but there are also times when you want to gild the lily. With two kinds of fragrant rice, a splash of coconut milk, and crunchy almonds, this version certainly does the trick. If you like more coconut flavor, add ⅓ cup/45 g shredded dried coconut, toasted in a skillet over medium heat until lightly browned.

COCONUT-ALMOND RICE

½ cup/100 g basmati rice

½ cup/100 g jasmine rice

1 Tbsp olive or canola oil

½ cup/70 g finely chopped yellow onion

1 garlic clove, minced

1¾ cups/420 ml reduced-sodium chicken broth

¼ cup/60 ml coconut milk (not cream of coconut)

½ tsp kosher salt

⅛ tsp freshly ground black pepper

½ cup/55 g sliced almonds, toasted (see page 44)

2 Tbsp unsalted butter, thinly sliced

1 Put the basmati and jasmine rice in a medium bowl and add enough cold water to cover by 1 in/2.5 cm. Let stand for 15 minutes. Drain well.

2 Heat the oil in a medium saucepan over medium heat. Add the onion and garlic and cook, stirring often, until the onion softens, about 3 minutes. Add the drained rice and stir well to coat with the oil. Add the broth, coconut milk, salt, and pepper and bring to a boil over high heat. Reduce the heat to very low and cover. Simmer until the rice is tender and has absorbed the liquid, about 20 minutes. Remove from the heat and let stand, covered, for 5 minutes.

3 Add the toasted almonds and butter and mix until the butter has melted. Serve hot.

MAKES 4 SERVINGS

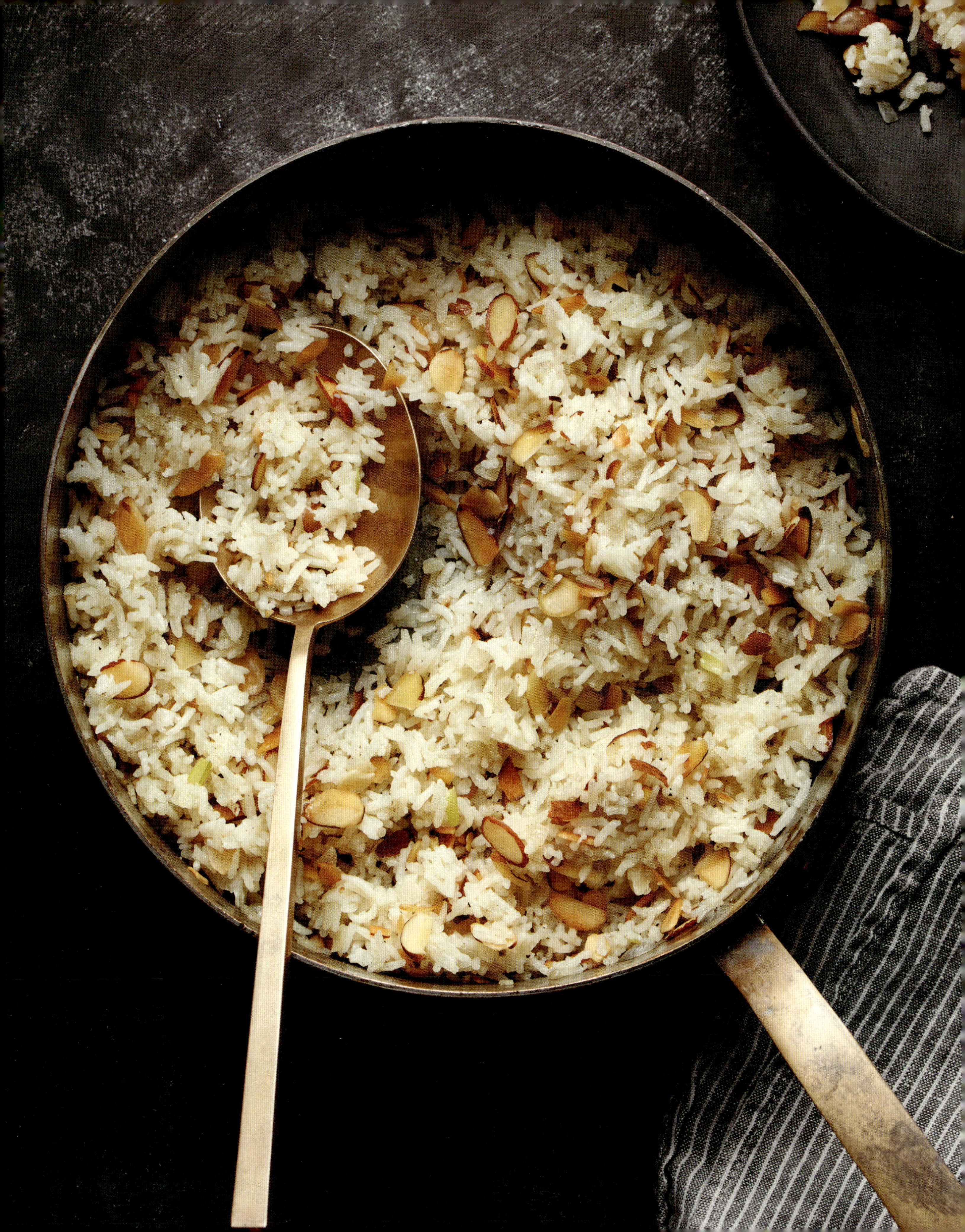

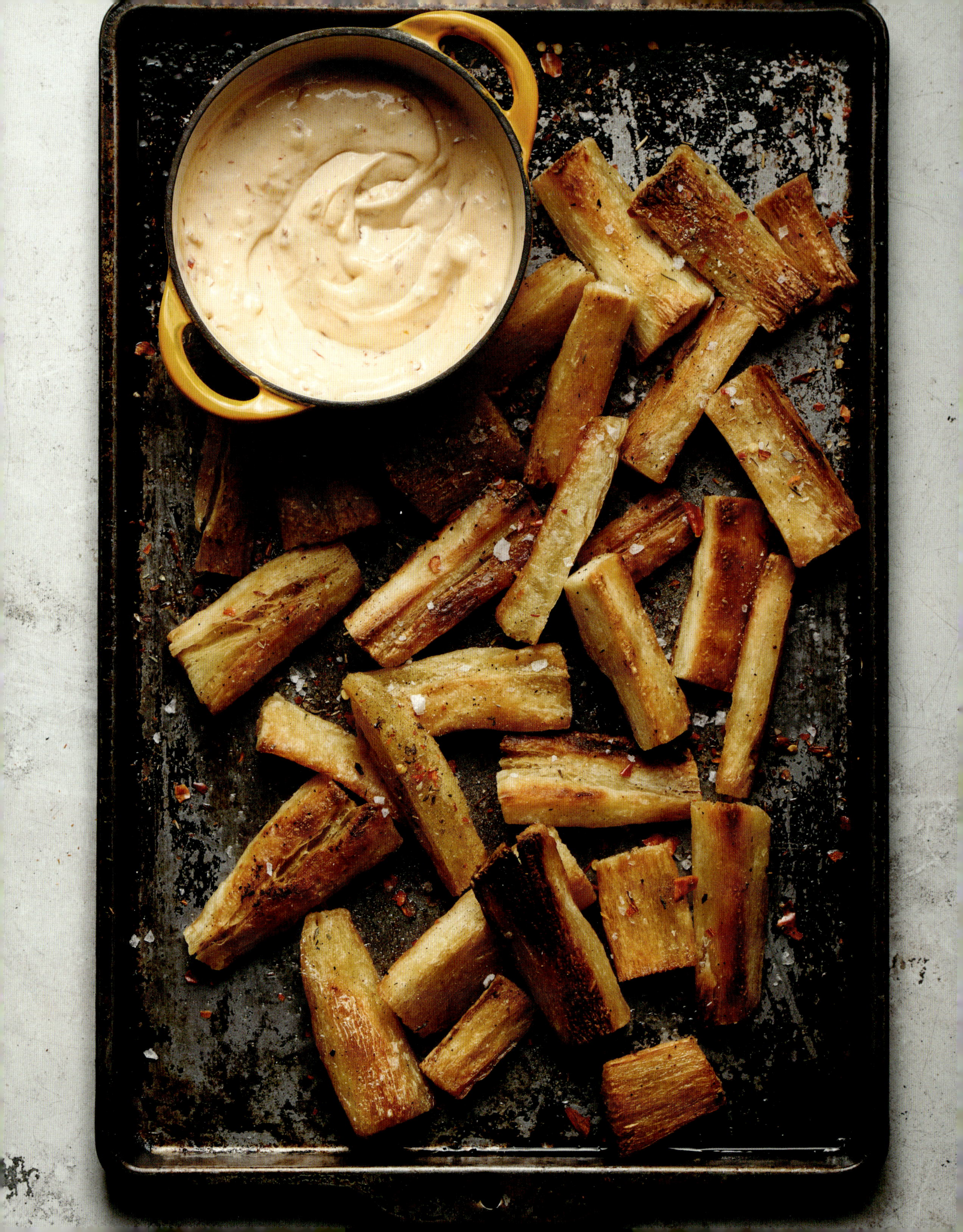

Sure, potato fries are great, but other starchy vegetables are also fry worthy. Yuca is a ubiquitous Caribbean tuber with a tough skin that makes it a challenge to peel. Frozen peeled yuca, sold at Latino markets and many supermarkets, is a better alternative. The yuca is oven-cooked to make golden wedges with a crunchy exterior, perfect for dipping in chipotle aïoli.

CRISPY YUCA OVEN FRIES

One 24-oz/680-g bag thawed frozen yuca (cassava)

2 Tbsp olive oil

1 tsp Dry Jerk Seasoning (page 213) or commercial jerk seasoning

1 green onion, white and green parts, cut on the diagonal into very thin slices

Chipotle Aïoli (page 210)

1 Cut each yuca chunk lengthwise into wedges about 2½ in/6 cm long and 1 in/2.5 cm wide. Trim off any visible cord running lengthwise in the yuca. (It is usually removed in frozen yuca, but some remnants might remain.)

2 Transfer the wedges to a medium saucepan and add enough lightly salted water to cover. Bring to a boil over high heat. Reduce the heat to medium and simmer just until the yuca is barely tender when pierced with the tip of a small, sharp knife, about 5 minutes. Drain and rinse under cold running water. Pat dry on paper towels. The fries can be stored at room temperature for up to 2 hours.

3 Position a rack in the top third of the oven and preheat the oven to 400°F/200°C.

4 Toss the yuca on a large rimmed baking sheet with the oil and spread in a single layer. Roast, flipping the fries halfway through cooking, until golden brown and tender, 30 to 40 minutes.

5 Sprinkle the fries on the baking sheet with the jerk seasoning and toss well to coat. Transfer to a serving bowl and sprinkle with the green onions. Serve hot, with the aïoli on the side.

MAKES 4 TO 6 SERVINGS

Bringing up the subject of perfect corn bread is one way to start an argument between Yankee and Southern cooks, as most folks south of the Mason-Dixon line like their corn bread without sugar in the batter. This version has just a hint of honey to balance the corn bread, but not so much that it turns into cake. Puréed fresh corn gives this corn bread its incredible flavor. A bit of the Jalapeño-Lime Butter on page 211 is a fine accompaniment.

MOIST CORN BREAD WITH FRESH CORN

2 large ears fresh corn, husked

½ cup/120 g full-fat sour cream

¼ cup/60 ml whole milk

2 Tbsp honey (optional)

1 large egg

1 cup/140 g yellow cornmeal, preferably stone-ground

¾ cup/105 g unbleached all-purpose flour

1 tsp baking powder

½ tsp baking soda

½ tsp kosher salt

4 Tbsp/55 g unsalted butter, cut up

1 Position a rack in the center of the oven and preheat the oven to 400°F/200°C.

2 Using a large knife, stand each corn ear on its stem end and cut down to remove the kernels from the cob. Starting at the bottom of the ear, scrape the knife blade up along the cob to extract the "corn milk." You should have about 1½ cups/255 g corn kernels and milk. Measure 1 cup/185 g and transfer it to a blender. Set the remaining corn aside to add to the batter later.

3 Add the sour cream, milk, honey, if using, and the egg to the blender and purée with the corn. Measure the corn liquid: you should have a scant 2 cups/480 ml (add more milk if necessary). Whisk the cornmeal, flour, baking powder, baking soda, and salt together in a medium bowl.

4 Put the butter in an 8-in/20-cm square baking dish. Bake until the pan is hot and the butter is melted, 3 to 5 minutes. Stir the butter into the corn mixture, leaving a thin layer of residual butter in the pan. Pour the corn mixture into the dry ingredients and stir just until combined. It's okay if the batter looks a bit lumpy. Fold in about two-thirds of the reserved corn kernels. Spread the batter evenly in the hot pan and sprinkle the remaining corn kernels on top.

5 Bake until the corn bread is golden brown and a wooden toothpick inserted in the center comes out clean, about 25 minutes. Let cool in the pan on a wire rack for 15 minutes. Cut into squares and serve warm.

MAKES 9 SERVINGS

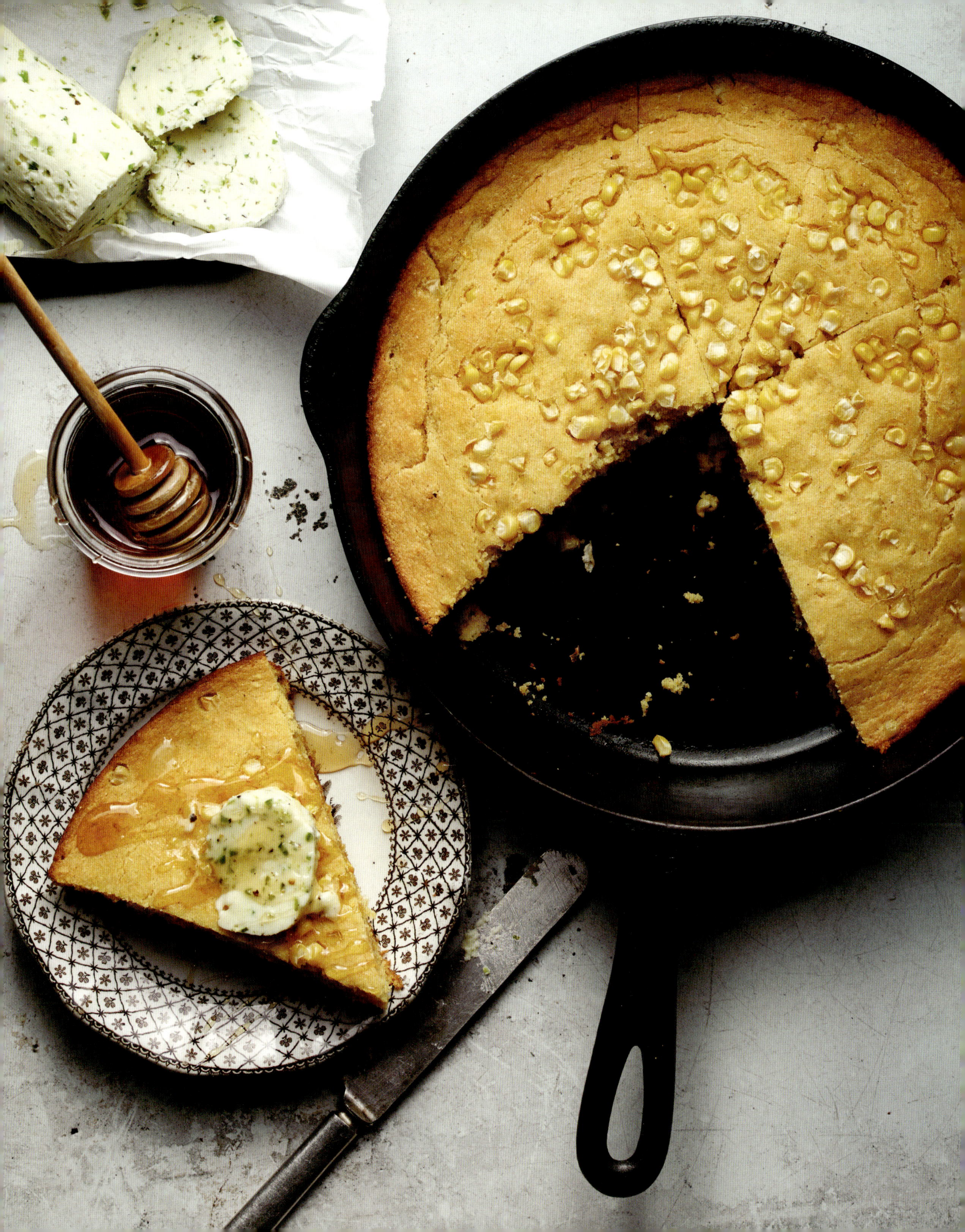

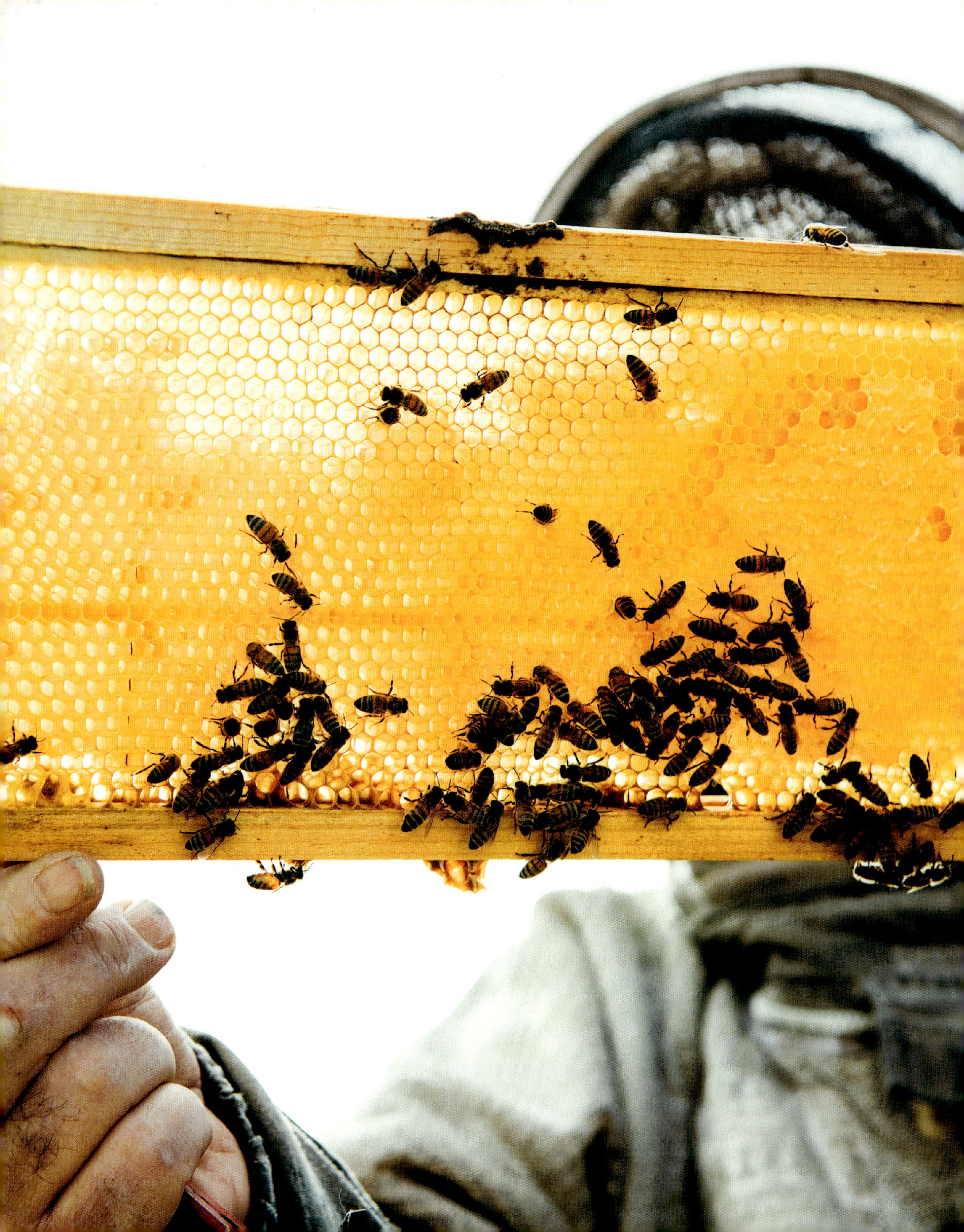

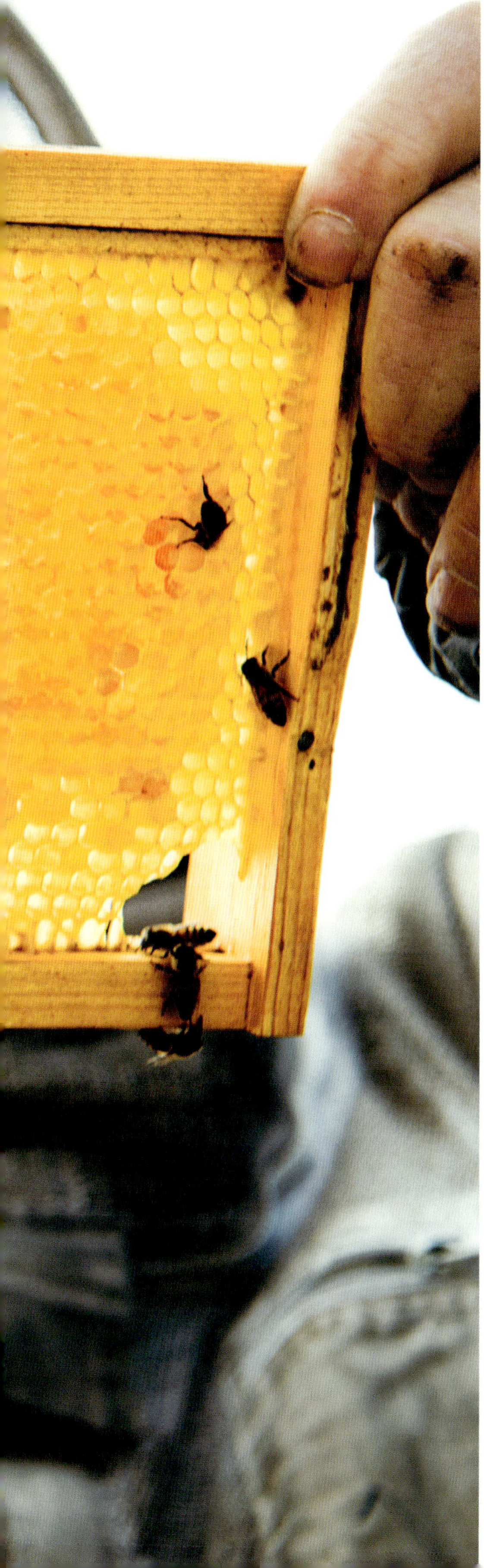
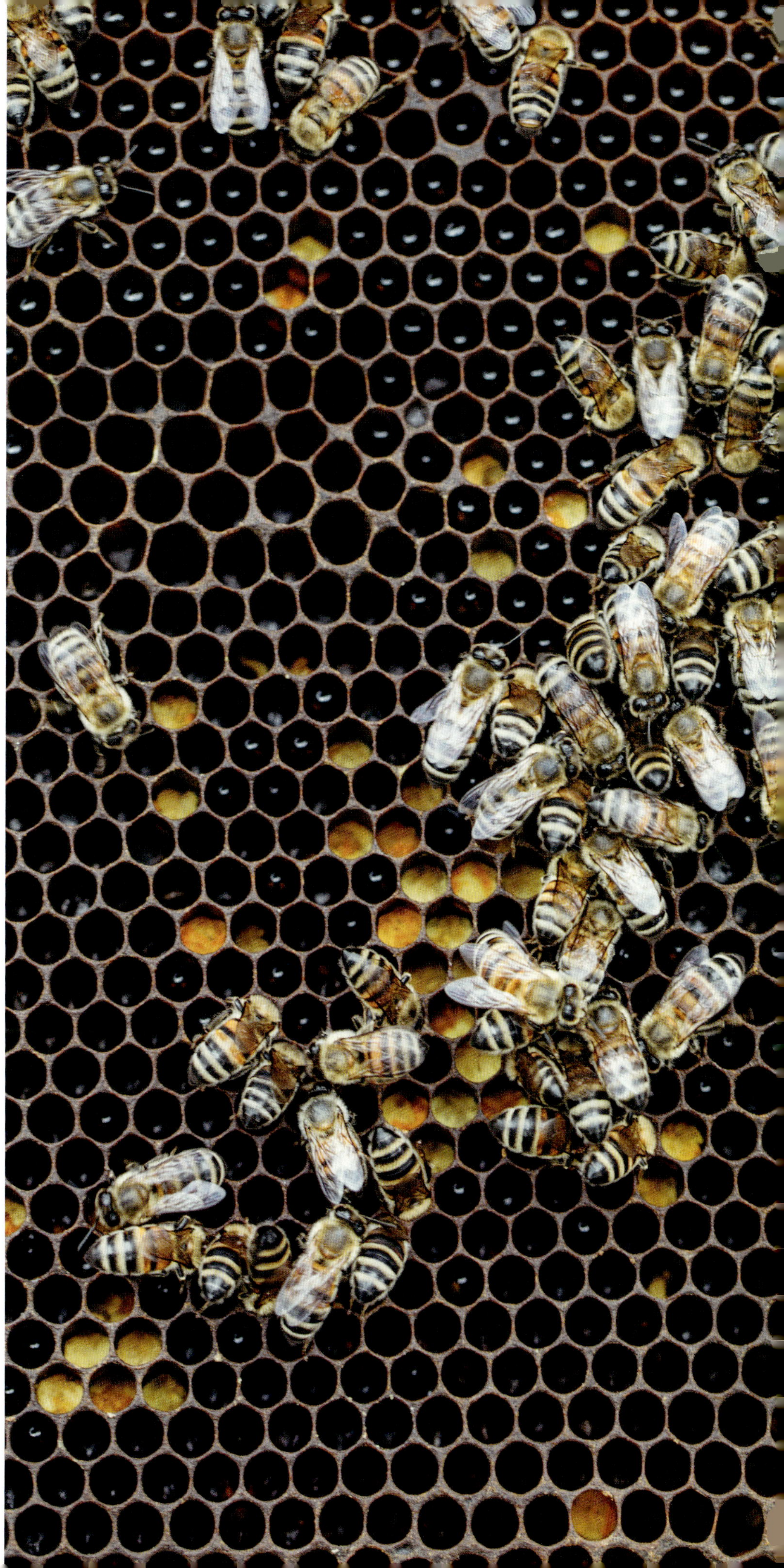

As popular as corn bread is with Southern cooks, hush puppies (which are made of corn bread batter fried by the spoonful) have their fans, too. Serve these nuggets crisp and piping hot with your choice of dip. While the sauces listed are good, so is a bowl of honey spiked with some red pepper sauce. Be sure to let the oil reheat to deep-frying temperature between batches.

JALAPEÑO AND BEER HUSH PUPPIES

1 cup/140 g unbleached all-purpose flour

1 cup/140 g yellow cornmeal, preferably stone-ground

1 Tbsp sugar

2 tsp baking powder

1 tsp kosher salt

½ cup/120 ml dark or lager beer

2 large eggs, beaten to blend

2 Tbsp shredded yellow onion (use the large holes on a box grater)

2 Tbsp seeded and minced jalapeño chile

Vegetable oil, for deep-frying

Comeback Sauce (page 157) or Chipotle Aïoli (page 210), for dipping

1 Whisk the flour, cornmeal, sugar, baking powder, and salt together in a medium bowl. Make a well in the center of the dry ingredients and add the beer and eggs. Stir just until combined. Fold in the onion and jalapeño. Set aside while heating the oil.

2 Preheat the oven to 200°F/95°C. Pour 2 in/5 cm oil into a large, heavy saucepan and heat over high heat to 350°F/180°C. Line a large rimmed baking sheet with paper towels.

3 In batches and without crowding, using a 1-Tbsp/15-ml portion scoop dipped into the oil, drop balls of the batter into the hot oil. (Or use two long-handled spoons, dipped in oil, to shape Tbsp-sized mounds of batter.) Deep-fry, turning any hush puppies that do not turn over by themselves, until crisp and golden brown, about 2½ minutes. Using a wire spider or slotted spoon, transfer the hush puppies to the paper towels and keep warm in the oven while deep-frying the remaining hush puppies. Serve immediately, with the sauce for dipping.

MAKES ABOUT 2 DOZEN

Whether breakfast, lunch, or dinner, any meal that has a basket of fresh-baked biscuits on the table automatically goes up a notch in quality. Gulf Coast cooks swear that soft-wheat flour (not easy to get outside of the region) makes the best biscuits, so this recipe uses a combination of nationally available flours for low gluten and extra tenderness. Cutting rectangular biscuits eliminates scraps that can toughen when rerolled.

FLAKY BUTTERMILK BISCUITS

2 cups/280 g unbleached all-purpose flour, plus more for rolling dough

1 cup/130 g cake flour

1 Tbsp sugar

2 tsp baking powder

1 tsp baking soda

¾ tsp fine sea salt

6 Tbsp/85 g cold unsalted butter, cut into ½-in/12-mm cubes

6 Tbsp/85 g chilled vegetable shortening, cut into ½-in/12-mm pieces

1¼ cups/300 ml buttermilk, as needed

1 Position a rack in the center of the oven and preheat the oven to 425°F/220°C.

2 Sift the unbleached and cake flours, sugar, baking powder, baking soda, and salt together into a medium bowl. Add the butter and shortening and stir to coat them with the flour mixture. Using a pastry blender or two dinner knives, cut in the fats until the mixture resembles coarse crumbs with some pea-sized pieces of fat. Stir in enough of the buttermilk to make a soft dough and mix just until it clumps together.

3 Scrape the dough out onto a well-floured work surface. Using floured hands, pat the dough into a rectangle about 14 in by 8 in/ 35.5 by 20 cm wide and about ¼ in/6 mm thick. Slide a long metal icing spatula or knife under the dough to loosen it, if necessary. Fold the dough in thirds, like a letter, folding the left side over first, and brushing off any excess flour. Turn the dough so the long open flap faces you. Flour the surface again and repeat the patting into a rectangle. Now, fold the right and left sides in to meet in the center of the rectangle. Brush off any excess flour and fold the dough in half vertically to make a packet with four layers—it will look like a thick book.

4 Flour the surface again and turn the dough so the long open flap faces you. Pat the dough into a rectangle about 12 by 6 in/ 30.5 by 15 cm and 1 in/2.5 cm thick. Using a large sharp knife, quickly and firmly cut the dough in half horizontally and then vertically into 6 strips to make 12 rectangular biscuits.

5 Transfer the biscuits, spacing them well apart, to an ungreased rimmed baking sheet. Bake until the biscuits have risen and are golden brown, about 20 minutes. Serve warm.

MAKES 1 DOZEN

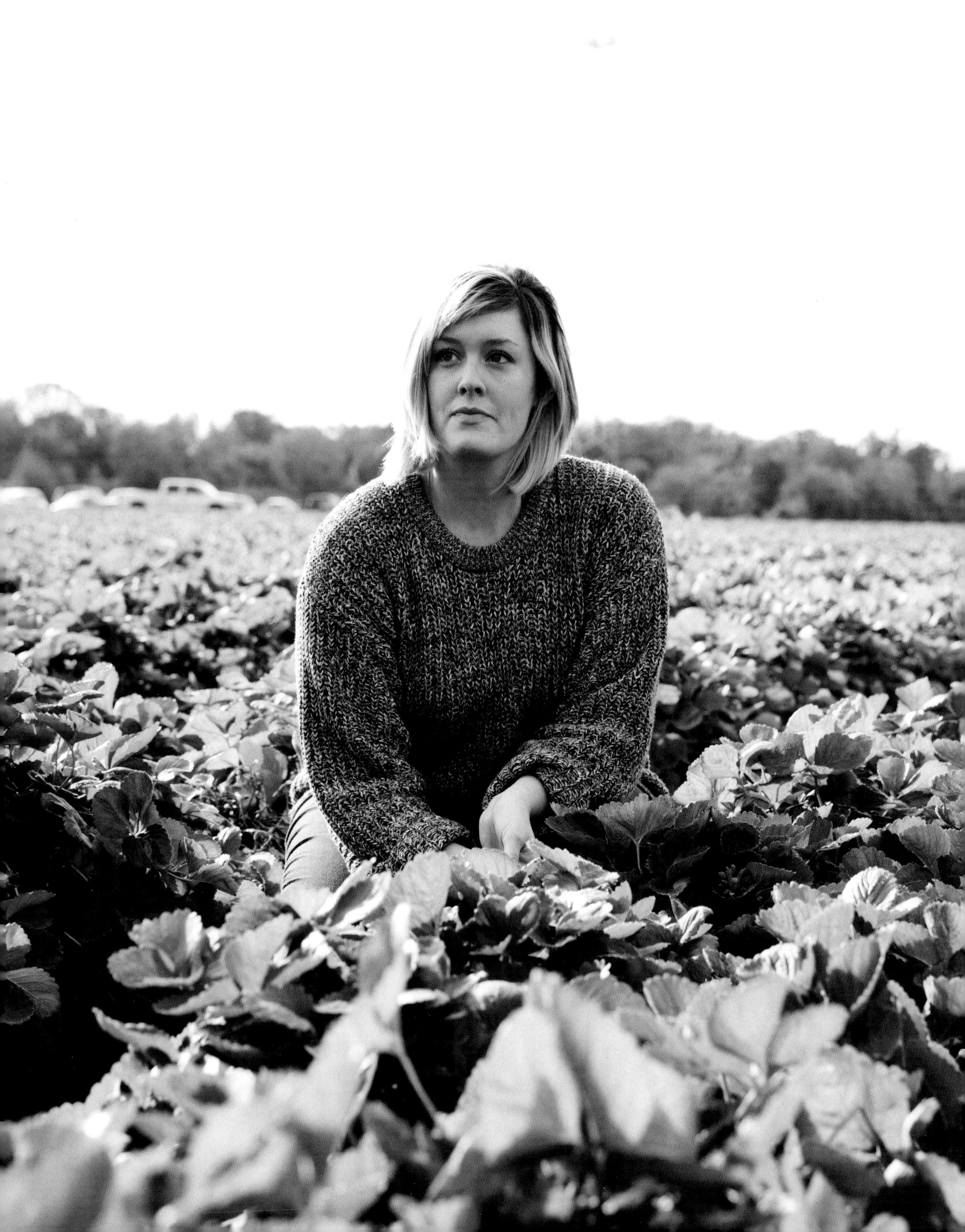

GEORGEA SNYDER, FARMERS' MARKET ADVOCATE

Georgea Snyder is a woman with a mission. As the market manager of Tampa's Downtown Market, which was established in 2008, she wants to educate consumers about the food on their plates. Florida is a well-known agricultural paradise for oranges, grapefruit, watermelons, tomatoes, green beans, cucumbers, and squash, but most of this produce travels to the rest of the nation. Georgea is advancing the farm-to-table movement in Tampa, now that both home cooks and professional chefs are demanding locally grown produce.

A native Floridian, Georgea returned to her home roots after earning a degree at the Culinary Institute of America and working in New York City's fabled Greenmarket program. She oversees the approximately twenty farm and craft booths at the Thursday market that operates in the heart of Tampa's commercial district. When she first started working there, she learned that some of the farmers were not actually growing their produce but were instead buying it from a third party. Now, she says, the vendors are mostly small businesses that "are committed to the method of producing the food."

Even though a farmers' market may not be brick-and-mortar, it has some of the same expenses as traditional grocery stores. "We rent our land from the parks district, and we have salaries to pay and education programs to run," Georgea explains. As a trained chef, she plans to give cooking classes to teach her customers how to use the bounty in their backyards (such as fruit from the many papaya trees in her neighborhood) and, of course, what they purchase at the markets: "Between the local farms and the seafood in the gulf, Tampans have a real opportunity to experience farm-to-table eating—and ocean-to-table, too."

DESSERTS

The famous sweets of the Southern Coast often showcase the region's fruits, especially strawberries, citrus, and tropical fare like mangoes. Local peanuts and pecans find their way into many baked goods, too, adding flavor and a bit of crunch. From tall layer cakes to creamy flan, this chapter will tempt you with the best of Southern desserts.

187
PEANUT BUTTER CAKES WITH SALTED PEANUT FROSTING

188
CHOCOLATE-RUM CAKE

190
MANGO ICEBOX CHEESECAKE WITH GINGERSNAP CRUST

192
TRES LECHES STRAWBERRY SHORTCAKE

193
HUMMINGBIRD QUICK BREAD

195
KEY LIME PIE WITH WHITE CHOCOLATE TOPPING

196
SWEET POTATO PIE WITH BOURBON WHIPPED CREAM

200
PEACH-BLACKBERRY BUCKLE

202
FLORIDA STRAWBERRY SHORTCAKES WITH LIME WHIPPED CREAM

203
PECAN-CHOCOLATE BARS

204
ORANGE-CINNAMON FLAN

Peanuts are not really nuts, but legumes (they were originally called ground peas). They thrive in the sandy soil of the South and have been an important crop there since the Civil War. Peanut butter used to be a local product, but became a national phenomenon in the 1920s. Both the batter and the frosting of this moist, old-fashioned cake is made with peanut butter. Be prepared for everyone to ask for seconds.

PEANUT BUTTER CAKE WITH SALTED PEANUT FROSTING

CAKE

1 cup/280 g creamy peanut butter (not natural style)

½ cup/115 g unsalted butter, at room temperature

1 cup/200 g granulated sugar

½ cup/100 g packed light brown sugar

3 large eggs, at room temperature

1 tsp vanilla extract

2 cups/280 g unbleached all-purpose flour

1 tsp baking soda

¼ tsp fine sea salt

1½ cups/360 ml buttermilk, at room temperature

FROSTING

¾ cup/220 g creamy peanut butter (not natural style)

6 Tbsp/85 g unsalted butter, at room temperature

3 cups/300 g confectioners' sugar

1 tsp vanilla extract

½ cup/120 ml whole milk, as needed

¾ cup/85 g coarsely chopped salted peanuts (see Note)

1 To make the cake: Position the oven rack in the center of the oven and preheat the oven to 350°F/180°C. Butter two 9-by-1½-inch/23-by-4-cm round cake pans. Line the bottoms of the pans with waxed paper. Coat the pans with flour and tap out the excess flour.

2 Beat the peanut butter and butter together in a large bowl with an electric mixer on medium-high speed until creamy, about 1 minute. Gradually beat in the granulated sugar and brown sugar and continue beating, stopping occasionally to scrape down the sides of the bowl with a rubber spatula, until the mixture is light in color and texture, about 3 minutes. One at a time, beat in the eggs, followed by the vanilla.

3 Sift the flour, baking soda, and salt together in a large bowl. With the mixer on low speed, add the flour mixture in thirds, alternating with two equal additions of the buttermilk, and mix, scraping down the bowl as needed, just until the batter is smooth. Divide the batter evenly among the cake pans and smooth the tops.

4 Bake until a wooden toothpick inserted into the center of the cakes comes out clean, 35 to 40 minutes. Let the cakes cool in the pans on wire racks for 10 minutes. Run a knife around the insides of the pans and invert and unmold the cakes onto the racks. Remove the paper, turn over, and let cool completely.

5 To make the frosting: Beat the peanut butter and butter in a medium bowl with an electric mixer on medium speed until combined. Add the confectioners' sugar and beat on low speed until crumbly. Beat in the vanilla. Gradually beat in milk just until the frosting is smooth. Increase the speed to high and beat until fluffy, about 30 seconds.

6 Add a 1-Tbsp dab of frosting in the center of a serving platter. Place a cake layer, bottom side up, on the platter. Slide strips of waxed paper under the cake to protect the platter from the frosting. Spread about ¾ cup/180 ml of the frosting over the cake. Top with the second layer, top side up. Using an offset metal spatula occasionally dipped in hot water, spread the top and then the sides of the cake with the frosting. Press the chopped peanuts onto the sides of the cake. (The cake can be refrigerated, loosely covered with plastic wrap, for up to 1 day. Remove from the refrigerator about 30 minutes before serving.) Remove the paper strips. Slice and serve the cake.

MAKES 8 TO 10 SERVINGS

NOTE: If you wish, substitute ¾ cup/125 g miniature semisweet chocolate chips for the chopped peanuts, or a combination of equal parts peanuts and chocolate chips.

If you've ever been on a Caribbean cruise, you might have brought home a rum cake from one of your ports of call. This moist dark chocolate cake is very easy to make—just mix, pour, and bake. While it has an easy glaze, this cake is so good that you really only need a dusting of confectioners' sugar, or perhaps a dollop of whipped cream. For even more depth of flavor, let the cake age overnight before serving.

CHOCOLATE-RUM CAKE

CAKE

2 Tbsp plain dried bread crumbs, for the pan (see Notes)

¾ cup/70 g Dutch-processed cocoa (see Notes)

2 cups/400 g granulated sugar

1¾ cups/245 g unbleached all-purpose flour

2 Tbsp cornstarch

2 tsp baking soda

1 tsp baking powder

1 tsp fine sea salt

1 cup/240 ml buttermilk

½ cup/120 ml canola or vegetable oil

½ cup/120 ml golden rum

½ cup/120 ml cool brewed coffee (medium or light roast)

2 large eggs, at room temperature

2 tsp vanilla extract

GLAZE

1 cup/100 g confectioners' sugar

3 Tbsp Dutch-processed or natural cocoa

2 Tbsp unsalted butter, melted

2 Tbsp hot water, as needed

¼ cup/45 g miniature chocolate chips

Whipped cream or vanilla ice cream, for serving

1 To make the cake: Position a rack in the center of the oven and preheat the oven to 350°F/180°C. Butter the inside of a 10-in/25-cm fluted tube pan, dust with crumbs, and tap out the excess crumbs.

2 Sift the ¾ cup/70 g cocoa, the sugar, flour, cornstarch, baking soda, baking powder, and salt together into a large bowl. Whisk the buttermilk, oil, rum, and coffee together in another bowl. Add the eggs and vanilla and whisk to combine. Add the buttermilk mixture to the dry ingredients. Mix with an electric mixer on medium-low speed, stopping to scrape down the sides of the bowl occasionally with a rubber spatula, until well combined, about 3 minutes. The batter will be thin. Scrape into the prepared pan.

3 Transfer the pan to the oven. (If using a heavy pan or one with a dark nonstick coating, immediately reduce the temperature to 325°F/165°C.) Bake until a long, thin wooden skewer inserted into the center of the cake comes out clean, 40 to 50 minutes. Let the cake cool in the pan on a wire rack for 15 minutes.

4 Run a dinner knife around the inside of the pan and the tube to release the cake. Using your fingertips, gently pull the cake away from the sides of the pan and the tube to release it a bit more. Invert and unmold the cake onto the cake rack and let cool completely.

5 To make the glaze: Whisk the confectioners' sugar, cocoa, and melted butter together in a medium bowl. Gradually whisk in enough hot water to make a smooth icing a little thicker than heavy cream.

6 Place the cake on a wire rack set in a rimmed baking sheet. Drizzle the glaze over the cake, letting the glaze run down the sides. Sprinkle the chips over the cake top. Let stand until the glaze sets, about 30 minutes. Wrap the cake tightly in plastic wrap. Store at room temperature until ready to serve, up to 3 days. Cut into wedges and serve with the whipped cream.

MAKES 12 SERVINGS

NOTES: This very moist cake needs a special pan treatment to allow easy unmolding, even with nonstick pans. If the pan is prepared with the usual butter and flour, the batter can soak right into the coating, making the cake difficult to unmold. A sprinkling of dried bread crumbs forms a barrier that allows the cake to be unmolded more easily. This trick works with all Bundt cakes.

Dutch-processed cocoa has been treated with alkali to reduce its acidity and give baked goods a darker color. Dröste is a brand found in many supermarkets and specialty foods stores. Natural cocoa, such as Hershey's, has not been treated and is not ideal for this recipe.

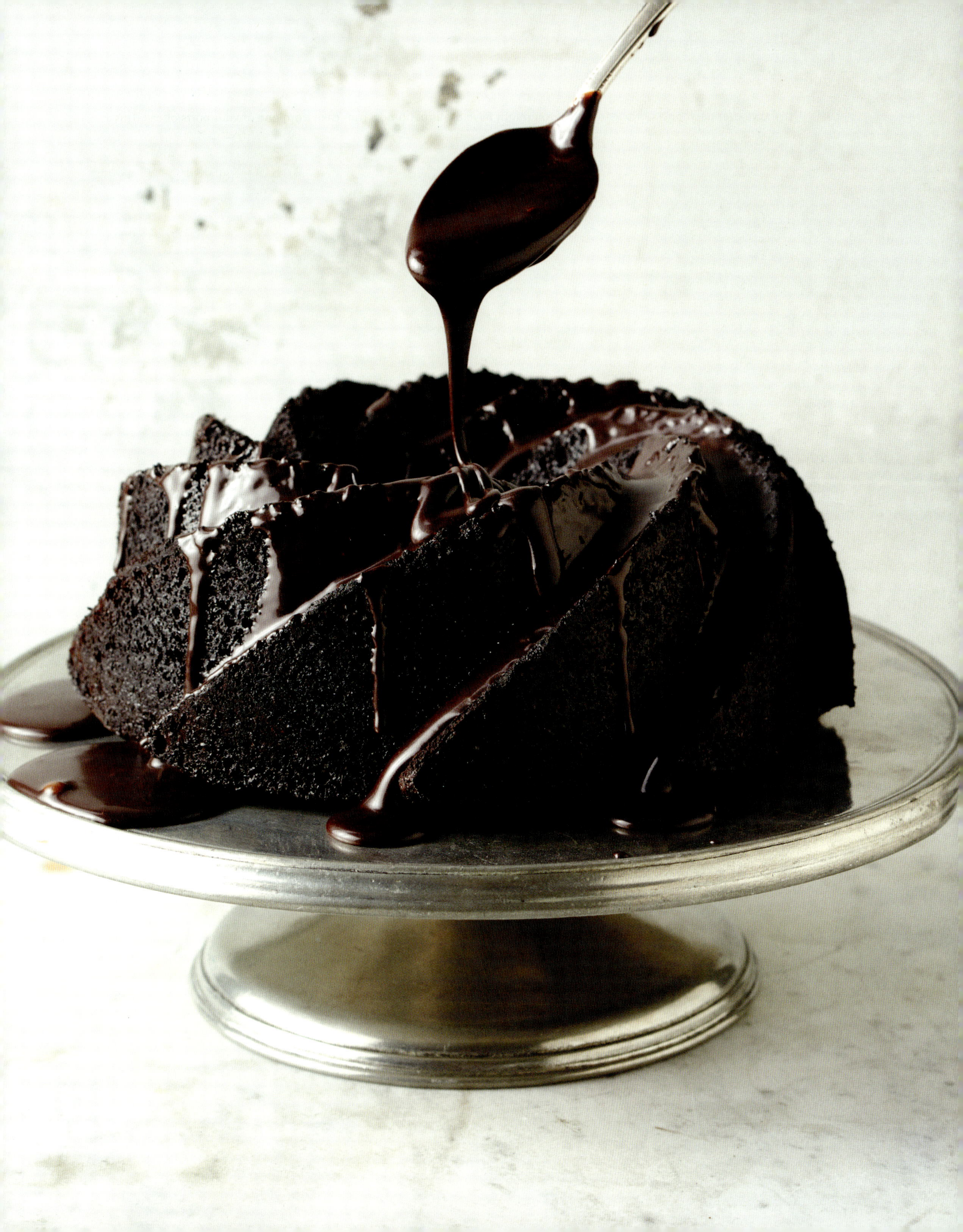

Cool and refreshing, with a beautiful crown of mango slices in a gold-orange glaze, this creamy cheesecake is bound to go to the top of your list of favorite desserts. It requires a minimum of baking, which is all the better for cooks in warm-weather locales. For the best flavor, the mangoes must be ripe (they'll "give" slightly when squeezed), so if you purchase hard fruit, allow a few days to ripen at room temperature.

MANGO ICEBOX CHEESECAKE WITH GINGERSNAP CRUST

CRUST

1¼ cups/115 g finely crushed gingersnap cookies

3 Tbsp unsalted butter, melted

1 Tbsp granulated sugar

4 ripe mangoes

FILLING

2 Tbsp fresh lime juice

2 Tbsp mango liqueur, golden rum, or water

2¼ tsp (1 envelope) unflavored gelatin

1 lb/455 g cream cheese, at room temperature

1 cup/100 g confectioners' sugar

½ cup/120 ml heavy cream

TOPPING

½ cup/120 ml plus ¼ cup/60 ml mango nectar (also called mango juice; available in the Latino or juice aisle of most supermarkets)

1 tsp unflavored gelatin

1 To make the crust: Position a rack in the center of the oven and preheat the oven to 350°F/180°C. Lightly spray a 9-by-3-in/23-by-7.5-cm springform pan with oil.

2 Mix the crushed cookies, melted butter, and sugar together in a medium bowl to combine well. Press the mixture firmly and evenly into the bottom of the pan, bringing it about ½ in/12 mm up the sides. Place on a large rimmed baking sheet. Bake until the crust smells toasty, 10 to 15 minutes. Let the crust cool completely.

3 Using a large, sharp knife, peel and pit the mangoes, reserving any trimmings from the flesh clinging to the pits. Process the trimmings and enough of the mangoes in a blender to make 1 cup/240 ml purée for the filling. Cover and refrigerate the remaining mangoes.

4 To make the filling: Mix the lime juice and liqueur in a ramekin or custard cup. Sprinkle the gelatin over the lime mixture and let stand until the gelatin softens, about 3 minutes. Bring a small skillet with ½ in/12 mm water to a simmer over high heat and reduce the heat to very low. Place the ramekin in the water and stir constantly until the gelatin dissolves, about 1 minute. Remove the ramekin from the water and let the mixture cool slightly. Set the skillet of water aside.

5 Place a small bowl in the freezer to chill. Beat the cream cheese and confectioners' sugar in a large bowl with an electric mixer on medium speed until smooth. Beat in the dissolved gelatin and mango purée. Whip the heavy cream with an electric hand mixer in the chilled bowl until it forms soft peaks. Fold the whipped cream into the cream cheese mixture and spread in the pan. Cover with plastic wrap and refrigerate until chilled and set, at least 2 hours or up to 1 day.

6 To make the topping: Pour the ½ cup/120 ml of the mango nectar into a 1-cup/240-ml glass measuring cup. Sprinkle the 1 tsp gelatin on top. Let stand until the gelatin softens, about 3 minutes. Reheat the water in the skillet. Place the cup in the water and stir constantly until the gelatin dissolves, about 1 minute. Remove the cup from the heat and stir in the ¼ cup/60 ml nectar to cool the gelatin mixture.

7 Cut the reserved mangoes into ½-in/12-mm dice and transfer to a medium bowl. Pour in the gelatin mixture and mix gently. Spoon the topping evenly over the chilled cheesecake. Cover again and refrigerate until the topping is set, at least 2 hours or up to 1 day.

8 To serve, run a dinner knife around the inside of the springform pan to loosen the cheesecake, then remove the sides of the pan. Dip a thin, sharp knife into hot water and slice the cheesecake. Serve chilled.

MAKES 8 TO 10 SERVINGS

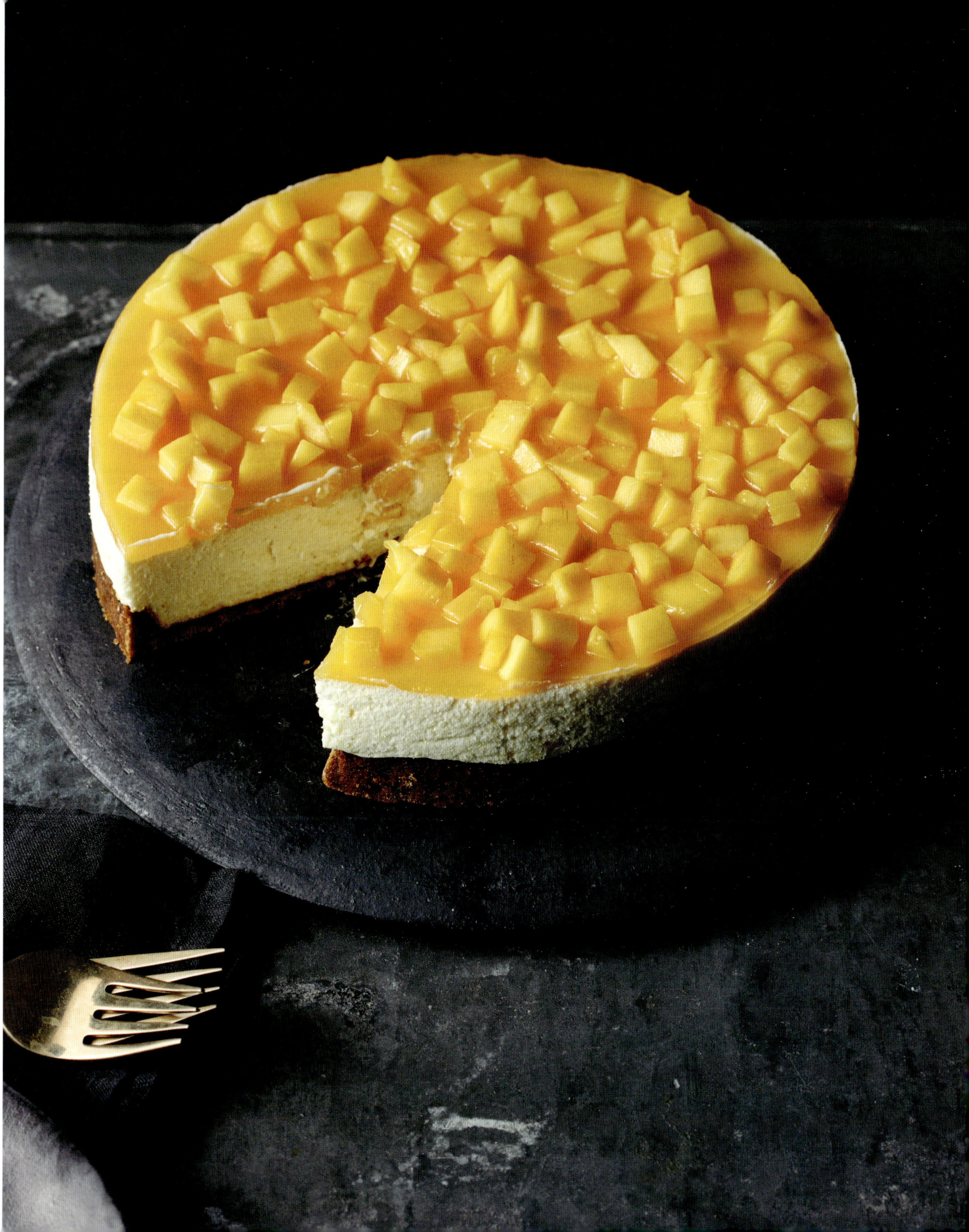

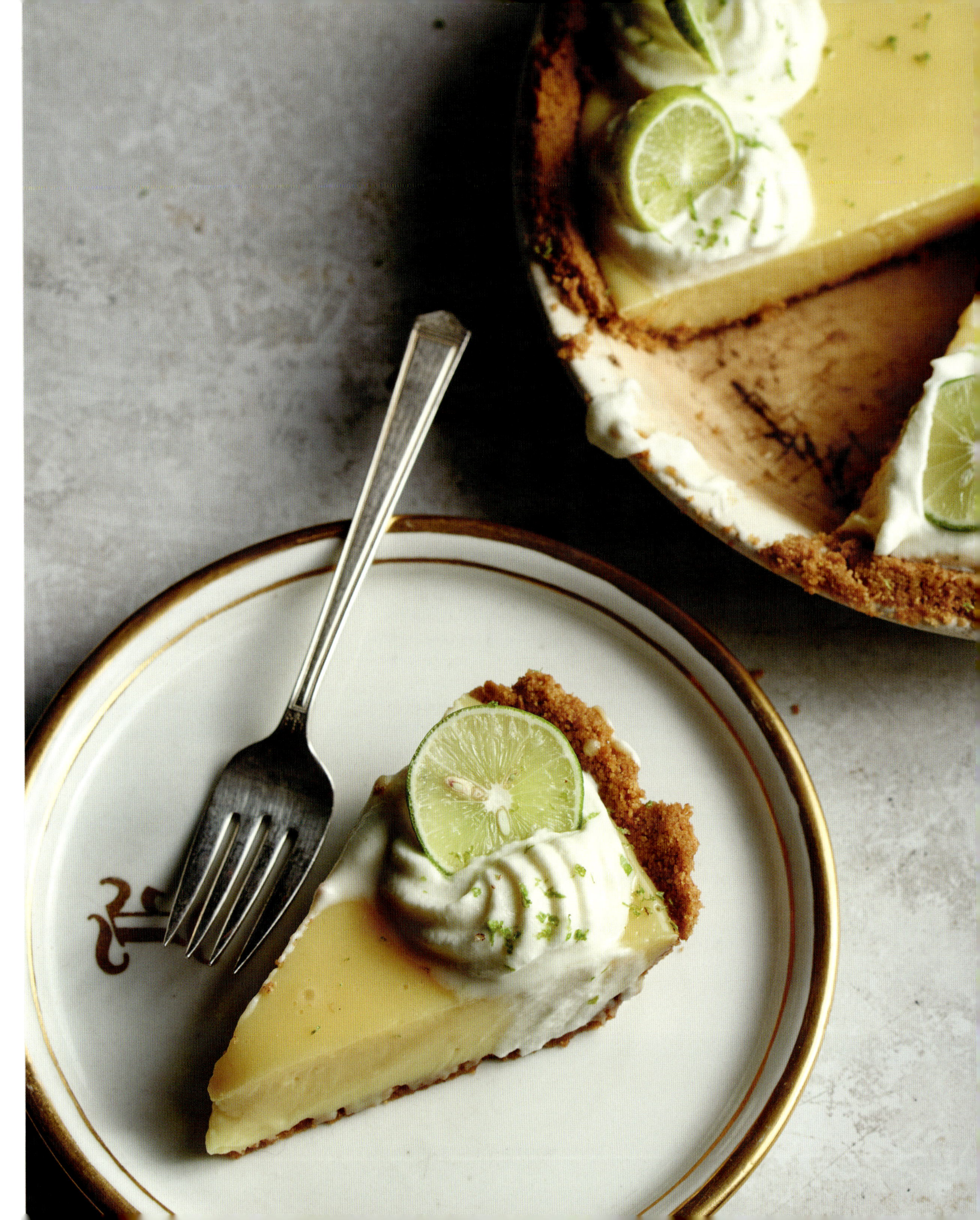

For decades, the Florida Keys, and especially its terminus, Key West, were truly the end of the world, or at least the end of the southern United States. It was not easy to transport food and other supplies, so local products (like Key limes) and foods with long shelf lives (like condensed milk and cookies) became essential foods. Here is Florida's most well-known dessert, with a generous amount of filling and a billowy white chocolate topping.

KEY LIME PIE WITH WHITE CHOCOLATE TOPPING

FILLING

Two 14-oz/390-g cans sweetened condensed milk

8 large egg yolks

1 cup/240 ml fresh lime juice, preferably Key lime

CRUST

4 Tbsp/55 g unsalted butter, melted

1¼ cups/120 g crushed vanilla wafer cookies

2 Tbsp granulated sugar

White Chocolate Topping (page 213)

2 limes (more if using Key limes), for garnish

1 To make the filling: Whisk the condensed milk and yolks together in a medium bowl. Gradually whisk in the lime juice. Let the mixture stand while preparing the crust. (The reaction of the lime juice with the condensed milk will slightly thicken the filling.)

2 Position a rack in the center of the oven and preheat the oven to 350°F/180°C.

3 To make the crust: Brush a 9-by-1½-in/23-by-4-cm pie dish with some of the melted butter. Mix the cookie crumbs and sugar together in a medium bowl and stir in the remaining melted butter. Press the crumb mixture firmly and evenly in the bottom and up the sides of the pie dish. Place the pie dish on a rimmed baking sheet. Bake just until the crust is set and smells toasty, about 10 minutes.

4 Strain the filling through a sieve into another bowl and pour into the pie crust. Return to the oven and immediately reduce the temperature to 300°F/150°C. Bake until the filling is barely set and jiggles in the center when the pie is gently shaken, 20 to 25 minutes. Let cool on a wire rack until tepid, about 1 hour. Refrigerate, uncovered, until chilled, at least 2 hours or up to 1 day.

5 Make the White Chocolate Topping and transfer the topping to a pastry bag fitted with a ½-in/12-mm star tip, such as Ateco 826. Pipe the topping around the circumference of the chilled pie. Using a Microplane, finely grate the zest of half a lime over the topping. Slice the remaining limes into 8 thin rounds. Insert the rounds, equally spaced, into the topping. Slice the pie and serve it chilled.

MAKES 8 SERVINGS

Key Limes

Key limes have pale, yellowish skin and a more rounded, tangy taste than Persian limes. They are also much smaller than Persian limes, only about the size of a walnut, so you will need at least 40 limes (about 1½ lb/680 g), to make the 1 cup/240 ml juice needed for this recipe. On the West Coast, Key limes are sometimes labeled Mexican limes. They are excellent in such cocktails as Mojitos and Margaritas, but you'll need three Key limes to equal one Persian lime. Bottled Key lime juice can have a chemical flavor and should be avoided.

Although sweet potato pie graces many a Thanksgiving or Christmas table, you don't need a holiday as an excuse to make this iconic Southern dessert. It may look like pumpkin pie, but the gently spiced filling has an earthier flavor and less custardy texture. Although many sweet potato pie recipes use boiled potatoes, this can lead to a waterlogged filling that never sets—microwaving is much easier and faster.

SWEET POTATO PIE WITH BOURBON WHIPPED CREAM

PASTRY DOUGH

1½ cups/210 g unbleached all-purpose flour, plus more for rolling out dough

1 Tbsp granulated sugar

¼ tsp fine sea salt

6 Tbsp/85 g cold vegetable shortening, cut into ½-in/12-mm cubes

3 Tbsp cold unsalted butter, cut into ½-in/12-mm cubes

¼ cup/60 ml ice-cold water

1 large egg yolk

½ tsp cider vinegar

FILLING

6 small orange-fleshed sweet potatoes or yams, such as Louisiana or jewel, scrubbed, about 2 lb/910 g

6 Tbsp/90 g unsalted butter, sliced

⅔ cup/165 ml heavy cream

½ cup/100 g granulated sugar

½ cup/100 g packed light brown sugar

2 large eggs, beaten

Grated zest of 1 lemon

½ tsp ground cinnamon

½ tsp ground nutmeg

WHIPPED CREAM

1 cup/240 ml heavy cream

1 Tbsp confectioners' sugar

1 Tbsp bourbon (optional)

½ tsp vanilla extract

1 To make the dough: Whisk the flour, sugar, and salt in a large bowl until combined. Add the shortening and butter. Using a pastry blender, rapidly cut the fats into the flour mixture until it is the consistency of coarse bread crumbs with some pea-sized pieces.

2 Whisk the cold water, egg yolk, and vinegar together in a liquid-measuring cup. Gradually stir enough of the water mixture into the flour mixture so that the dough begins to clump together. You may not need all of the liquid. Knead the dough briefly in the bowl and gather it into a ball. Shape the dough into a thick disk and wrap in plastic wrap. Refrigerate just until chilled, about 1 hour. (The dough can be refrigerated for up to 1 day. If too hard to roll out, let it stand at room temperature for about 10 minutes to soften slightly.)

3 Position a rack in the bottom third of the oven and preheat the oven to 400°/200°C. Heat a rimmed baking sheet in the oven.

4 Unwrap the dough. On a lightly floured work surface, roll the dough into a round about 13 in/33 cm in diameter and ⅛ in/3 mm thick. You should see flattened flakes of fat in the dough. Fit the dough into a 9-in/23-cm pie pan, preferably Pyrex. Trim the overhanging dough to a ½-in/12-mm overhang. Fold the edge of the dough under so it is flush with the edge of the pan and flute the edges. Prick the dough all over with a fork. Freeze or refrigerate the piecrust for 10 to 15 minutes.

5 Line the dough with a sheet of aluminum foil. Fill the foil with pie weights or dried beans. Place the pan on the hot baking sheet and bake until the dough looks set and is beginning to brown, about 15 minutes. Remove the foil and weights. Continue baking, pricking the dough with a fork if it bubbles up, until it looks dry but not completely baked, about 5 minutes more. Remove from the oven.

6 Meanwhile, make the filling: Pierce each sweet potato with a fork. Place on the turntable of a microwave and cook on high (100 percent power) until tender, 7 to 10 minutes, depending on the microwave wattage. (Or bake on a baking sheet in the preheated 400°F/200°C oven until tender, about 50 minutes.) Let stand for 5 minutes. Protecting your hand with a kitchen towel, peel the sweet potatoes and transfer the flesh to a small bowl. Mash the sweet potatoes; you should have 2 cups/450 ml.

7 Add the butter to the sweet potatoes and beat with a hand-held electric mixer on medium speed until the mixture is smooth. Add the heavy cream, granulated sugar, brown sugar, eggs, lemon zest, cinnamon, and nutmeg and mix just until combined. Pour into the warm pie shell.

8 Return the pie to the oven and bake for 15 minutes. Reduce the heat to 350°F/180°C and cook until the filling is evenly puffed and looks set when the pie is gently shaken, 35 to

45 minutes more. Transfer the pie to a wire rack and let cool completely, at least 3 hours. (The pie can be covered and refrigerated for up to 1 day.)

9 To make the whipped cream: Whip the cream, confectioners' sugar, bourbon, if using, and vanilla together in a chilled medium bowl until stiff peaks form. Cut the pie into wedges and serve, topping each serving with a dollop of the topping.

MAKES 8 SERVINGS

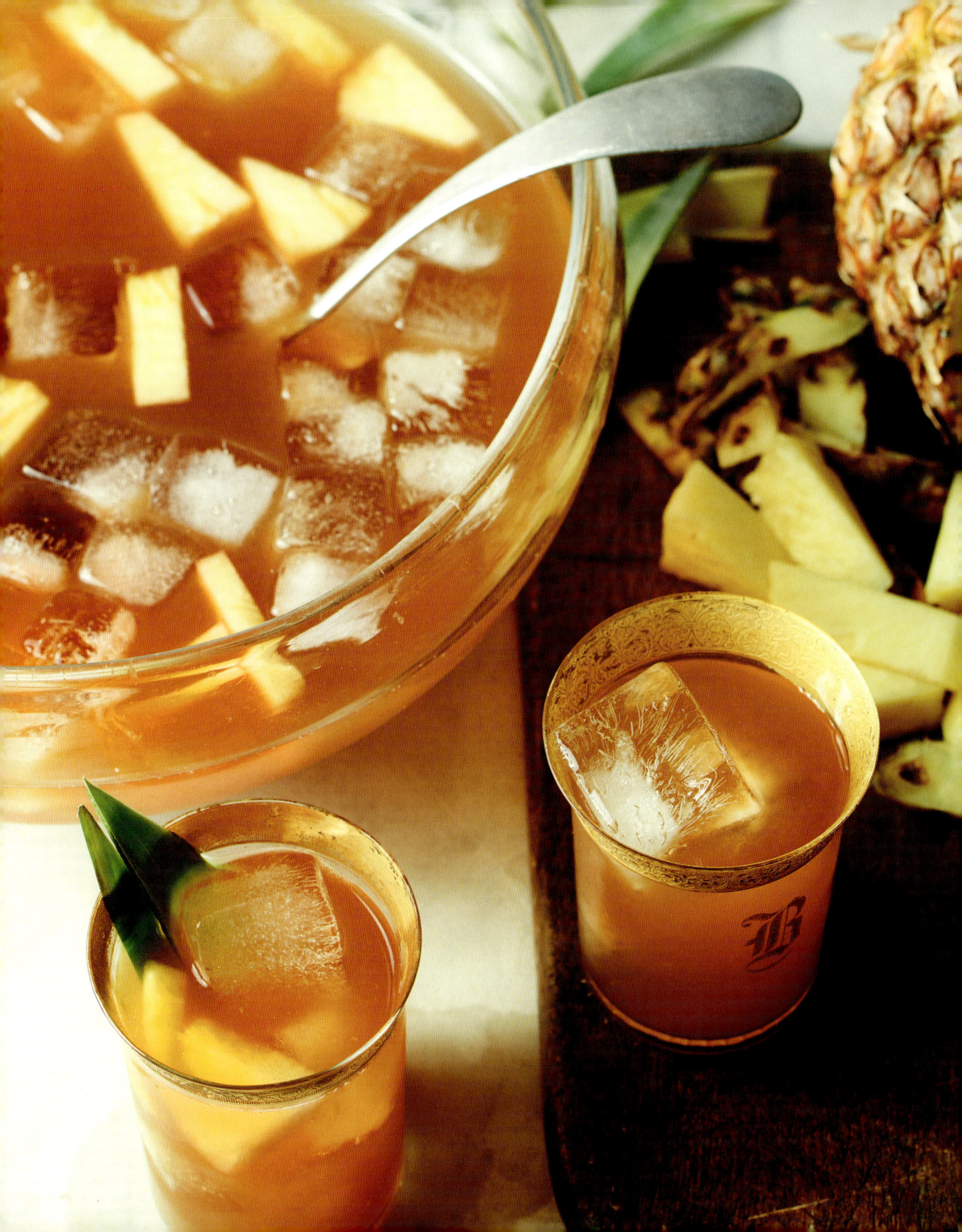

Serve one of our communal punches with long straws and watch the party begin. There is no way you can't have fun sipping this tropical concoction of rum, melon liqueur, and two fruit juices, mixed with fresh pineapple. Be sure the pineapple is good and ripe so it adds its sweet-tart juices to the brew.

KEYS BREEZE PUNCH

1⅜ cups/330 ml dark rum, preferably Pyrat Xo

1⅜ cups/330 ml melon liqueur, preferably Midori

⅔ cup/165 ml fresh orange juice

⅔ cup/165 ml sweetened cranberry juice

¼ pineapple, peeled, cored, and cut into bite-size chunks

SPECIAL EQUIPMENT: One small punch bowl, at least 6 cups/1.4 L; 6 to 8 long straws

1 Stir the rum, melon liqueur, orange juice, and cranberry juice together in a small punch bowl. Add the pineapple and large ice cubes. Let stand for 5 minutes to chill.

2 Serve immediately, with the straws.

MAKES 6 TO 8 SERVINGS

No zombie jokes, please. This punch is the kind of drink that made the tiki craze last for over twenty years during the mid-twentieth century—and why it came back. If you've never made your own grenadine, now's your chance. If you can't find passion fruit vodka, use an equal amount of plain vodka and ½ cup/120 ml unsweetened passion fruit juice.

VOODOO PUNCH

HOMEMADE GRENADINE

½ cup/120 ml unsweetened pomegranate juice

½ cup/100 g sugar, preferably superfine

PUNCH

1⅜ cups/330 ml passion fruit–flavored vodka, preferably SKYY

½ cup/120 ml fresh lemon juice

½ cup/120 ml Homemade Grenadine, above

1¼ fl oz/37.5 ml fresh orange juice

1¼ fl oz/37.5 ml dark orange liqueur, preferably Grand Marnier

½ fl oz/15 ml orange bitters

1⅜ cups/330 ml chilled club soda

4 orange slices

4 lemon slices

SPECIAL EQUIPMENT: One small punch bowl, at least 6 cups/1.4 L; 6 to 8 long straws

1 To make the grenadine: Shake the ingredients in a covered jar until the sugar is dissolved. (Makes about ⅔ cup/160 ml. The mix can be refrigerated for up to 1 week.)

2 Stir the passion fruit vodka, lemon juice, grenadine, orange juice, orange liqueur, and bitters together in a small punch bowl. Add large ice cubes and let stand for 5 minutes to chill. Add the club soda with the orange and lemon slices and stir gently. Serve immediately, with the straws.

MAKES 6 TO 8 SERVINGS

There should be a warning attached to this recipe, because once you make it, you will want to make it every day peaches and berries are in season. A buckle is made of cake-like batter topped or mixed with sliced fresh fruit and or berries; when baked, the cake "buckles" up through the cooked fruit. Of course, you can substitute other stone fruits and berries for the peaches and blackberries.

PEACH-BLACKBERRY BUCKLE

2 ripe peaches, peeled and cut into ½-in/12-mm slices

One 6-oz/170-g container fresh blackberries (about 1⅓ cups)

½ cup/100 g packed light brown sugar

½ cup/115 g unsalted butter, thinly sliced

1¼ cups/175 g unbleached all-purpose flour

⅔ cup/130 g granulated sugar

1 tsp baking powder

⅛ teaspoon fine sea salt

¾ cup/180 ml whole milk

1 large egg, beaten

½ tsp vanilla extract

Vanilla ice cream, for serving

1 Position a rack in the center of the oven and preheat the oven to 350°F/180°C.

2 Toss the peaches, blackberries, and brown sugar together in a medium bowl and set aside while making the batter so the peaches can give off some juices.

3 Scatter the butter in an 8-by-11-in/20-by-28-cm baking dish. Place in the oven and heat until the butter is melted, about 5 minutes. Remove the dish from the oven.

4 Whisk the flour, sugar, baking powder, and salt together in a medium bowl and make a well in the center. Pour in the milk, egg, and vanilla and whisk just until the batter is smooth. Pour the batter evenly over the melted butter in the dish, but do not stir together. Arrange the peaches and blackberries on the batter and drizzle the juices in the bowl over them.

5 Bake until the buckle is golden brown, 50 to 60 minutes. Let cool for 10 minutes. Serve warm, with ice cream.

MAKES 6 SERVINGS

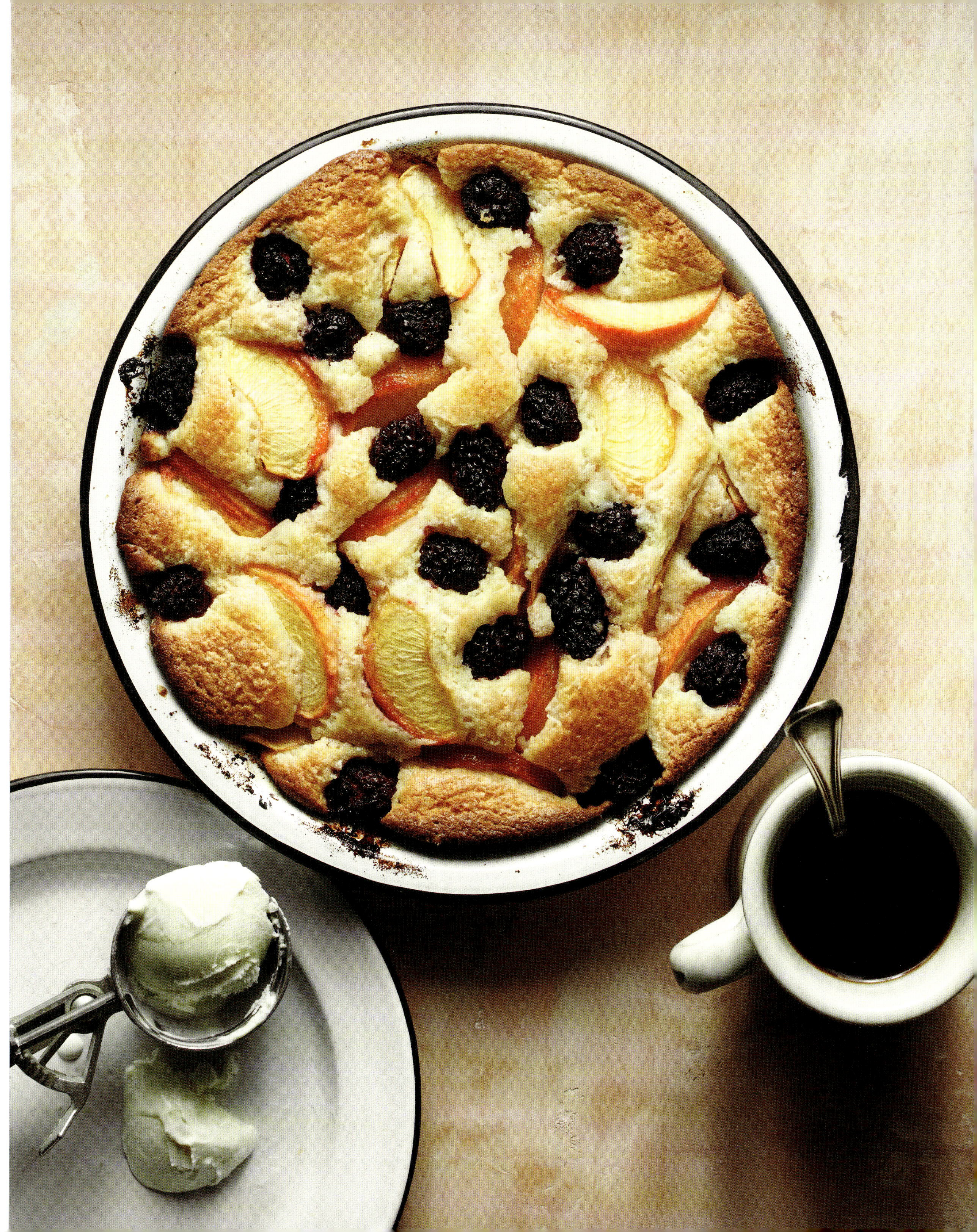

An extra-rich custard in a pool of brown caramel sauce, flan is one of the most beloved of Latino desserts. Sweet almost to the point of sinfulness, it is a great dish for entertaining because it must be made well ahead of serving in order to chill. Here is a recipe from Florida, where both orange groves and Latino cooks flourish.

ORANGE-CINNAMON FLAN

CARAMEL

1¼ cups/250 g sugar

CUSTARD

One 14-oz/430-g can condensed sweetened milk

One 12-oz/340-g can evaporated milk

1 cup/240 ml whole milk

Zest of ½ orange, removed from the orange in strips with a vegetable peeler

One 2-in/5-cm cinnamon stick

2 large eggs, plus 4 large egg yolks

1 tsp vanilla extract

1 To make the caramel: Have ready one 9-in/23-cm metal cake pan with 2 in/5 cm sides. Bring the sugar and ⅓ cup/75 ml water to a boil in a small saucepan over high heat, stirring to dissolve the sugar. When the syrup boils, stop stirring and cook, occasionally swirling the pan by the handle, until the caramel is amber in color and very lightly smoking, about 5 minutes. Carefully pour the caramel into the cake pan. Protecting your hands with pot holders, quickly tilt and rotate the cake pan to coat the bottom and sides of the pan as well as possible with caramel.

2 Position a rack in the center of the oven and preheat the oven to 350°F/180°C.

3 To make the custard: Combine the condensed milk, evaporated milk, whole milk, orange zest, and cinnamon stick in a medium saucepan and bring to a simmer over medium heat, stirring often to keep the sugars in the mixture from scorching. Remove from the heat and let steep for 15 minutes. Strain the mixture through a fine-mesh sieve into a medium bowl, pressing hard on the zest with the back of a spoon.

4 Whisk the eggs, egg yolks, and vanilla together in a medium bowl. Gradually whisk in the warm milk mixture. Strain the custard through the sieve back into the bowl that held the milk mixture and pour into the cake pan. Place the cake pan in a larger roasting pan. Pour hot water into the roasting pan to come about one-third up the sides of the cake pan.

5 Bake until the custard is set and moves as a unit when the cake pan is gently shaken, about 1 hour. Remove the flan from the roasting pan and let cool to room temperature. Cover the flan with plastic wrap and refrigerate until chilled, at least 4 hours or up to 1 day.

6 Run a dinner knife around the inside of the pan to loosen the flan, being sure to reach the bottom on the pan to break the custard's suction. Cover with a round serving platter. Holding the platter and cake pan together, invert them and give them a strong shake to unmold the flan with its caramel. Serve chilled.

MAKES 6 TO 8 SERVINGS

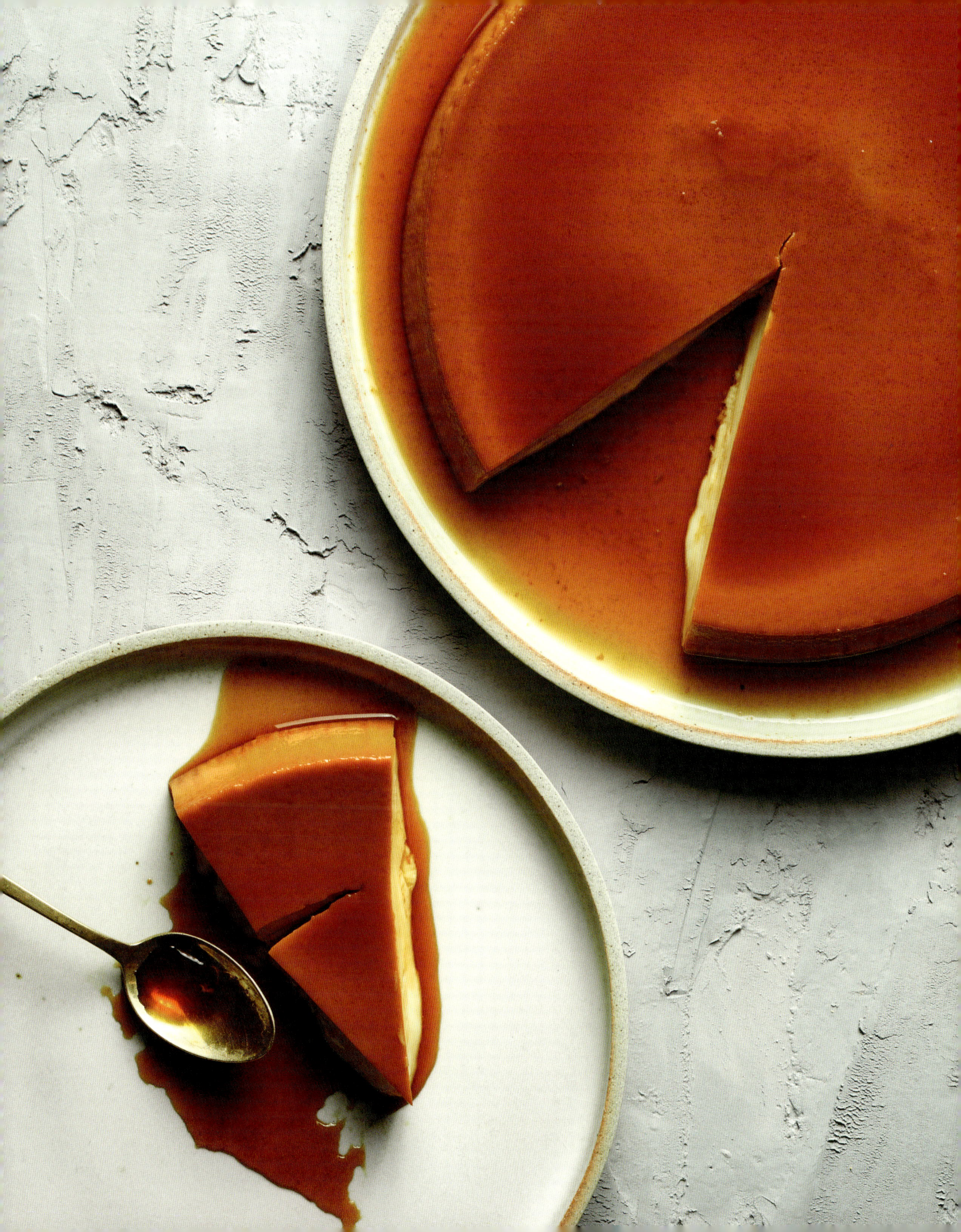

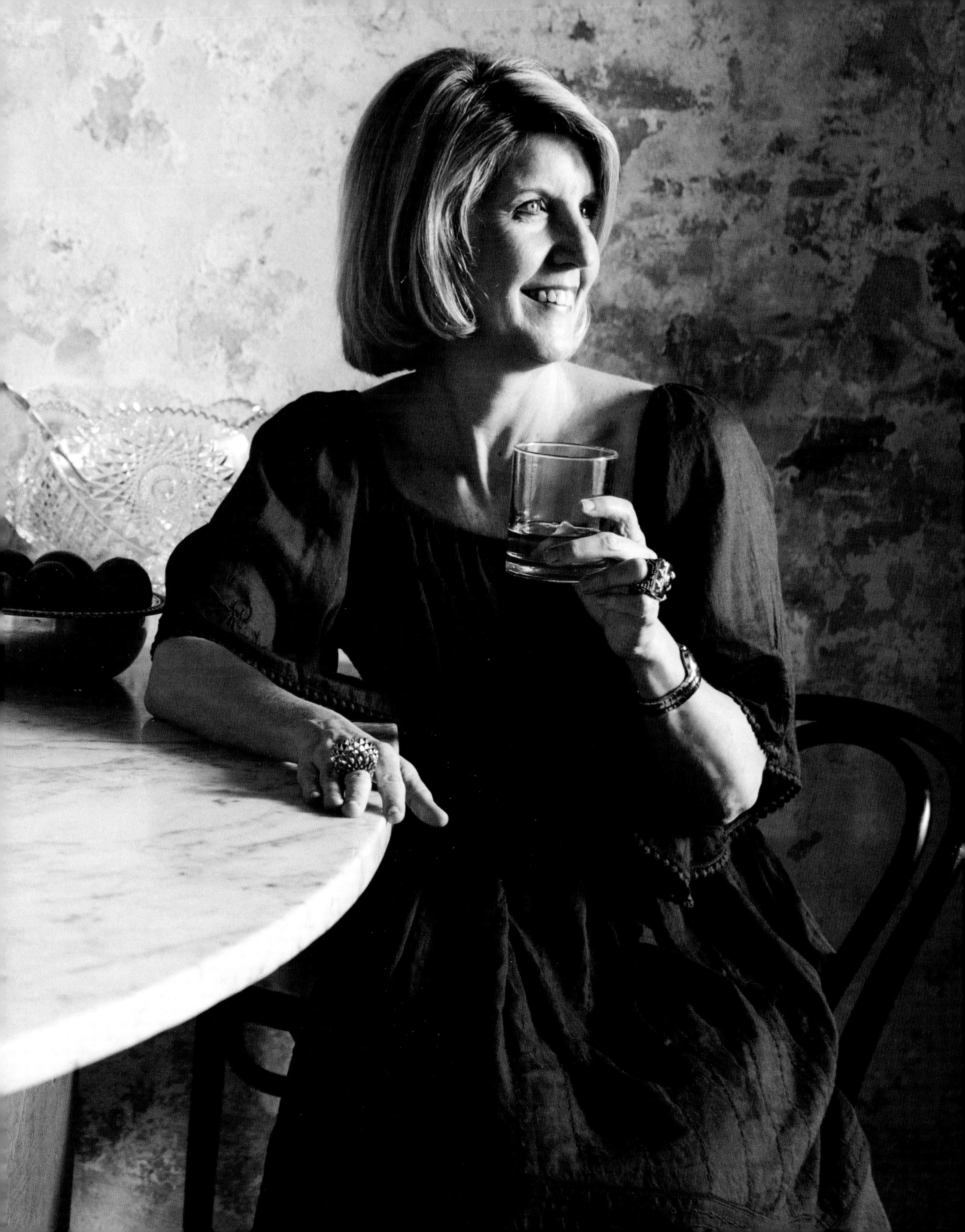

ANN TUENNERMAN, MRS. COCKTAIL

Perched on a rattan stool, sipping a hand-crafted Sazerac at Cane and Table, a Caribbean-themed restaurant near the French Market, an elegant blonde woman regards her drink and says, "The Sazerac is history in a glass." She should know. As the founder of Tales of the Cocktail, the annual spirits-industry gathering held each summer in New Orleans, Ann Tuennerman (a.k.a. Mrs. Cocktail) is one of the libation's biggest fans. In fact, in 2008, she lobbied to make the Sazerac the Official Cocktail of New Orleans, the first city in the country to designate an official cocktail. (For the early history of the Sazerac, see page 109.)

Tales of the Cocktail had modest beginnings. In 2001, Ann was leading walking tours of the city's best eateries and watering holes, taking her followers on a cultural and historical journey informed by the famous drinks invented in her hometown, including, of course, the Sazerac. "To celebrate the first anniversary of the tour," she explains, "I invited some spirits professionals to join in. The word of mouth from those 150 people made Tales of the Cocktail the success it is today."

Now in its fourteenth year, TOTC attracts about eighteen thousand attendees from thirty-five countries. It is, first and foremost, an educational event with seminars, demonstrations, and discussions on all aspects of the alcoholic-beverages trade. Members of the international cocktail community—from bartenders to distillers—come to New Orleans every summer as it is the leading place for exchanging ideas and establishing trends in the business.

"Mid-July used to be the leanest time of the year for New Orleans bars and restaurants," says Ann. "Now, they're packed with people from around the world. While the event is a celebration of cocktails, it's also a celebration of the Crescent City and everything the city has to offer."

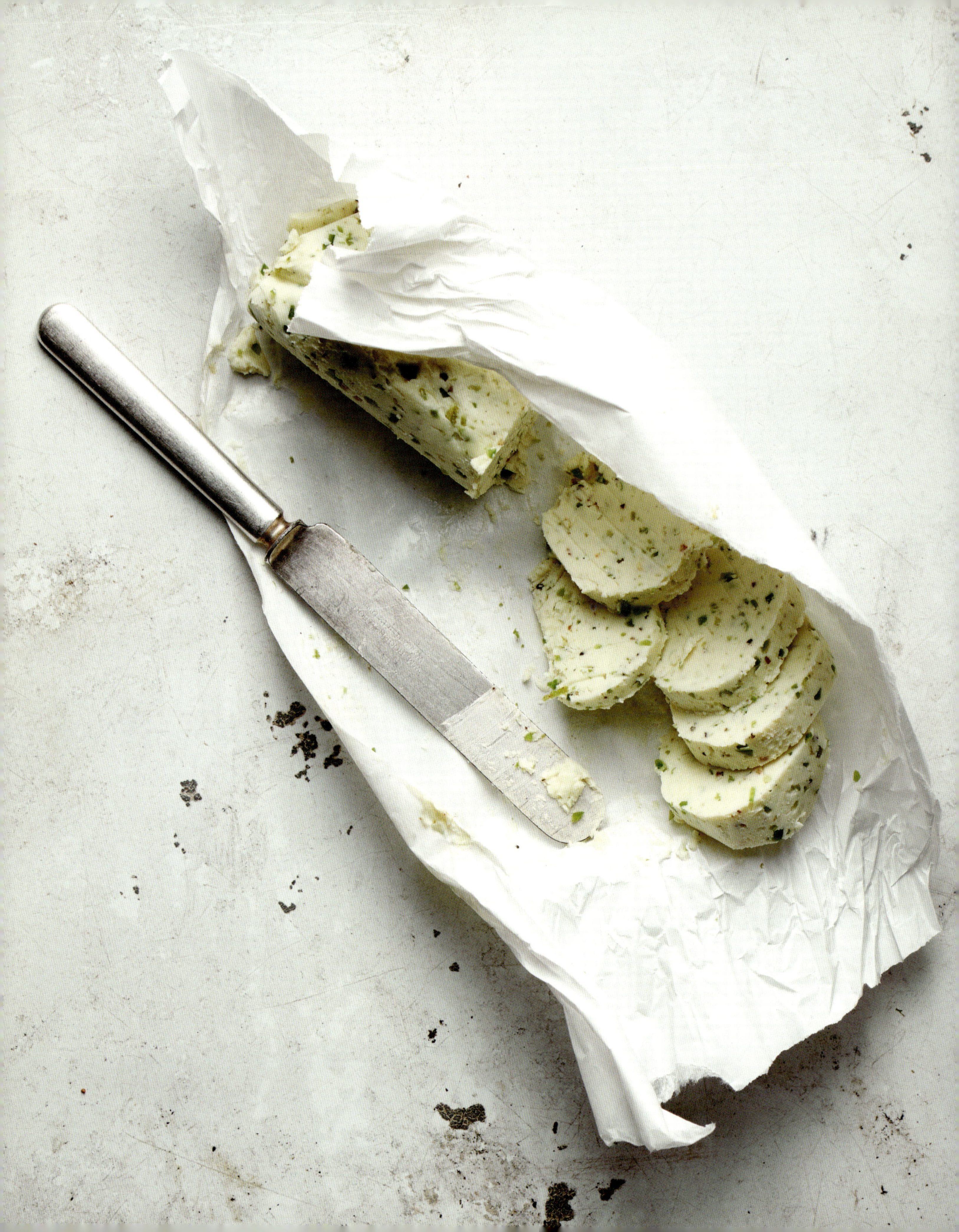

BASICS

CRISPY ONIONS

We use these onion rings to garnish sandwiches like the Pulled Pork Sandwiches on page 146. The secret to crisp onion rings is a soak in ice water before coating and frying.

1 large sweet onion, such as Vidalia or Walla Walla, about 14 oz/400 g, cut into thin slices and separated into rings

Vegetable oil, for deep-frying

1 cup/140 g all-purpose flour

1 Tbsp sugar

¼ tsp fine sea salt

1 Put the onion rings in a medium bowl and add ice water to cover. Let stand at room temperature for 1 to 2 hours. Drain well, discarding any unmelted ice cubes.

2 Preheat the oven to 200°F/95°C. Line a large baking sheet with paper towels. Pour 2 in/5 cm oil into a large, heavy saucepan and heat over high heat to 375°F/190°C on a deep-frying thermometer.

3 Whisk the flour, sugar, and salt together in a large bowl. Pat the onion rings dry with paper towels. In batches, without crowding, toss the onion rings in the flour mixture, coating them thoroughly but lightly. Add the rings to the hot oil and deep-fry, stirring occasionally, until golden brown, about 3 minutes. Using a wire spider or a slotted spoon, transfer to the wire rack to drain. Keep warm in the oven while deep-frying the remaining rings.

MAKES ABOUT 10 GARNISH SERVINGS

ISLAND SLAW

Coleslaw, like its cousin, potato salad, has many incarnations. This minimally sweetened version, from our restaurants, is especially versatile, and is a component in Blackened Fish Tacos, page 154.

1 cup/240 ml mayonnaise

2 Tbsp rice vinegar

2 Tbsp drained and chopped pickled ginger for sushi

1 tsp celery seeds

1 tsp sugar

1 small head green cabbage, cored and shredded, about 6 cups/450 g

2 cups/205 g peeled and julienned jicama (use a V-slicer or mandoline)

½ red onion, cut into thin half-moons

¼ cup/20 g coarsely chopped fresh cilantro

Hawaiian pink or kosher salt and freshly ground white pepper

Whisk the mayonnaise, rice vinegar, pickled ginger, celery seeds, and sugar together in a large bowl. Add the cabbage, jicama, red onion, and cilantro and mix well. Season to taste with the salt and pepper. Cover and refrigerate until chilled, at least 2 hours or up to 2 days. Serve chilled.

MAKES 8 SERVINGS; ABOUT 8 CUPS/2 L

BASIC RICE

When your gumbo or étouffée calls for plain white rice, this is the recipe to use. For a boost of flavor, substitute reduced-sodium chicken broth for the water. This makes a fairly large batch, but leftovers refrigerate well and are easy to reheat in the microwave.

2 cups/400 g long-grain rice

1 tsp kosher salt

1 bay leaf

Combine the rice, salt, and bay leaf and 4 cups/960 ml water in a medium saucepan. Bring to a boil over high heat. Reduce the heat to medium-low and cover tightly. Simmer until the rice is tender and has absorbed the liquid, about 20 minutes. Remove from the heat and let rest for 5 minutes. Fluff with a fork, discard the bay leaf, and serve hot.

MAKES ABOUT 4 CUPS/620 G

DON'T EVEN
THINK
OF SMOKING
Cigarettes
HERE
SE BUSCA
(813)402-6316
SPORT.S

ROASTED GARLIC

Roasting garlic in oil gives the cloves a mellow, nutty flavor. There are many ways to roast a head of garlic, but this one yields individual cloves, which are more attractive and take less time to cook than an entire head. At the restaurant, we use pre-peeled garlic cloves (sold raw in the refrigerated produce section at the supermarket), but you can peel them yourself, if you prefer.

2 large, plump heads garlic, or about 24 peeled garlic cloves

⅓ cup/75 ml olive oil, plus more as needed

1 Position a rack in the center of the oven and preheat the oven to 375°F/190°C. Break the garlic heads into cloves. Lightly crush the cloves under the flat side of a knife and remove the peels, keeping the cloves as intact as possible. Transfer to a small baking dish and add the oil. Bake until the garlic is tender and turns light beige, 30 to 40 minutes. Let the garlic cool in the dish.

2 Transfer the garlic and oil to a small covered container. Add enough oil to completely cover the garlic. Leave the garlic intact until ready to mash. Just before using, mash the garlic with a fork. (The garlic can be covered and refrigerated for up to 1 month.)

MAKES ABOUT 3 TBSP ROASTED GARLIC PURÉE

DRY JERK SEASONING

Jamaican jerk can either be a wet marinade (see page 72) or a dry spice mixture, as shown here. Both always contain onion, chiles, thyme, and such warm spices as allspice and cinnamon. Our favorite commercial brand is PepperMary Island Jerk Rub, available at www.peppermary.com.

2 tsp sugar

1 tsp granulated onion

1 tsp dried thyme

1 tsp ground allspice

1 tsp kosher salt

½ tsp dried oregano

½ tsp freshly grated nutmeg

½ tsp red pepper flakes

½ tsp granulated garlic

¼ tsp ground cloves

Whisk all of the ingredients together in a small bowl. Transfer to a covered jar and store in a cool, dark place for up to 3 months.

MAKES ABOUT 3 TBSP

CAJUN SEASONING

You may see Cajun seasoning at the supermarket, but too often it is just gussied-up salt and pepper. This one is on the spicy side, but with distinct herbal flavors, too. Our favorite commercial brand is PepperMary Cajun Blend, available at www.peppermary.com.

2 tsp cayenne pepper

1½ tsp freshly ground black pepper

1½ tsp granulated garlic

1½ tsp granulated onion

1½ tsp dried thyme

1½ tsp dried oregano

1 tsp kosher salt

Whisk all of the ingredients together in a bowl. Transfer to a covered jar and store in a cool, dark place for up to 3 months.

MAKES ABOUT 3 TBSP

WHITE CHOCOLATE TOPPING

This creamy topping is designed for the Key Lime Pie on page 195, but it is also perfect as an accompaniment to chocolate cake, strawberry shortcake, or any recipe that calls for whipped cream. Choose a high-quality white chocolate and check the ingredients label to be sure it includes cocoa butter and not other tropical fats like palm kernel oil.

1 cup/240 ml heavy cream

2 oz/55 g white chocolate, finely chopped

2 tsp confectioners' sugar

½ tsp vanilla extract

1 Heat ¼ cup/60 ml of the cream in a small saucepan over medium heat until simmering. Remove from the heat. Add the white chocolate and whisk until melted and the mixture is smooth. Transfer to a small bowl and let stand until lukewarm, about 15 minutes.

2 Chill a medium bowl in the freezer or refrigerator. Pour in the remaining ¾ cup/180 ml cream and add the confectioners' sugar and vanilla. Beat with a hand-held electric mixer on high speed just until the mixture forms soft peaks. Add the cooled white chocolate mixture. With the mixer on low speed, beat just until the topping forms stiff peaks. Do not overbeat, or the topping could separate. (The topping can be covered and refrigerated for up to 1 day.)

MAKES ABOUT 2½ CUPS/600 ML, ENOUGH FOR ONE 9-INCH PIE

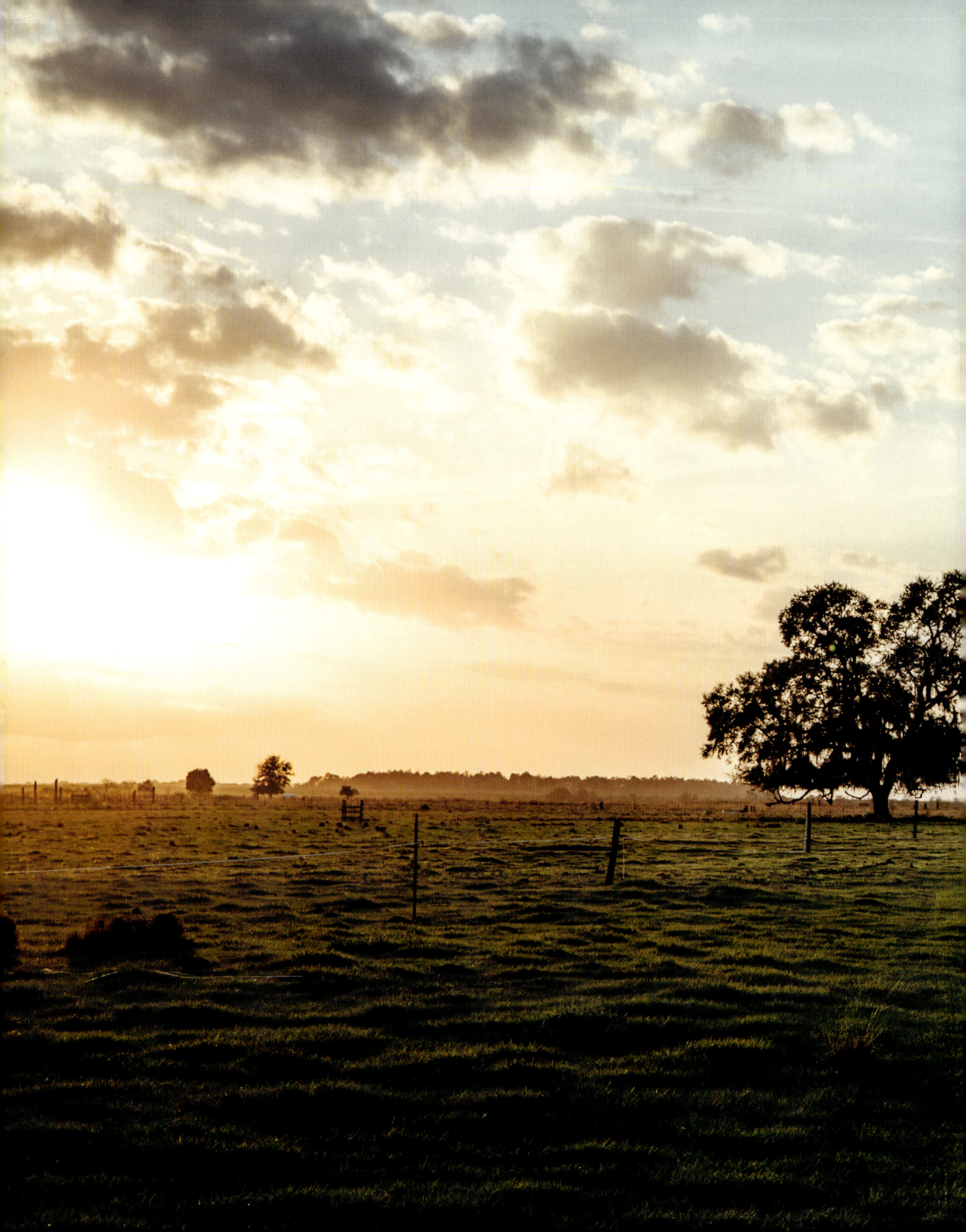

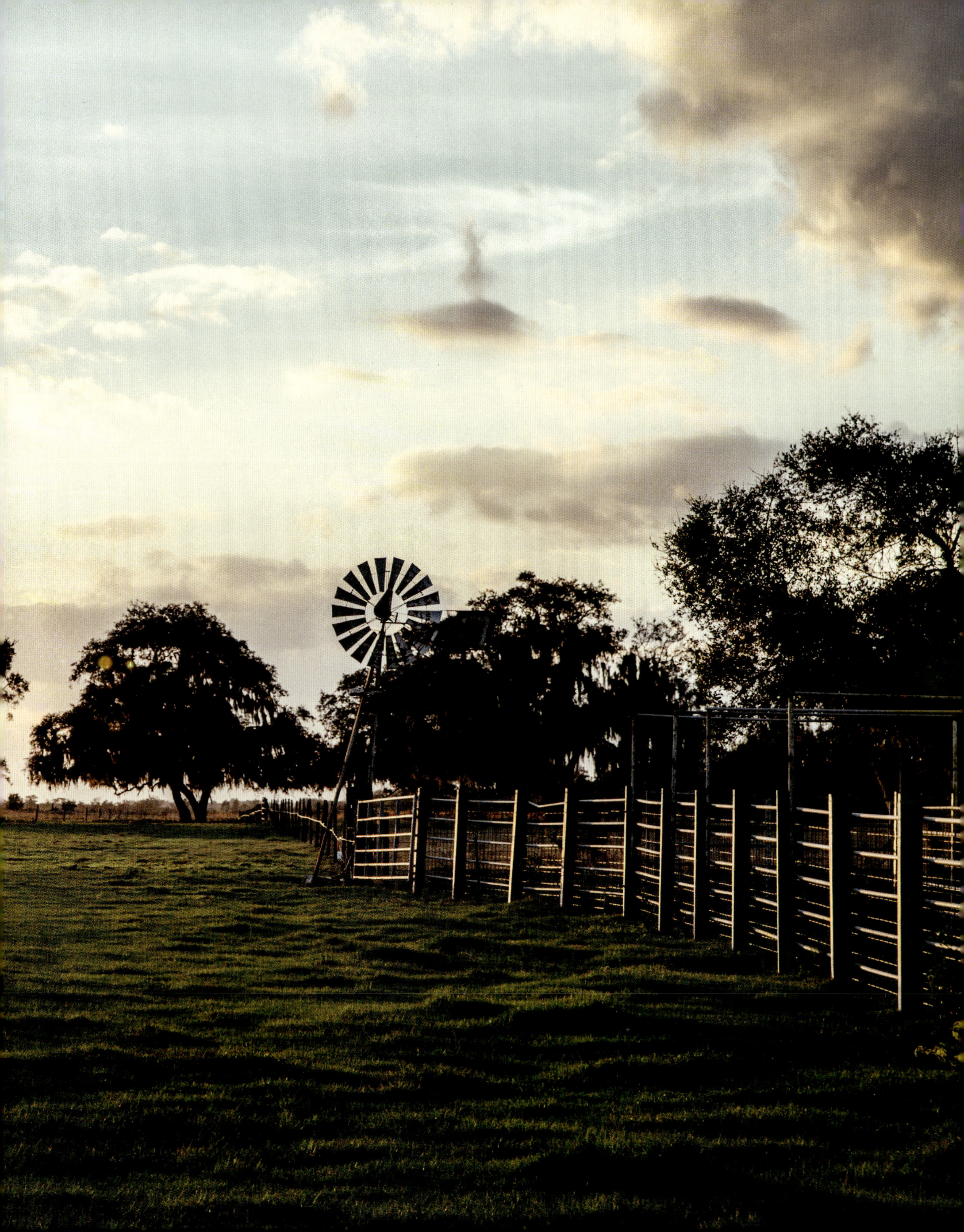

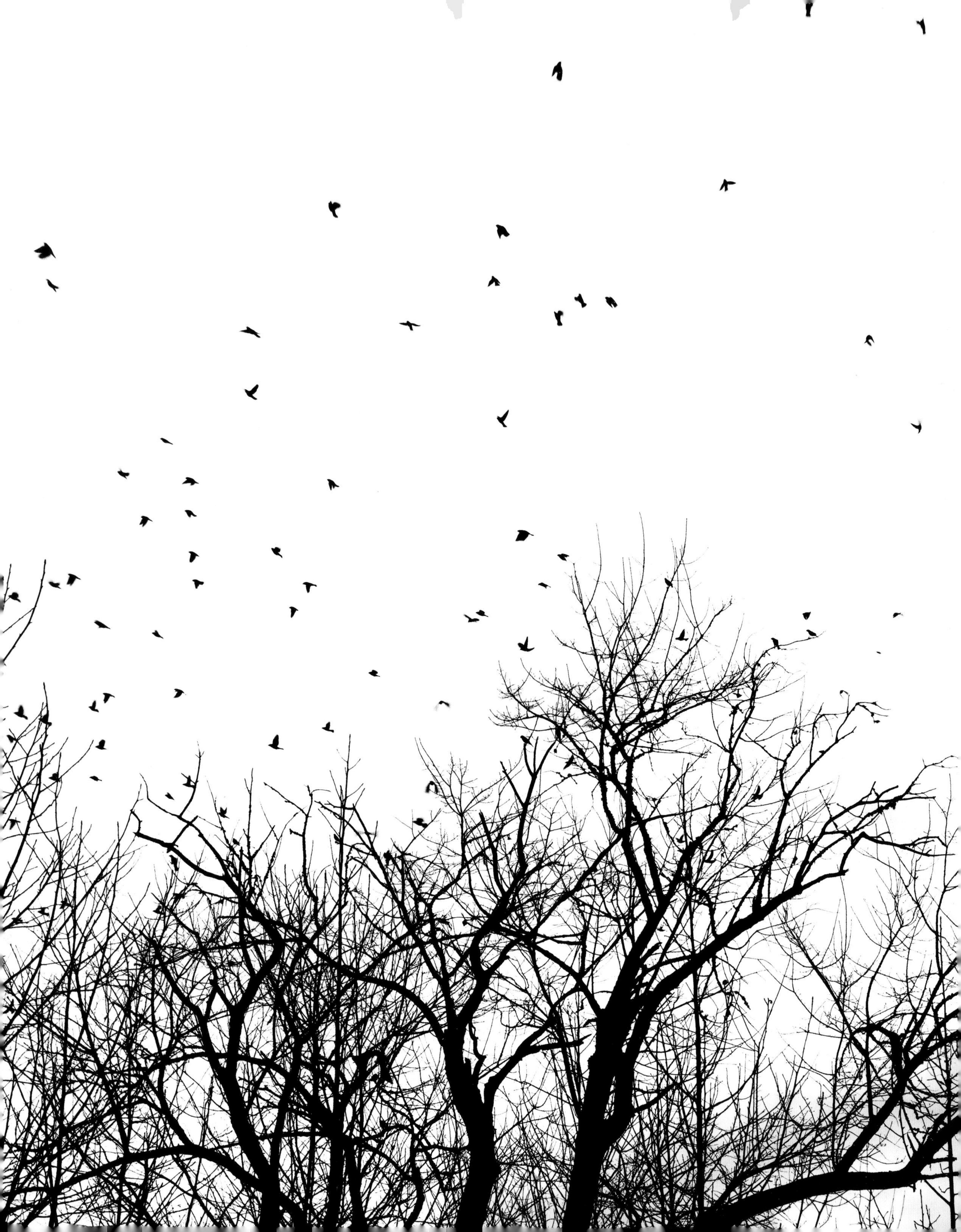

ACKNOWLEDGMENTS

Offering a relaxing and welcoming atmosphere at each of our Tommy Bahama restaurants is a highly rewarding team effort—and the same holds true with producing a cookbook to share our favorite recipes. With pleasure we acknowledge the individuals and businesses who collaborated to bring you this second book in the Cooking with Tommy Bahama series.

We were delighted to once again have renowned chef and writer Rick Rodgers lend his talents and wisdom to the project, including tailoring some of our popular restaurant recipes for the home kitchen. We appreciate the photography team of Peden + Munk for creating beautiful recipe shots that look good enough to eat, and for discovering exquisite locations that give you a visual taste of the Gulf Coast. And many thanks to Toni Tajima, designer extraordinaire, for making the pages look gorgeous.

Heartfelt thanks to the creative styling team, led by prop stylists Amy Wilson and Nicolette Owen and food stylist Alison Attenborough, with assistance from food assistants Sandy Ta, Tina Dang, and Shelly Petericia Ellis; prop assistants Nina Lalli and Nicole Louie; photo assistant Rob Petrie; on-location production assistants Jessica Fender and Curt Leimbach; location photo assistant Craig Mulcahy; camera operator Thomas Nakasone; and studio assistant Asmite Gherezgiher, assisted by Marley Wong.

A rich part of this endeavor was meeting some wonderful people who shared their stories and insights with us. Thanks and handshakes all around to Joey Fonseca of Des Allemands Outlaw Katfish Company, Leonard Horak of Circle 6 Farm & Ranch, Louis Michot of the Lost Bayou Ramblers, Georgea Snyder of Tampa Downtown Market, and Ann Tuennerman of Tales of the Cocktail.

We commend and value the efforts of our own team members in bringing these recipes from our kitchens to yours. Props to Andy Comer, Don Donley, Rob Goldberg, Eric Karp, Catherine Mirabile, Melinda Porter, Thomas Prowell, and Curtis Smith—and thank you to our chief executive officer Doug Wood for his support and endorsement of this touchstone project. Thanks as well to independent producer Katherine Prato, who worked with our team from start to finish line.

We appreciate the opportunity to again collaborate with Chronicle Books, and our thanks to the excellent team assembled to produce this book: Mike Ashby, Amy Bauman, Ken DellaPenta, Pamela Geismar, Catherine Huchting, Laurel Leigh, Carolyn Miller, Beth Steiner, and Beth Weber.

And to our guests and readers of this book: thank you for being the impetus for this ongoing series of adventurous cookbooks. We sincerely hope you find inspiration within these pages to share with family and friends.

INDEX

A

Aïoli, 210
    Chipotle Aïoli, 210
Almonds
    Coconut-Almond Rice, 174
    Grilled Chicken and Mango Salad, 44
    toasting, 44
Ambrosia, Fresh, with Sour Cream Dressing, 51
Anaya, Ignacio "Nacho," 25
Arroz con Pollo y Chorizo, 80
Asian Chili Sauce, 126
Asparagus
    Chicken Fricassee with Spring Vegetables and Chive Dumplings, 79
Avocados
    Chopped Chicken Taco Salad with Chipotle Ranch Dressing, 43
    Grilled Chicken Tortas with Chipotle Aïoli, 138
    Seafood Avocado Cocktail, 22
    Spiked Guacamole with Fire-Roasted Pepper Salsa, 28

B

Bacon
    Bacon and Bourbon Jam Crostini with Goat Cheese, 27
    Bacon BBQ Burgers, 139
    Collard Greens with Bacon and Garlic, 164
    cooking, 158
    Corn-Bacon Hash, 105–6
    Fried Green Tomato and Pimento Cheese BLTs, 158
    Shrimp and Sausage Gumbo with Slow Roux, 57
    Smothered Green Beans, 163
    The Ultimate Texas Chili, 90
Bananas
    Hummingbird Quick Bread, 193
Bars, Pecan-Chocolate, 203
Beans
    Black Bean Soup with Sherry, 63
    Chopped Chicken Taco Salad with Chipotle Ranch Dressing, 43
    Cuban Black Bean Soup with Chorizo Sofrito, 63
    Quinoa Succotash, 170
    Smothered Green Beans, 163
    Super Nachos with Skirt Steak, Black Beans, and Queso Sauce, 25
    Texas Caviar, 31
Beef
    Bacon BBQ Burgers, 139
    Beef Debris Po' Boys with Gravy, 145
    Creole Surf and Turf with Spicy Mustard Sauce, 87
    Cuban "Hamburgers" with Chorizo and Shoestring Potatoes, 142
    Jamaican Beef Patties, 94
    Picadillo-Stuffed Acorn Squash, 96
    Ropa Vieja, 91
    Smoked and Baked Texas Brisket, 88
    Super Nachos with Skirt Steak, Black Beans, and Queso Sauce, 25
    The Ultimate Texas Chili, 90
Beer
    BBQ Shrimp with Spicy Beer Sauce, 129
    Jalapeño and Beer Hush Puppies, 182
    The Ultimate Texas Chili, 90
Bell peppers
    Fire-Roasted Pepper Salsa, 28
    Red Pepper Jam, 24
    Roasted Red Pepper Cream, 74–75
    roasting, 74
Biscuits, Flaky Buttermilk, 183
Bisque, Crab, 61
Blackberries
    Blackberry Brandy BBQ Sauce, 99
    Peach-Blackberry Buckle, 200
Black-eyed peas
    Texas Caviar, 31
BLTs, Fried Green Tomato and Pimento Cheese, 158
Bourbon
    Bacon and Bourbon Jam Crostini with Goat Cheese, 27
    Bourbon-Brined Pork Chops with Peach Glaze and Corn-Bacon Hash, 105–6
    Bourbon-Mint Lemonade, 140
    Bourbon Whipped Cream, 196–97
    Sazerac, 109
Brandy
    Blackberry Brandy BBQ Sauce, 99
    Hurricane, 55
    Sazerac, 109
Bread. *See also* Sandwiches
    Bacon and Bourbon Jam Crostini with Goat Cheese, 27
    Hummingbird Quick Bread, 193
    Moist Corn Bread with Fresh Corn, 178
    Muffaletta Salad with Olive Vinaigrette, 47
Buckle, Peach-Blackberry, 200
Burgers
    Bacon BBQ Burgers, 139
    Cuban "Hamburgers" with Chorizo and Shoestring Potatoes, 142
Burritos, "Wet" Chicken, with Red Sauce, 137
Butter, Jalapeño-Lime, 211

C

Cabbage
    Coleslaw with Poppy Seed Dressing, 52
    Island Slaw, 209
    Lamb Shanks Adobo Soft Tacos, 151
Cajun Seasoning, 213
Cakes
    Chocolate-Rum Cake, 188
    Mango Icebox Cheesecake with Gingersnap Crust, 190

Peanut Butter Cake with Salted Peanut
  Frosting, 187
Caribbean Mahi Mahi with Quinoa
  Succotash, 117
Carrots
  Coleslaw with Poppy Seed Dressing, 52
  Jamaican Curry Lamb, 107
  Quinoa Succotash, 170
  Roast Chicken Asado with Root
    Vegetables, 67
Catfish, 135
  Crispy Fish Fillet Sandwiches with Island
    Tartar Sauce, 152–53
Cheese
  Baby Spinach with Lime-Mustard
    Vinaigrette and Sweet and Spicy
    Pecans, 50
  Bacon and Bourbon Jam Crostini with
    Goat Cheese, 27
  Bacon BBQ Burgers, 139
  Baked Grits with Spicy Mushrooms and
    Cheese, 168
  Cheese-Stuffed Chicken Breasts with
    Roasted Red Pepper Cream, 74–75
  Crab Enchiladas in Green Sauce, 125
  Creamy Macaroni and Cheese with
    Parmesan Crust, 169
  Fried Green Tomato and Pimento Cheese
    BLTs, 158
  Grilled Chicken and Mango Salad, 44
  Horiatiki Greek Salad with Marinated
    Grilled Shrimp, 48
  Lamb Shanks Adobo Soft Tacos, 151
  Mango Icebox Cheesecake with
    Gingersnap Crust, 190
  Muffaletta Salad with Olive Vinaigrette, 47
  Old-School Cuban Sandwiches with Garlic
    Mayonnaise, 149
  Savory Tomato and Cheese Pie, 39
  Shrimp and Andouille with
    Cheese Grits, 132
  Southern Vegetable Gratin, 167
  Super Nachos with Skirt Steak, Black
    Beans, and Queso Sauce, 25
  "Wet" Chicken Burritos with
    Red Sauce, 137
  Zesty Pimento Cheese (aka Zesty Pub
    Cheese), 37
Chicken, 65
  Arroz con Pollo y Chorizo, 80
  Cheese-Stuffed Chicken Breasts with
    Roasted Red Pepper Cream, 74–75
  Chicken Breasts with Jerk Marinade, 72

Chicken Fricassee with Spring Vegetables
  and Chive Dumplings, 79
Chopped Chicken Taco Salad with
  Chipotle Ranch Dressing, 43
Fried Chicken with Iced Tea Brine, 71
Grilled Chicken and Mango Salad, 44
Grilled Chicken Tortas with
  Chipotle Aïoli, 138
Grilled Chicken Wings with Mole Rub, 83
Grilled Jerk Chicken, 72
Hickory BBQ Chicken with Sweet and
  Sticky Root Beer Sauce, 68
Roast Chicken Asado with Root
  Vegetables, 67
Tandoori-Style Chicken, 78
Tortola Tortilla Soup, 58
"Wet" Chicken Burritos with
  Red Sauce, 137
Chiles, 85
  Chipotle Aïoli, 210
  Chipotle Ranch Dressing, 43
  Dry Jerk Seasoning, 213
  Jalapeño and Beer Hush Puppies, 182
  Jalapeño-Lime Butter, 211
  Jerk Marinade, 72
  Leap of Faith, 77
  roasting, 74
  Salsa Verde, 125
Chili, The Ultimate Texas, 90
Chocolate
  Chocolate-Rum Cake, 188
  Pecan-Chocolate Bars, 203
Church Supper Potato Salad, 56
Cilantro Oil, 211
Circle 6 Farm & Ranch, 65
Citrus fruits, 17. See also individual fruits
Cocktails
  Bourbon-Mint Lemonade, 140
  Daiquiri, 77
  equipment for, 32
  Hemingway La Floridita, 33
  Hibiscus-Ginger Punch, 140
  Hurricane, 55
  Key Lime Martini, 33
  Keys Breeze Punch, 199
  Leap of Faith, 77
  Margarita, 55
  Mojito, 109
  in pitchers and punch bowls, 32
  Sazerac, 109, 207
  Tales of the Cocktail, 207
  tips for, 32
  Voodoo Punch, 199

Coconut
  Crab Cakes with Coconut Crust, 21
  Fresh Ambrosia with Sour Cream
    Dressing, 51
  Hummingbird Quick Bread, 193
Coconut milk
  Coconut-Almond Rice, 174
  Jamaican Curry Lamb, 107
  Jamaican Fish Rundown, 120
Cognac
  Sazerac, 109
Cointreau
  Margarita, 55
Coleslaw
  Coleslaw with Poppy Seed Dressing, 52
  Island Slaw, 209
Collard greens, 161
  Collard Greens with Bacon and Garlic, 164
Conch Fritters with Red Pepper Jam, 24
Corn. See also Cornmeal; Grits
  Corn-Bacon Hash, 105–6
  Grilled Corn Salsa, 58
  Moist Corn Bread with Fresh Corn, 178
  Quinoa Succotash, 170
  Southern Vegetable Gratin, 167
  Texas Caviar, 31
Cornmeal
  Fried Green Tomato and Pimento Cheese
    BLTs, 158
  Jalapeño and Beer Hush Puppies, 182
  Moist Corn Bread with Fresh Corn, 178
  Oyster Po' Boys with Mississippi
    Comeback Sauce, 157
Crab, 21
  Crab Bisque, 61
  Crab Cakes with Coconut Crust, 21
  Crab Enchiladas in Green Sauce, 125
  Crab-Stuffed Shrimp with Two Sauces,
    126–28
  Seafood Avocado Cocktail, 22
Crayfish
  Crayfish Étouffée, 119
  Crayfish Stock, 210
Crema, 125
Creole Surf and Turf with Spicy Mustard
  Sauce, 87
Crostini, Bacon and Bourbon Jam, with Goat
  Cheese, 27
Cuban Black Bean Soup with
  Chorizo Sofrito, 63
Cuban "Hamburgers" with Chorizo and
  Shoestring Potatoes, 142

INDEX | 219

Cuban Sandwiches, Old-School, with Garlic Mayonnaise, 149
Cucumbers
    Horiatiki Greek Salad with Marinated Grilled Shrimp, 48
    Tzatziki, 110
Cultural Research Institute of Arcadia, 41

D
Daiquiri, 77
Demerara Syrup, Rich, 109
Des Allemands Outlaw Katfish Company, 135
Desserts
    Chocolate-Rum Cake, 188
    Florida Strawberry Shortcakes with Lime Whipped Cream, 202
    Hummingbird Quick Bread, 193
    Key Lime Pie with White Chocolate Topping, 195
    Mango Icebox Cheesecake with Gingersnap Crust, 190
    Orange-Cinnamon Flan, 204
    Peach-Blackberry Buckle, 200
    Peanut Butter Cake with Salted Peanut Frosting, 187
    Pecan-Chocolate Bars, 203
    Sweet Potato Pie with Bourbon Whipped Cream, 196–97
    Tres Leches Strawberry Shortcake, 192
Dill-Yogurt Sauce, 115
Dumplings, Chive, Chicken Fricassee with Spring Vegetables and, 79

E
Enchiladas, Crab, in Green Sauce, 125
Escarole
    Horta, 121
Étouffée, Crayfish, 119

F
Farmers' markets, 65, 185
Fish
    Baked Grouper with Dill-Yogurt Sauce, 115
    Blackened Fish Tacos, 154
    Caribbean Mahi Mahi with Quinoa Succotash, 117
    catfish, 135
    Crispy Fish Fillet Sandwiches with Island Tartar Sauce, 152–53
    Jamaican Fish Rundown, 120
    Marinated Swordfish with Skordalia and Horta, 121
    Tuna in Veracruz Sauce, 122
Flan, Orange-Cinnamon, 204
Florida Strawberry Shortcakes with Lime Whipped Cream, 202
Fonseca, Joey, 135
Fritters, Conch, with Red Pepper Jam, 24

G
Garlic
    Aïoli, 210
    Garlic Mayonnaise, 149
    Roasted Garlic, 213
Grand Marnier
    Margarita, 55
    Voodoo Punch, 199
Grapefruit, 17
    Leap of Faith, 77
Greek Lamb Souvlaki with Vegetable Kebabs and Tzatziki, 110
Greek Salad, Horiatiki, with Marinated Grilled Shrimp, 48
Grenadine, Homemade, 199
Grilling tips, 19
Grits
    Baked Grits with Spicy Mushrooms and Cheese, 168
    Shrimp and Andouille with Cheese Grits, 132
Grouper
    Baked Grouper with Dill-Yogurt Sauce, 115
    Crispy Fish Fillet Sandwiches with Island Tartar Sauce, 152–53
    Jamaican Fish Rundown, 120
Guacamole, Spiked, with Fire-Roasted Pepper Salsa, 28
Gumbo, Shrimp and Sausage, with Slow Roux, 57

H
Ham
    Muffaletta Salad with Olive Vinaigrette, 47
    Old-School Cuban Sandwiches with Garlic Mayonnaise, 149
Hemingway La Floridita, 33
Hibiscus-Ginger Punch, 140
Honey Onions, 152
Horak, Leonard, 65
Horiatiki Greek Salad with Marinated Grilled Shrimp, 48
Horta, 121
Hot sauces, 85
Hughes, Lena B. Smithers, 17
Hummingbird Quick Bread, 193
Hurricane, 55
Hush Puppies, Jalapeño and Beer, 182

I
Island Slaw, 209

J
Jamaican Beef Patties, 94
Jamaican Curry Lamb, 107
Jamaican Fish Rundown, 120
Jams
    Bacon and Bourbon Jam, 27
    Red Pepper Jam, 24
Jerk
    Chicken Breasts with Jerk Marinade, 72
    Dry Jerk Seasoning, 213
    Grilled Jerk Chicken, 72
    Jerk Pork Tenderloin with Pineapple-Rum Sauce, 102–4
Jicama
    Island Slaw, 209

K
Key lime liqueur
    Key Lime Martini, 33
Key limes, 195
    Key Lime Pie with White Chocolate Topping, 195
Keys Breeze Punch, 199

L
Lamb
    Greek Lamb Souvlaki with Vegetable Kebabs and Tzatziki, 110
    Jamaican Curry Lamb, 107
    Lamb Shanks Adobo Soft Tacos, 151
Leap of Faith, 77
Lemons, 17
    Bourbon-Mint Lemonade, 140
    Meyer Lemon Vinaigrette, 211
Limes, 17
    Jalapeño-Lime Butter, 211
    Key, 195
    Key Lime Martini, 33
    Key Lime Pie with White Chocolate Topping, 195
    Lime-Mustard Vinaigrette, 50
    Lime Sour Cream, 154
    Lime Whipped Cream, 202
    Mojito, 109
Lost Bayou Ramblers, 41

M

Macadamia nuts
　Grilled Chicken and Mango Salad, 44
　toasting, 44
Macaroni and Cheese, Creamy, with Parmesan Crust, 169
Mahi Mahi, Caribbean, with Quinoa Succotash, 117
Mangoes
　Grilled Chicken and Mango Salad, 44
　Mango Icebox Cheesecake with Gingersnap Crust, 190
　Mango Salsa, 102–4
Maraschino liqueur
　Hemingway La Floridita, 33
Margarita, 55
Martini, Key Lime, 33
Mayonnaise, Garlic, 149
Melon liqueur
　Keys Breeze Punch, 199
Michot, Louis, 41
Mississippi Comeback Sauce, 157
Mofongo, Sweet Potato, 172
Mojo, 67
Mole Rub, 83
Muffaletta Salad with Olive Vinaigrette, 47
Mushrooms
　Baked Grits with Spicy Mushrooms and Cheese, 168
　Quinoa Succotash, 170

N

Nachos, Super, with Skirt Steak, Black Beans, and Queso Sauce, 25
Nuts. *See also individual nuts*
　toasting, 44

O

Oil, Cilantro, 211
Okra
　Shrimp and Sausage Gumbo with Slow Roux, 57
　Spicy Pickled Okra, 34
Olives
　Horiatiki Greek Salad with Marinated Grilled Shrimp, 48
　Muffaletta Salad with Olive Vinaigrette, 47
　Picadillo-Stuffed Acorn Squash, 96
　Ropa Vieja, 91
　Veracruz Sauce, 122
Onions
　Crispy Onions, 209
　Honey Onions, 152
　Pickled Onions, 50, 151
Oranges, 17
　Fresh Ambrosia with Sour Cream Dressing, 51
　From-Scratch Sour Mix, 55
　Keys Breeze Punch, 199
　Mojo, 67
　Orange-Cinnamon Flan, 204
　Voodoo Punch, 199
Oyster Po' Boys with Mississippi Comeback Sauce, 157

P

Peaches
　Bourbon-Brined Pork Chops with Peach Glaze and Corn-Bacon Hash, 105–6
　Peach-Blackberry Buckle, 200
Peanut Butter Cake with Salted Peanut Frosting, 187
Peas. *See also* Black-eyed peas; Pigeon peas
　Arroz con Pollo y Chorizo, 80
　Chicken Fricassee with Spring Vegetables and Chive Dumplings, 79
　Corn-Bacon Hash, 105–6
Pecans
　Hummingbird Quick Bread, 193
　Pecan-Chocolate Bars, 203
　Sweet and Spicy Pecans, 50
　toasting, 50
Picadillo-Stuffed Acorn Squash, 96
Pickles
　Pickled Onions, 50, 151
　Spicy Pickled Okra, 34
Pico de Gallo, 154
Pies
　Key Lime Pie with White Chocolate Topping, 195
　Savory Tomato and Cheese Pie, 39
　Sweet Potato Pie with Bourbon Whipped Cream, 196–97
Pigeon peas
　Arroz con Pollo y Chorizo, 80
　Yellow Rice and Peas, 173
Pimento Cheese, Zesty, 37
Pineapple
　Fresh Ambrosia with Sour Cream Dressing, 51
　Hummingbird Quick Bread, 193
　Keys Breeze Punch, 199
　Pineapple-Rum Sauce, 102–4
Plantains
　Sweet Potato Mofongo, 172
Po' boys
　Beef Debris Po' Boys with Gravy, 145
　Oyster Po' Boys with Mississippi Comeback Sauce, 157
Poppy Seed Dressing, 52
Pork. *See also* Bacon; Ham; Sausage
　Baby Back Ribs with Blackberry Brandy BBQ Sauce, 99
　Bourbon-Brined Pork Chops with Peach Glaze and Corn-Bacon Hash, 105–6
　Jerk Pork Tenderloin with Pineapple-Rum Sauce, 102–4
　Old-School Cuban Sandwiches with Garlic Mayonnaise, 149
　Puerto Rican Pork Roast, 100–101
　Pulled Pork Sandwiches with Blackberry Brandy BBQ Sauce, 146
　shoulder, 100
Potatoes
　Church Supper Potato Salad, 56
　Cuban "Hamburgers" with Chorizo and Shoestring Potatoes, 142
　Jamaican Curry Lamb, 107
　Roast Chicken Asado with Root Vegetables, 67
　Skordalia, 121
Puerto Rican Pork Roast, 100–101
Punch
　Hibiscus-Ginger Punch, 140
　Keys Breeze Punch, 199
　Voodoo Punch, 199

Q

Quinoa Succotash, 170

R

Raisins
　Picadillo-Stuffed Acorn Squash, 96
Ranch Dressing, Chipotle, 43
Raspberries
　Fresh Ambrosia with Sour Cream Dressing, 51
Ribs, Baby Back, with Blackberry Brandy BBQ Sauce, 99
Rice
　Arroz con Pollo y Chorizo, 80
　Basic Rice, 209
　Coconut-Almond Rice, 174
　Shrimp and Sausage Gumbo with Slow Roux, 57
　Yellow Rice and Peas, 173
Root Beer Sauce, Sweet and Sticky, 68
Ropa Vieja, 91

Rum
- Chocolate-Rum Cake, 188
- Daiquiri, 77
- Hemingway La Floridita, 33
- Hibiscus-Ginger Punch, 140
- Hurricane, 55
- Keys Breeze Punch, 199
- Mojito, 109
- Pineapple-Rum Sauce, 102–4

Rundown, Jamaican Fish, 120

Rye whiskey
- Sazerac, 109

S

Salad dressings. See also Vinaigrettes
- Chipotle Ranch Dressing, 43
- Poppy Seed Dressing, 52

Salads
- Baby Spinach with Lime-Mustard Vinaigrette and Sweet and Spicy Pecans, 50
- Chopped Chicken Taco Salad with Chipotle Ranch Dressing, 43
- Church Supper Potato Salad, 56
- Coleslaw with Poppy Seed Dressing, 52
- Fresh Ambrosia with Sour Cream Dressing, 51
- Grilled Chicken and Mango Salad, 44
- Horiatiki Greek Salad with Marinated Grilled Shrimp, 48
- Island Slaw, 209
- Muffaletta Salad with Olive Vinaigrette, 47
- Texas Caviar, 31

Salsas
- Fire-Roasted Pepper Salsa, 28
- Grilled Corn Salsa, 58
- Mango Salsa, 102–4
- Pico de Gallo, 154
- Salsa Verde, 125

Sambal olek, 128

Sandwiches
- Bacon BBQ Burgers, 139
- Beef Debris Po' Boys with Gravy, 145
- Crispy Fish Fillet Sandwiches with Island Tartar Sauce, 152–53
- Cuban "Hamburgers" with Chorizo and Shoestring Potatoes, 142
- Fried Green Tomato and Pimento Cheese BLTs, 158
- Grilled Chicken Tortas with Chipotle Aïoli, 138
- Old-School Cuban Sandwiches with Garlic Mayonnaise, 149
- Oyster Po' Boys with Mississippi Comeback Sauce, 157
- Pulled Pork Sandwiches with Blackberry Brandy BBQ Sauce, 146

Sauces. See also Salsas
- All-American BBQ Sauce, 211
- Asian Chili Sauce, 126
- Blackberry Brandy BBQ Sauce, 99
- Dill-Yogurt Sauce, 115
- hot, 85
- Island Tartar Sauce, 152
- Mississippi Comeback Sauce, 157
- Mojo, 67
- Pineapple-Rum Sauce, 102–4
- Red Sauce, 137
- Roasted Red Pepper Cream, 74–75
- Sweet and Sticky Root Beer Sauce, 68
- Tzatziki, 110
- Veracruz Sauce, 122

Sausage
- Arroz con Pollo y Chorizo, 80
- Cuban Black Bean Soup with Chorizo Sofrito, 63
- Cuban "Hamburgers" with Chorizo and Shoestring Potatoes, 142
- Muffaletta Salad with Olive Vinaigrette, 47
- Shrimp and Andouille with Cheese Grits, 132
- Shrimp and Sausage Gumbo with Slow Roux, 57

Sazerac, 109, 207

Seasonings
- Cajun Seasoning, 213
- Dry Jerk Seasoning, 213

Sesame seeds, toasting, 83

Sherry, Black Bean Soup with, 63

Shortcakes
- Florida Strawberry Shortcakes with Lime Whipped Cream, 202
- Tres Leches Strawberry Shortcake, 192

Shrimp, 113
- BBQ Shrimp with Spicy Beer Sauce, 129
- Crab-Stuffed Shrimp with Two Sauces, 126–28
- Creole Surf and Turf with Spicy Mustard Sauce, 87
- Horiatiki Greek Salad with Marinated Grilled Shrimp, 48
- Seafood Avocado Cocktail, 22
- Shrimp and Andouille with Cheese Grits, 132
- Shrimp and Sausage Gumbo with Slow Roux, 57
- Shrimp Stock, 210

Simple Syrup, 33

Skordalia, 121

Smoke, adding, 19

Snyder, Georgea, 185

Soups
- Black Bean Soup with Sherry, 63
- Crab Bisque, 61
- Cuban Black Bean Soup with Chorizo Sofrito, 63
- Shrimp and Sausage Gumbo with Slow Roux, 57
- Tortola Tortilla Soup, 58

Sour cream
- Lime Sour Cream, 154
- Sour Cream Dressing, 51

Sour Mix, From-Scratch, 55

Souvlaki, Greek Lamb, with Vegetable Kebabs and Tzatziki, 110

Spinach
- Baby Spinach with Lime-Mustard Vinaigrette and Sweet and Spicy Pecans, 50
- Crab-Stuffed Shrimp with Two Sauces, 126–28

Squash
- Picadillo-Stuffed Acorn Squash, 96
- Southern Vegetable Gratin, 167

Stocks
- Crayfish Stock, 210
- Shrimp Stock, 210

Strawberries
- Florida Strawberry Shortcakes with Lime Whipped Cream, 202
- Tres Leches Strawberry Shortcake, 192

Succotash, Quinoa, 170

Sweet potatoes
- Sweet Potato Mofongo, 172
- Sweet Potato Pie with Bourbon Whipped Cream, 196–97

Swordfish, Marinated, with Skordalia and Horta, 121

Syrups
- Rich Demerara Syrup, 109
- Simple Syrup, 33

T

Tacos
- Blackened Fish Tacos, 154
- Lamb Shanks Adobo Soft Tacos, 151
- Taco Salad, Chopped Chicken, with Chipotle Ranch Dressing, 43

Tales of the Cocktail, 207

Tampa's Downtown Market, 185
Tandoori-Style Chicken, 78
Tartar Sauce, Island, 152
Tea Brine, Iced, Fried Chicken with, 71
Tequila
    Leap of Faith, 77
    Margarita, 55
Texas Caviar, 31
Tomatillos, 125
    Salsa Verde, 125
Tomatoes
    Beef Debris Po' Boys with Gravy, 145
    Chopped Chicken Taco Salad with Chipotle Ranch Dressing, 43
    Crayfish Étouffée, 119
    Fried Green Tomato and Pimento Cheese BLTs, 158
    Horiatiki Greek Salad with Marinated Grilled Shrimp, 48
    Jamaican Fish Rundown, 120
    Muffaletta Salad with Olive Vinaigrette, 47
    Oyster Po' Boys with Mississippi Comeback Sauce, 157
    Pico de Gallo, 154
    Savory Tomato and Cheese Pie, 39
    Smothered Green Beans, 163
Veracruz Sauce, 122
"Wet" Chicken Burritos with Red Sauce, 137
Tortas, Grilled Chicken, with Chipotle Aïoli, 138
Tortilla chips
    Chopped Chicken Taco Salad with Chipotle Ranch Dressing, 43
    Spiked Guacamole with Fire-Roasted Pepper Salsa, 28
    Super Nachos with Skirt Steak, Black Beans, and Queso Sauce, 25
    Texas Caviar, 31
Tortillas
    Blackened Fish Tacos, 154
    Crab Enchiladas in Green Sauce, 125
    Lamb Shanks Adobo Soft Tacos, 151
    Tortola Tortilla Soup, 58
    "Wet" Chicken Burritos with Red Sauce, 137
Tortola Tortilla Soup, 58
Tres Leches Strawberry Shortcake, 192
Tuennerman, Ann, 207
Tuna in Veracruz Sauce, 122
Tzatziki, 110

V
Vanilla-spice liqueur
    Key Lime Martini, 33
Veracruz Sauce, 122
Vinaigrettes
    Lime-Mustard Vinaigrette, 50
    Meyer Lemon Vinaigrette, 211
    Olive Vinaigrette, 47
Vodka
    Key Lime Martini, 33
    Voodoo Punch, 199

W
White Chocolate Topping, 213

Y
Yogurt
    Dill-Yogurt Sauce, 115
    Tzatziki, 110
Yuca Oven Fries, Crispy, 177
Yuzu, 128

Z
Zucchini
    Southern Vegetable Gratin, 167

Photo Credits

We'd like to thank the following people and businesses for helping us with the photography in this cookbook.

Chef Aaron Burgau (pictured on page 8) of Patois Restaurant in New Orleans, who treated us to the crawfish boil featured on pages 2 and 118, and to the folks at the Paradigm Gardens urban farm who participated.

La Segunda Central Bakery has been the place to go in Ybor City, Florida, for authentic Cuban bread and sandwiches for four generations. The shots on pages 13, 26, and 101 are from their kitchen.

Nick Detrich, managing partner of Cane & Table—a great spot for rum-based cocktails and our location for the shots on pages 54 and 206. The place evokes old Havana.

Billy Keith Williams and Darrell Williams and the very fine folks at D&K Farms in Plant City, Florida, let us walk their fields to photograph the shots on pages 166 and 185.

Beekeepers Pat & Jan Allen helped us wrangle the shots on pages 180 and 181 without getting stung. Thanks!

Ybor City was once named Cigar Capital of the world, and Tabanero Cigars is keeping that legacy alive. We were grateful to spend a pleasant afternoon there capturing the shot on page 212.

A local tradition, Brocato's Sandwich Shop (pages 14–15) in Tampa, Florida, has been in business since 1948. The garage pictured on page 38 belongs to seed collector Louis Michot (see page 41). Pages 92–93 show views of Circle 6 Farm & Ranch (see page 65). The photo on pages 130–131 is of catfish wrangler Joey Fonseca (see page 135) on his boat in the bayou.

Thanks to all!

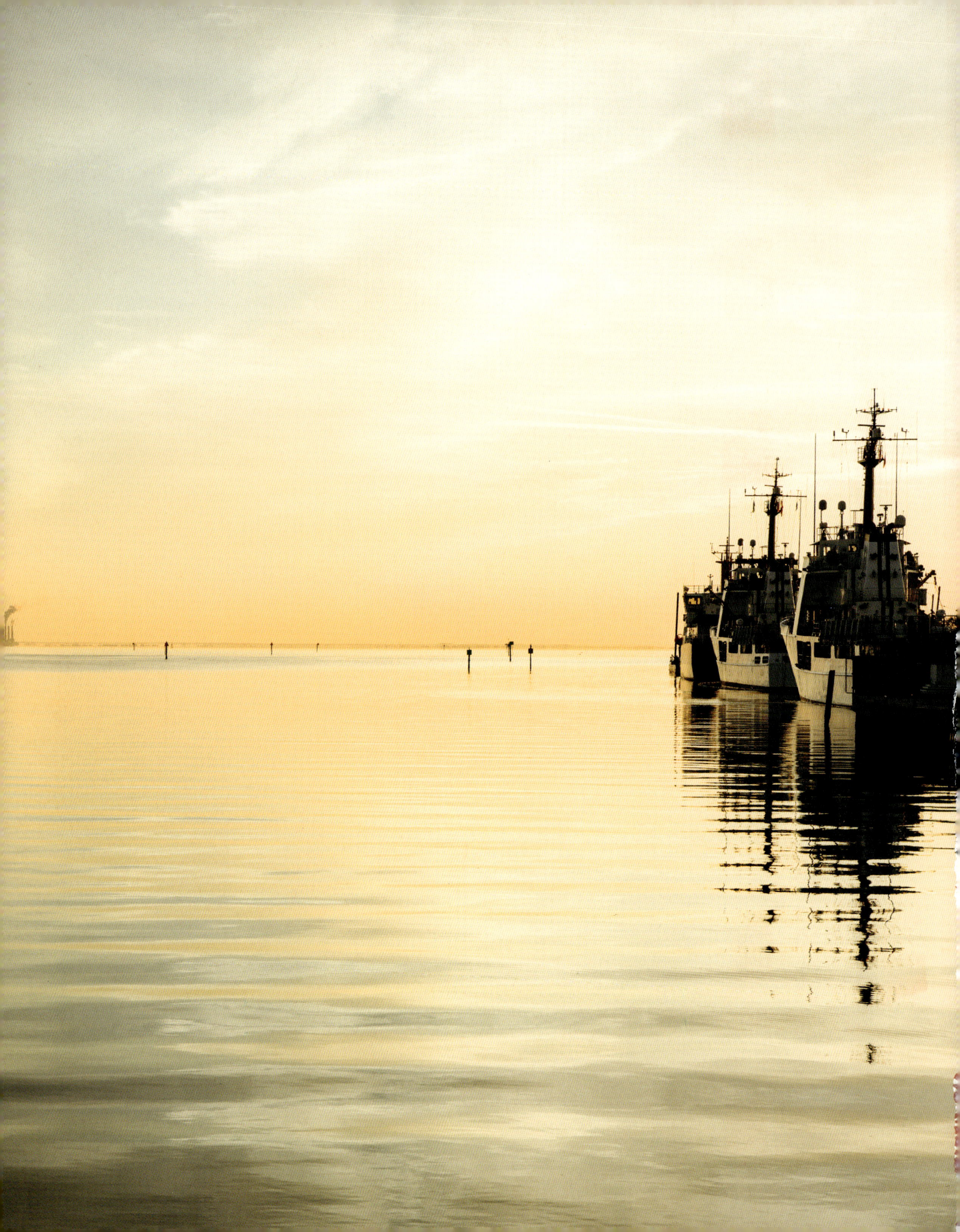

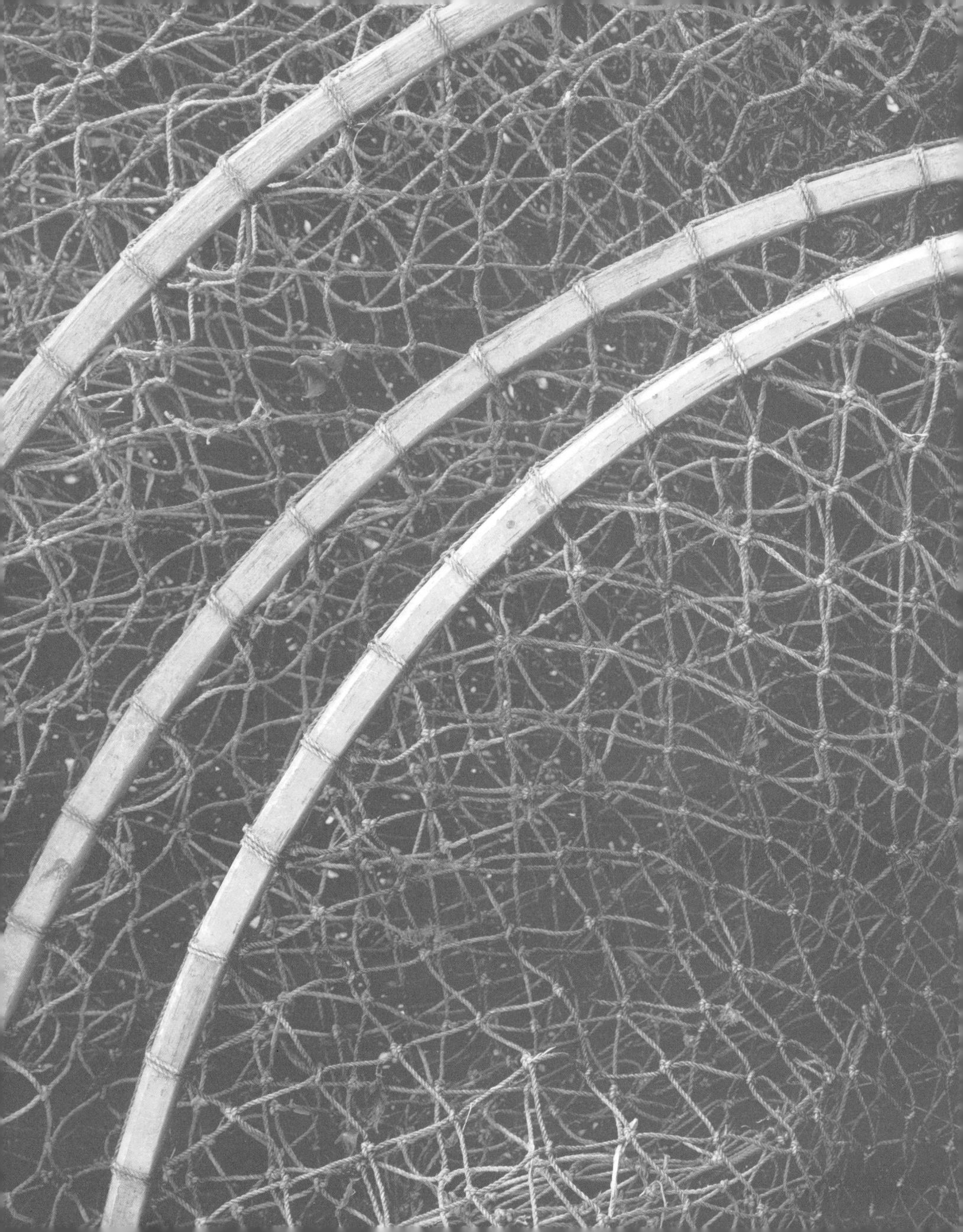